CW01425553

PUBLICATIONS OF THE

ARMY RECORDS SOCIETY

VOL. 34

MILITARY INTELLIGENCE
FROM GERMANY
1906–1914

SUBJECT   Penal Law.

8220 16,000 2—10 H W V

From M.A.Berlin.   No. 1231. Date 23-8-11., 19 .

Replying to your No. CXI/7921   Date 12-8-11., 19 .

M. O. 2.(c).

P

(1). Passing under an assumed name is not in itself considered an offence under German law. It is , for instance , permissible to give an assumed name at an hotel. If, however, a theft or something of that sort takes places at the hotel and you are asked your name by an official, it is an offence (a minor one punishable with a small fine) to give a wrong name.

It is also a minor offence to enter your name falsely in any public register. (birth, death, marriage, etc.)

(2). Being in disguise is not considered an offence if unconnected with another offence, unless it amounts to what is called "Grosser Unfug ". For instance, if a lady prefers to walk about in the Grunewald in male attire, there is no law to prevent her doing so. If, however, a man with a big beard walks down the Wilhelmstrasse in lady's clothes and causes a commotion,he can be punished.

(3). The same rules apply when the two cases are in conjunction.

Alick Russell .

Lieutenant-Colonel.

General Staff.

The rule with regard to attire is that men should wear "sichtbare Hosen" and ladies " unsichtbare Hosen".

a.R.

Report by Lieutenant Colonel Alick Russell on German penal law (Russell Memorandum no. 1231, 23 August 1911). Source: KV 3/1.

MILITARY INTELLIGENCE FROM GERMANY 1906–1914

Edited by

MATTHEW S. SELIGMANN

Published by

THE HISTORY PRESS
for the
ARMY RECORDS SOCIETY
2014

First published in the United Kingdom in 2014 by
The History Press · The Mill · Brimscombe Port · Stroud ·
Gloucestershire · GL5 2QG

Copyright © The Army Records Society, 2014

All rights reserved. No part of this publication may be reproduced,
stored in a retrieval system, or transmitted, in any form, or by any means,
electronic, mechanical, photocopying, recording or otherwise, without
the prior permission of the publisher and copyright holders.

British Library Cataloguing in Publication Data
A catalogue record for this book is available from the British Library.

ISBN 978-0-7509-6071-7

Typeset in Ehrhardt.
Typesetting and origination by
The History Press.
Printed and bound in England.

The Army Records Society was founded in 1984 in order to publish original records describing the development, organisation, administration and activities of the British Army from early times.

Any person wishing to become a Member of the Society should consult our website for details of the procedure. Members receive at least one volume per annum and are entitled to purchase back volumes at reduced prices.

The Council of the Army Records Society wish it to be clearly understood that they are not answerable for opinions or observations that may appear in the Society's publications. For these the responsibility rests entirely with the Editors of the several works.

The Society's website can be found at
www.armyrecordssociety.org.uk

ARMY RECORDS SOCIETY
COUNCIL FOR 2013–2014

PRESIDENT
Professor Sir Michael Howard OM CH CBE MC DLitt FBA

VICE-PRESIDENTS
Field Marshal Sir John Chapple GCB CBE DL MA FSA FRSA
Professor John Gooch BA PhD FRHistS

HONORARY SECRETARY
Jim Beach MBE BA MA MSc PhD

HONORARY TREASURER
Simon House BA ACMA

MEMBERSHIP SECRETARY
Timothy Bowman BA PhD FRHistS

COUNCILLORS
Professor Ian Beckett BA PhD FRHistS (Chairman)
Niall Barr MA PhD FRHistS
Huw Bennett BSc(Econ) MSc(Econ) PhD
Jonathan Boff MA PhD
Colonel Hugh Boscawen BA
Professor Mark Connelly BA PhD
Professor David French BA PhD FRHistS
Professor Matthew Hughes JP BA MSc PhD FRHistS
Lieutenant General Sir Alistair Irwin KCB CBE MA
Spencer Jones BA MPhil PhD
Alistair Massie MA DPhil
Simon Robbins BA MA PhD
Matthew Seligmann MA DPhil FRHistS
Professor Edward Spiers MA PhD FRHistS
Professor Sir Hew Strachan DL MA PhD FRSE FRHistS
Major General John Sutherell CB CBE DL BA
Andrew Syk BA LLB MA DPhil

Contents

Acknowledgements

I would like to thank everyone who has helped in the production of this volume. Documents from the Royal Archives are reproduced by gracious permission of Her Majesty Queen Elizabeth II. Permission to quote from documents in the Hamilton papers is courtesy of the Trustees of the Liddell Hart Centre for Military Archives. Crown Copyright material in the National Archives and elsewhere is reproduced under the Open Government Licence.

Introduction

This volume is a study of the *overt* gathering of military intelligence on Germany by the British Army in the immediate run up to the First World War. In an era, such as today's, when states spend vast sums *covertly* gathering information by all the means at their disposal and have massive agencies employing numerous people devoted entirely to this task, the idea that this was not always the case and that secret intelligence work was once a much more marginal part of the data collection process than is now the case is intrinsically counter-intuitive. Nevertheless, prior to 1914 – and especially prior to 1909, when Britain did not even have a dedicated secret service – the systematic acquisition of military information on potential rivals was largely in the hands of a very small group of people, whose identity was known to the foreign powers in question and whose activities were entirely open and legitimate. These people were the officers who served as military attachés in foreign capitals. Their role has frequently been noted,[1] but often in an unduly dismissive fashion. Paul Kennedy, for example, in a ground-breaking chapter on British intelligence before 1914, described the reports of the British military attachés as 'humdrum' and argued that the restrictions the German authorities placed upon their work meant that they only 'conveyed to London what the German army was prepared to permit the rest of the world to learn. They did not penetrate far below the deliberately exposed surfaces.'[2] The object of this volume is to demonstrate that this was not the case. Contrary both to Kennedy's argument and also to the additional suggestion from another leading historian that British military

---

1   The classic texts are Lothar Wilfred Hilbert, 'The Role of Military and Naval Attachés in the British and German Service with particular reference to those in Berlin and London and Their Effect on Anglo-German Relations, 1871–1914' (PhD, University of Cambridge, 1954) and Alfred Vagts, *The Military Attaché* (Princeton, 1967).

2   Paul M. Kennedy, 'Great Britain before 1914', in Ernest R. May (ed.), *Knowing One's Enemies: Intelligence before the Two World Wars* (Princeton, 1984), pp. 179–80.

intelligence-gathering was largely 'passive' and that no fixed system was in place for most of the pre-war years,[3] it will provide documentary evidence that conclusively demonstrates that Britain's military attachés provided, as was the intention behind their appointment, both a steady stream of technical information on the German armed forces and regular reliable appraisals of the mood of the German military authorities in respect to peace and war. As will also be shown, these were vital sources that played a substantial role in shaping the British picture of Germany and the intentions of its rulers, a fact that poses some obvious questions about how and why Britain's military attachés came to be in Germany in the first place.

Diplomatic Realignments and Britain's Need for Military Intelligence on Germany

In the pre-First World War era Britain conceived itself as more of a maritime power than a military one. This was probably not obvious to the various independent peoples in Africa, Asia and the Pacific that succumbed during this period to British colonial rule, often at the point of a rifle wielded by a British soldier. However, in European terms the army that Britain maintained was a small one and the wars it fought, which, after 1856, were entirely in other continents, were in comparative terms trivial affairs. This is not to say that the British Empire did not have military potential – it had huge resources and, given time, it could mobilize much larger forces, as the Second South African War demonstrated – but its obvious totem of armed strength was not its army, but the Royal Navy. Countries seeking to modernize their fleets – countries as diverse as Japan, Chile, Greece and the Ottoman Empire – frequently looked to Britain for guidance. By the same token, countries wishing to learn from or about the foremost military power increasingly turned to the Prusso-German Empire. One means of doing this was to send a serving officer to the German capital to report on the progress of military affairs there. Such officers, attached as they were to their country's diplomatic mission in Berlin, were formally known as military attachés. Their role, entirely overt, was two-fold: to represent their country's army in the diplomatic, ceremonial and court functions of the

---

3   Nicholas P. Hiley, 'The Failure of British Espionage against Germany, 1907–1914', *Historical Journal* 26 (1983), p. 868.

German Empire and to gain such intelligence as they could acquire by legitimate means from their hosts.

Britain might have been more of a naval than a military power, but it was active enough in military affairs to find the stationing of a military attaché in the major European capitals an essential matter. Thus, in 1860 the first British military attaché had been sent to Berlin, albeit at that time only temporarily, the post ultimately being given a more permanent footing in 1864. Representing the British army at the court of Europe's premier military power, a posting which provided its holder with the opportunity to observe the world's most formidable army on manoeuvre and to discuss military matters with the continent's leading practitioners of the art and science of land warfare, was not without prestige or import. Consequently, officers of standing and distinction – for example, Sir Garnet Wolseley's[4] military secretary, Colonel (later Major General Sir) Leopold Swaine[5] – were often nominated for the role and served with enthusiasm. In addition, so long as Britain and Germany enjoyed amicable diplomatic relations, as they did for most of the late nineteenth century, the post was generally a congenial one. However, the diplomatic transformation that occurred at the start of the twentieth century fundamentally changed the nature and significance of this role. The emergence of the Anglo-German antagonism and the subsequent alignment of Britain with France and Russia meant that the military attaché in Berlin was no longer seen merely as a source of general information on the broad spectrum of military matters, but rather as a gatherer of specific intelligence on a country with which Britain might one day be at war, however unwelcome this prospect might be. Determining whether or not Germany was really a hostile power in a military sense, what its intentions were with regard to the British Empire and its continental partners and whether or not the capabilities of its armed forces would permit it to secure its political aspirations by force of arms should it decide to do so, suddenly became key questions that in some respects the military attaché was best placed to answer.

---

4 Field Marshal Sir Garnet Wolseley, 1st Viscount Wolseley (1833–1913), distinguished British soldier, best known for his campaigns in the colonial realm especially Africa.

5 Major General Sir Leopold Victor Swaine (1840–1931). In a long and distinguished military career, he was notable for serving as military attaché in three capitals, St Petersburg, Constantinople and Berlin.

The Role of the Military Attaché in Berlin in an Era of Crises

This volume provides documentary evidence as to how the British military attachés in Berlin answered these questions in the eight years leading up to the outbreak of the First World War in 1914. This period has been selected for a specific set of reasons. Most obviously, the immediate run up to the start of the fighting was the era when tensions between the powers were often at their greatest and when the road to war was most vigorously being forged. While, of course, historians' opinions on the matter do vary considerably, the cycle of great power confrontations that ultimately culminated in the July crisis of 1914 and then in war is generally deemed to have commenced with the eruption of the First Moroccan Crisis, a major Franco-German spat which ran from 31 March 1905, when Kaiser Wilhelm II landed in Tangier, through to 31 May 1906, when the Algeciras conference, the meeting which settled the dispute, came to a close. By starting in the spring of 1906, this volume examines a world shaped by the First Moroccan Crisis and can provide a picture of how this new tenser diplomatic and military environment was perceived by those charged with providing an intelligence picture of it.[6]

The choice of 1906–1914 as the chronological parameters for this volume also gives it another specific form of cohesion, one centred on personality. Military attachés generally served four-year terms. This span allowed the holder of the post sufficient time to develop the necessary contacts in his host nation to perform the intelligence functions that were required of him, but at the same time was not so long as to narrow the holder's perspective through the process generally known as 'going native'. The eight years from 1906 to 1914 thus correspond to the tenures of two British officers, Colonels Frederic Trench[7] and the Hon. Alexander

---

6   The First Moroccan Crisis was conceived by Friedrich von Holstein, the head of the Political Department of the German Foreign Office, as a means of breaking the newly formed Entente Cordiale and separating Britain from France before this new friendship crystallized into something more significant. In reality it had the opposite effect. By challenging the two powers it pushed them together and helped start the process of transforming an agreement over colonial boundaries into something akin to a *de facto* alliance.

7   Frederic John Arthur Trench (1857–1942). An artillery officer, he was educated at Geneva University before entering the Royal Military Academy. He was gazetted second lieutenant in 1876, captain in 1884, major in 1893, and lieutenant colonel in 1902. He received a brevet colonelcy in 1905, receiving substantive rank in 1908. He served in the Zulu War of 1879, being mentioned in despatches on account of his conduct at the Battle of Ulundi. He also served in the Second South African War, where he was once again mentioned in despatches. In the latter stages of the South African War he acted as a press censor in headquarters, a role sometimes viewed as training for intelligence work. He was attached to the German forces in South-West Africa from May 1905 to March 1906, when he took up his appointment in Berlin. This would be his last post. He retired on its expiry and devoted himself to campaigning for compulsory military service in preparation for the war he felt sure would come.

4

('Alick') Russell.[8] Consequently, the volume contains the considered view, built up over time by two British observers of German military affairs. As will be explained later, both Trench and Russell developed a clear, albeit different, view about the meaning and implications of Germany's military policies and relayed their analyses back to London in a series of sometimes forthright dispatches.

Of course, the question might well be asked: would not the volume have had a similar cohesion if, say, three rather than two military attachés had been its focus, a decision that would have had the added benefit of extending the chronological range to include such significant events as the German reaction to the signing of the Entente Cordiale. While there would be much to such an approach, it was not taken because of the particular circumstances surrounding the tenure of Count Edward Gleichen, Trench's predecessor as military attaché in Berlin. Gleichen was a distinguished officer, a good linguist and a distant relative of both King Edward VII and Kaiser Wilhelm II.[9] On the face of it, therefore, he appeared to be an inspired choice for the Berlin role. Unfortunately, his personal relationship with the Kaiser was never a close one and, in fact, the two fell out spectacularly when Gleichen was only half way through his term.[10] As a result, at the insistence of the Reich government, Gleichen had to be transferred from Berlin to another post – Washington, DC – after only three years in the German capital and he was effectively

---

8 The Hon. Alexander ('Alick') Victor Frederick Villiers Russell (1874–1965). A Guards officer, he spent much of his childhood at the British Embassy in Berlin, where his father was the ambassador. He was subsequently educated at Wellington and then Sandhurst. He served in the South African War, where he was twice mentioned in dispatches. In January 1908, after a spell as battalion and then regimental adjutant in the Grenadier Guards, he was appointed as General Staff Officer, 3rd grade, in the section of the Military Operations directorate (MO2c) responsible for German affairs, perfect preparation for his desired post of Military Attaché in Berlin, where he served from 1910 to the outbreak of war in 1914. After the war he served as Military Attaché in Switzerland and then Chile before becoming one of the British commissioners on the Hungarian–Rumanian Boundary Commission. He retired from the Army in 1926.

9 Count (later Lord) Albert Edward Wilfed Gleichen (1863–1937). Commissioned in the Grenadier Guards in 1881, he was promoted captain in 1892, major in 1898, lieutenant colonel in 1903, brevet colonel in 1906 and substantive colonel in 1907. He served in the Guards' Camel Regiment during the attempt to relieve General Gordon at Khartoum, before joining the Intelligence Section of the War Office in 1895. He went to Egypt as an intelligence office in 1896 and then to South Africa in 1899, where he was wounded at the engagement at Modder River. He was appointed military attaché in Berlin in October 1903, but transferred to Washington in January 1906 after falling out with the Kaiser. In 1907 he was appointed Assistant Director of Military Operations and placed in charge of MO2, the European section of that body. In 1911 he was appointed to command the 15th Brigade of the 5th Division, with which unit he served at the battles of Mons and Le Cateau in 1914. In 1915 he was promoted GOC 37th Division. He retired from the Army in 1919.

10 Some details of this can be found in Gleichen's memoirs. See Lord Edward Gleichen, *A Guardsman's Memories: A Book of Recollections* (London, 1932).

cut off from access to important sources of information well before that.[11] In short, his utility as an attaché was severely compromised. The result was that his reporting did not benefit from the same opportunities of time and access that existed for his successors. The cohesion that comes from selecting 1906–1914 as the span of this volume would not exist if 1903–1914 were chosen instead.

The Destruction and Survival of the Documentary Record

This would not be the only problem with extending the volume further back in time. It would also create difficulties in terms of the primary source base. The original top copies of all military attaché reports were sent, via the Foreign Office in London, to the War Office. Thus, the obvious location for the archived copies of the reports of the British military attaché in Berlin, who was, after all, a serving officer, and whose principal role was to provide information to the British army, would be the War Office files in the British National Archives. Unfortunately, almost none are to be found therein. The reasons for this are varied. To begin with, in the aftermath of the First World War the British Army found that it had accumulated an enormous number of paper records. Unable to maintain and store them all, the War Office took on extra clerical staff for the purpose of going through the accumulated mass of files and weeding out those that were of only peripheral value. While many of the temporary clerks employed for this purpose were conscientious about their work and expert judges of the records placed before them, as it subsequently transpired many others were not. Numerous important files were destroyed by those additional staff members who lacked the expertise to make a proper judgement as to what should be retained and what should be destroyed. The damage done to the War Office records by this process was considerable, but it was only the first stage in a sorry tale of destruction. When the Second World War started in 1939, record management was naturally relegated down the list of the Army's priorities. As a result, with only a few exceptions, old records in storage stayed in storage. This included a large mass of military intelligence documents that were kept in a depository in Arnside Street in the east end of London,

11 Matthew S. Seligmann, 'Military Diplomacy in a Military Monarchy? Kaiser Wilhelm II and the British Service Attachés in Berlin 1903–1914', in Wilhelm Deist and Annika Mombauer (eds), *The Kaiser: New Research on Wilhelm II's Role in Imperial Germany* (Cambridge, 2003).

a location that, as it happens, was flattened on the first day of the Blitz. Those War Office records that survived the inter-war weeding and the German bombs were eventually deposited in the Public Record Office (as the National Archives was then known). In theory, this was for posterity, but in 1965 the archivists responsible for these files decided that they were not in good order and a rearrangement was necessary. While there might well have been something to this judgement, the decision was also taken to utilize the process of rearranging and recataloguing to go through the files and dispose of the many allegedly unimportant documents contained therein. Thus, files that had already been extensively weeded and then bombed were further thinned out, with yet more irreplaceable and invaluable documents disposed of in the process.[12] The outcome of all of this destruction was that, whereas a full set of military attaché reports from Berlin would once have existed in the War Office files, almost none are to be found there today. One exception, a technical memorandum rather than a full report, that covers Alick Russell's encounter with Anton Fokker, appears to have survived serendipitously [document 77].

However, if there are very few copies of the dispatches from Berlin in the War Office papers, that does not mean that none exist anywhere. As was mentioned earlier, military attaché reports were sent to the War Office via the Foreign Office. Prior to 1906 the Foreign Office read the reports before their onward transmission, but only very infrequently did they keep a copy for themselves. In 1906, however, the Foreign Office introduced a new filing system. One helpful consequence of this administrative change was that it engendered a greater interest than had existed hitherto in keeping copies of any important documents that passed through the Foreign Office's hands. As Anglo-German relations were a matter of the highest significance, and as military attaché reports were an important adjunct to the analysis of diplomatic relations between these two states, the decision appears to have been taken part way through 1906 to retain a record of the more important of these dispatches. For the most part this was achieved by instructing the attaché to send in a duplicate copy of all his reports as a matter of routine. However, where this was not done, or where a single duplicate was not sufficient – say, for example, because the Foreign Office wished to send a copy on to another department – then the Foreign Office frequently had their own clerks type a duplicate of their own. By such means a large

---

12   Matthew S. Seligmann, 'Hors de Combat? The Management, Mismanagement and Mutilation of the War Office Archive', *Journal of the Society for Army Historical Research* 337 (Spring 2006), 52–8.

corpus of military attaché reports has been preserved for posterity; but, sadly, not all of them. Helpfully, however, the Foreign Office was not the only department to see the virtue of retaining those military attaché reports that came into their possession. On several occasions, copies of dispatches from Berlin were sent to the Committee of Imperial Defence, which chose to retain them in its files (an example is document 28 in this volume). Likewise, several reports from Berlin on the activities of the German army in Africa were forwarded by the Foreign Office to the Colonial Office [3, 6], which also kept them for subsequent reference. Interestingly, and most revealingly, a few also ended up with the Security Service, some examples of which are again to be found in this volume [39, 52, 65]. Finally, the establishment of the Independent Air Force in 1918 also led to the preservation of some military attaché reports. The reason for this was that, with the establishment of a separate Air Ministry, many of the files relating to aerial matters that previously belonged to the War Office were now surplus to the requirements of that body, but were vital to the work of the new organization. As a result, they were transferred en masse to the new department. Among these papers were several military attaché reports on the progress of German aviation [67, 84, 109].

The result of these various departmental record-keeping policies is that, whereas it is extremely difficult to locate copies of military attaché reports from Berlin before 1906, after this date quite a large number still exist, albeit not among the papers of the War Office. The date parameters of this volume, which reflect the tenures of Trench and Russell as well as the broader diplomatic context of the post-Moroccan Crisis world, are thus further determined by the availability of records, a matter that is itself a factor of serendipity, wartime enemy action and the adoption of particular filing systems. So, what do these reports show?[13]

The Reporting of Frederic Trench

In the case of Frederic Trench, the dominant leitmotif of his reports is their emphasis on the existence and influence in Germany of a strong strain of Anglophobia that permeated not just German society in general, but the army's officer corps as well. In some respects, this is quite surprising as, outwardly at least, Trench might have been expected to be highly sympathetic towards Germany. An artillery officer who had

---

13 The section that follows draws upon Matthew S. Seligmann, *Spies in Uniform: British Military and Naval Intelligence on the Eve of the First World War* (Oxford, 2006).

served in the Second South African War, Trench had been educated in Switzerland and, thus, spoke German perfectly. His selection for the post in Berlin was not, however, a reflection of his expertise, past service or linguistic attainments; rather it was determined by entirely personal considerations. In 1903, while in Gibraltar to collect the warrant and insignia of the Distinguished Service Order, Trench was introduced to the Kaiser, who was then partaking in one of his innumerable Mediterranean cruises. They appear to have developed something of a rapport because, a year later, Trench was invited to attend the annual German Army manoeuvres and the year after that, when the British government applied to send an army officer to South-West Africa to observe the German forces in action in their efforts to suppress the Herero, permission was given so long as the officer in question was Trench. Subsequently, when the need arose to supersede Count Gleichen, it was intimated, none too subtly, that Trench would be a welcome replacement. Given the disadvantages of not having a military attaché in Berlin who was fully *persona grata*, the British government acceded to this request. Thus, in effect, Trench was the Kaiser's nominee for the post.

That the Kaiser liked Trench and that the two got on well together was evident throughout the four years that Trench served in Berlin. However, if the Kaiser was hoping that this would lead to favourable reports from the British military attaché in Berlin – ones that minimized the German threat and spoke positively but soothingly about the German Army – he would have been sorely disappointed by what Trench was actually writing. While Trench was always scrupulously courteous to the Kaiser in person and was always careful to note in his reports the monarch's personal friendliness towards him at any official or court function [12], he was not so generous in his reflections on the goals of the German Army. This manifested itself in a number of different ways.

First of all, having come to Berlin straight from the conflict in German South-West Africa, it is perhaps unsurprising that Trench continued to send in dispatches about this conflict, albeit now from the perspective of how it was perceived from the German capital rather than from the battle front. As far as the military matters were concerned, this included some broad criticisms about the inability of the German Army to adapt properly to fighting in a colonial setting [4]. However, by the time Trench reached Berlin the fighting was almost over and so Trench was also interested in the contours of the peace. In this context, the evident and exaggerated cruelty of the German forces towards their defeated foe and the seeming indifference of the German authorities to whether captured Africans lived or died so long as they could be used as slave labour struck Trench forcibly [11]. His conclusion, which would acquire greater importance in later years, when the British government sought to condemn German colonial rule as barbaric and inhumane, was that the neglect and death were an act of deliberate policy [6]. Nothing illustrated this better than the death rate in the notorious concentration camp on Shark Island. A rocky outcrop in the South Atlantic with no shelter, confinement there, as Trench reported, spelt automatic death for many prisoners [16]. This was not the only thing that troubled Trench. The slow withdrawal of German forces after the pacification of the country was to his mind only explicable if the Germans wished to maintain an army in the region for some other purpose [11]. As the only other power in southern Africa was Britain, the implications of this were obvious and it was not without import that Trench frequently noted that Germany was casting envious eyes on the British possession of Walvis Bay (spelt Walfish or Walfisch by Trench), the only decent harbour in the region [9, 19].

In addition to his worries about the possibilities of aggressive German action in Africa, Trench also frequently reported that a strong motivating factor in German politics was Anglophobia, or, as he put it, the 'detestation of England' [32]. This was, in his opinion, not only widespread, but was conditioning Germans to see Britain as their 'world enemy' and a country in need of being defeated if Germany was to attain its rightful place in the world. What made this so alarming was that this opinion was not only held by outright chauvinists, but was shared by most army officers as well, many of whom openly expressed the view that war with England was 'not only inevitable but desirable' [37]. The result was that Germany was busily preparing for a future conflict with Britain. In the psychological realm the population was being mobilized by patriotic societies and pressure groups such as the Navy League, a large organization that made the overthrown of Britain its main goal [24]. In effect, therefore, mental preparations for war were proceeding alongside the material underpinnings of future conflict. Meanwhile, the fruits of new scientific discoveries were all being geared towards the invasion of Britain. The German enthusiasm for the airship, for example, was in Trench's dispatches a factor of their ability to circumvent Britain's island status and make aerial bombing and landing a possibility [35, 38]. This interest in new discoveries did not, of course, mean that the possibility of a more traditional seaborne assault was being ignored. Trench reported on the continuous work by the General Staff to perfect such a scheme [13] and on the espionage that was being undertaken to support it [23]. While there were no doubt numerous obstacles to such an invasion attempt, Trench was convinced that the Germans intended to circumvent at least some of these by ignoring the usual conventions of war, such as a declaration prior to any conflict [8]. A surprise attack – perhaps on the model of the Japanese coup against Port Arthur – might well be the first inkling Britain had of any war [29]. This, of course, was an option that the British Admiralty continually asserted was not open to Germany, but Trench thought otherwise. The nature of Germany's reserve forces, he explained, meant that an invasion force could be gathered and no one would be any the wiser about this [28].

Trench's belief that Germany harboured a desire to attack Britain and was making preparations to do so was supplemented by a range of technical appreciations of Germany's forces that drew attention to their outstanding capabilities and their constant striving to improve. This included the formation of special machine-gun companies [25, 34, 36], the use of motor vehicles [27] and dirigible airships [42, 43, 44]. In short Trench drew a picture of a formidable and technologically capable foe. This did not mean that Trench saw no chinks in the German armour. Possibly because he was an artillery officer himself, he was not always impressed by the manner in which German field artillery conducted itself on the manoeuvre ground, deprecating their inadequate use of indirect fire and proper cover [18]. While this was more of an exception than the rule, it was a serious shortcoming and it is to be noted that Trench would not be alone in identifying weaknesses in German preparations for the modern battlefield. Similar issues would, as we shall see below, be identified by his successor, Colonel Russell, while, even during Trench's tenure in Berlin, some of the more astute British officers who, like the attaché, were allowed to witness German tactical exercises, would make similar deductions. One of these was Lieutenant General Sir Ian Hamilton, formerly British observer with the Japanese forces in Manchuria during the Russo-Japanese War, then serving as GOC Southern Command. Invited to watch the manoeuvres of the Saxon Army in September 1909, he was anything but unmindful of the strengths of what he described as a 'potent instrument of war'. At the same time, however, like Trench, he was surprised to find attacks pressed forward 'with but the briefest indication of artillery preparation' and frankly astonished to witness 'guns gallop[ing] up into lines of charging bayonets to support ... the assault'. As he summed up the matter: 'The battlefield lately so up-to-date and modern suddenly presents … a reversion to the tactics of Frederick the Great.'[14]

The Reporting of Alick Russell

Trench departed Berlin in March 1910. His successor, Alick Russell, was no stranger to German affairs. The younger son of Lord Odo Russell, British Ambassador in Berlin, Russell was born in the German capital and grew up in Bismarck's Reich. Later as a major working in the Directorate of Military Operations at the War Office, he was one of the officers to receive and read Trench's reports. He was, thus, like Trench well equipped linguistically and by prior familiarity to serve as the British Army's representative in Berlin.

Russell arrived in Germany with entirely different ideas to his predecessor. Whereas Trench was impressed by the virulence of German Anglophobia and believed that this sentiment provided ample motive for and momentum behind German scheming to invade the British Isles, Russell was conscious instead of the German confidence in their own military might, especially in comparison to France [61, 63, 66]. This sense of security, Russell believed, was a major factor inclining Germany towards peace. As a result, he set no score by occasional belligerent comments, even from the highest source, instead laughing them off as ironic or humorous remarks [62].

This all changed, however, with the advent in July 1911 of the Second Moroccan Crisis, a renewal of the conflict between France and Germany over the question of empire in Africa that erupted when the German government sent the gun-boat *Panther* to the port of Agadir in support of German claims to influence in the region.[15] The spat, in which Britain was vigorously involved, ended with a German renunciation of political influence in the north African kingdom in return for some unimpressive tracts of land adjacent to their colony in the Cameroons. To Russell's expert eye, the belief of the German public that their government was outmanoeuvred by Britain and France in the crisis and that the outcome constituted a profound setback for German global ambitions and possibly even a major diplomatic defeat shattered the sense of confidence that

---

14 Hamilton, 'Report on Manoeuvres of the Saxon Army', sent to the War Office 2 November 1909. LHCMA: Hamilton 4/2/9

15 The best account in English remains Geoffrey Barraclough, *From Agadir to Armageddon: Anatomy of a Crisis* (London, 1982).

had previously ensured Germany maintained a peaceful disposition [68]. Instead, it was replaced by a sense of anxiety about Germany's position. Coupled with this was widespread, deep and abiding anger towards Britain [66, 68]. These sentiments, Russell concluded, were extremely dangerous because they predisposed the Germans towards taking the kind of drastic military action to alleviate their situation that they had formerly eschewed. Evidence of the country's growing belligerence was apparent in the succession of increases in the size and power of the German army that were pushed through the German parliament, the Reichstag, to considerable popular acclaim in both 1912 and 1913 [73, 91, 93]. These new Army Bills were major measures: not only did they increase the size of the forces available to Germany, but, as importantly, they increased its efficiency and hence its ability to strike quickly [80, 96, 98]. Did Germany intend to strike? In this context, Russell noted with some alarm throughout 1912 that there were all kinds of evidence that could lead to the conclusion that Germany was quietly preparing for war [75, 78, 87]. The tension dissipated a bit thereafter, but it is worth recording that in March 1914, Russell once again raised the possibility that Germany, whose relative advantage in mobilization time versus Russia would soon begin to diminish, might for this reason be tempted to strike [107]. If so, the likelihood, as most people recognized, was that Germany would strike through Belgium, and in this context Russell supplied extracts from press reports pointing in that direction [81]. He also noted the existence of misinformation on this point [103].

If Russell's analysis of Germany's ambitions and intentions differed from Trench's both in its initial form and in its subsequent direction, he was more in accord with his predecessor when it came to evaluating the German Army's technical development. One area where the Germans were clearly very busily innovating was aviation. The continuous work on airships could hardly be missed and Russell frequently reported on it [56, 69, 72, 83, 84, 97, 105]. However, the attaché was also conscious of the nation's progress with heavier than air flight [58, 67, 69, 89, 90, 108, 109]. Particularly interesting in this regard was Russell's encounter with Anton Fokker [77]. The Dutch aviation pioneer greatly impressed the attaché, who urged that measures be taken to keep a close eye on his work and his machines. Sadly, for Britain, this advice did not lead anywhere. Another area that Russell watched closely was the country's railway network, a key infrastructure component for mobilization and deployment [92, 106]. He reported developments both in the west of Germany [79] and in the east [88]. Like his predecessor, he also reported on motor vehicles [100].

As with his predecessor, Russell was not a blind admirer of the German Army. For all its qualities, he could see weakness. One of these was its sense of superiority over all others [66], a form of hubris that would prove its undoing on more than one occasion in the twentieth century. More significant, however, were some of its battlefield assumptions. If Trench had pointed to deficiencies in artillery, Russell, a Guards officer and a veteran of the war in South Africa, a conflict where concentration of fire played a major role, noted that the Germans seemed blithely unconcerned about the effects of modern firepower on the battlefield [69] and uncertain about the necessity and the means of obtaining fire superiority [54]. In comparison to the many strengths that he identified, it was, perhaps, a minor criticism, but it was a salient one.

Collective Overview

Taking the reports of Trench and Russell together, it is clear that a steady stream of information came from the British embassy in Berlin to London in the years before 1914. Some of this information concerned intelligence on technical matters and much of this was broadly accurate. However, the bulk of the material was an assessment of German ambitions and capabilities. Despite Russell's initial belief that Germany did not harbour any belligerent intentions, both ultimately agreed that Germany was a power with significant political ambitions and an aggressive agenda. In Trench's case, this was his view from the outset, one which even his close personal relations with the Kaiser could not stem. The main driver for Germany's hostile intent was the deep and widespread popular animus amongst Germans towards Britain, a country that was hated by the public and the officer caste alike for its dominant global position and the sense that it alone was blocking Germany's path to greatness. A direct assault on Britain was, thus, what Trench believed was in the minds of Germany's leaders. In his view, they possessed armed forces well equipped both intellectually and materially to achieve this. Initially, at least, Russell thought otherwise. While he later came to share aspects of Trench's analysis, the underlying thinking was different. Russell's opinion was that so long as Germany felt secure it would remain a peaceful nation. The problem was that in late 1911 the necessary confidence began to ebb away. A series of setbacks, starting with the disastrous outcome of the Second Moroccan Crisis, eroded the nation's self-belief and replaced it with a new insecurity. The German solution to this unexpected and previously unknown sentiment was to rearm with a view to regaining their security, if necessary by military means. Germany's highly capable armed forces – which would only get more capable as the fruits of rearmament bloomed – endowed Germany with the ability to make good on this idea. Hence Russell viewed with anxiety the increasing signs that Germany was getting ready for war. While he did not necessarily predict the inevitability of conflict, he was cognizant that its probability had increased and he said as much in his reports. If he did not share Trench's conviction that Anglophobia lay at the heart of the situation, he did grow to believe that Anglophobia was present and that a war party existed that would seek to use this to their own ends. Hence, in Russell's reports, as with Trench's, the road to war can clearly be seen. In this light, the British Army's preparations from the First Moroccan Crisis to the July Crisis make perfect sense.

Reception and Influence of the Attaché Reports

Of course, this raises the question of exactly how these reports were received upon reaching London. Their reception in those departments that routinely retained the reports along with the dockets in which the notes and minutes on them were written is relatively easy to gauge. For example, we know that the officials in the Foreign Office, who saw all of the despatches from the military attachés from Berlin, set great store upon them. A sample of the minutes penned in response to Colonel Trench's many expositions on the German threat illustrates this clearly.

One topic that frequently formed the subject of Trench's despatches was the idea that the German public was being mentally prepared for war. The response to such reports shows that the Foreign Office was clearly listening. When, for example, Trench sent in a despatch explaining that the German Navy League (*Flottenverein*) was mobilizing German public opinion for war against Britain [24], this news was greeted with absolute concurrence. 'There can be no doubt,' wrote one official, 'as to the great power wielded by the *Flotten Verein*. … From all its utterances it is fairly obvious that the driving motive of the *Flottenverein* is hostility to this country, & that it is ever working to educate German public opinion in that direction.'[16] In similar fashion, a subsequent report arguing that 'as far as mental preparation for war goes, this country is mobilized,

---

16   Minute on Trench MA 77, 20 December 1907. TNA: FO 371/260, f. 201.

so that, should it be determined to appeal to arms at any time before a relaxation of the tension takes place, all that will be necessary will be to give the word to start' [32] was also met with concurrence. 'Anyone who has been to Germany lately,' wrote Eyre Crowe, '… must agree that the feelings which Colonel Trench describes prevail throughout Germany.'[17] Significantly, the officials in the Foreign Office were not alone in this view. The despatch was considered important enough for them to forward it to other departments and individuals and, in this instance, we have documentary evidence about how its message was received. The Admiralty, for example, took careful note of what Trench was saying. The Director of Naval Intelligence, Edmond Slade, recorded that the situation Trench described was 'most serious and any hope of a diminution of will to maintain our superiority would only encourage Germany to take some step which both powers would ultimately bitterly regret'.[18] Another recipient was the Prime Minister, Herbert Henry Asquith, who was personally sent a copy by the Foreign Secretary, Sir Edward Grey. Asquith took some comfort from Britain's naval supremacy, which in his view provided a cushion against any German action in the immediate future. 'German opinion may be "mobilised",' he replied, 'but they know quite well that, so far as we are the objective, they cannot for a long time to come get within striking distance.' Nevertheless, he did not dispute Trench's underlying analysis. On the contrary, he accepted that the levels of hostility to Britain that were being forged in Germany did not bode well. As he went on, 'these reports do not encourage me to be sanguine as to an approaching *détente*.'[19]

If reports about Anglophobia and Germany's mental preparations for war were circulated and approved, Foreign Office officials greeted the attaché's many despatches about the German plans to invade Britain with similar broad concurrence. Thus, the suggestion that German officers regularly undertook 'reconnaissance' trips to Britain to prepare for a future invasion [23] was readily endorsed. 'There is evidently a good deal of work going on which can only be in preparation for a possible invasion', noted Walter Langley, one of the senior clerks, who went on to observe that 'the German General Staff at any rate do not exclude the possibility of an invasion taking place some day'.[20] An equally favourable minute was

---

17 Minute by Crowe on Trench, MA 107, 17 August 1908. TNA: FO 371/461, f. 463.
18 Minute by Slade, 9 September 1908. Quoted in Arthur J. Marder, *From the Dreadnought to Scapa Flow*. 5 vols (Oxford, 1961–70), I, p. 149.
19 Asquith to Grey, 28 August 1908. TNA: FO 800/100.
20 Minute by Langley on Trench MA 76, 15 December 1907. TNA: FO 371/263, f. 528.

penned on Trench's suggestion that public enthusiasm in Germany for airships had much to do with the general hatred of Britain and the belief that these new craft could be used to circumvent British naval supremacy and thereby facilitate an invasion by aerial rather than maritime means [38]. 'It has long been known here how violently Anglophobe Germany really is,' asserted G. H. Villiers, 'but there are still people in England who refuse to believe it. It is a pity that this despatch as it stands cannot be printed in big type in every newspaper in the British Empire.'[21] Concurrence was also shown towards Trench's assertion that German secrecy measures at manoeuvres were designed to hide the gathering of an invasion force [47]:

> As the Germans must be quite confident that their country is unassailable, and know that no country can possibly think of invading Germany, it is obvious that these precautions are being taken to enable them when the right moment arrives to launch their attack without indications of their intent being given.[22]

The unequivocally favourable response to Trench's numerous assertions that the German army was preparing to invade Britain was all the more remarkable given that the view was strongly disputed by the British Ambassador in Berlin, Sir Frank Lascelles. In April 1908 Trench produced a despatch entitled 'Should Warning Precede Hostilities?' which forcibly argued that Germany would attack Britain without prior declaration should the occasion arise [29]. In forwarding the report Sir Frank made no secret of his disagreement. 'Colonel Trench's views,' he wrote in a highly critical, not to say scathing covering letter, 'appear to me to be of a most unduly alarmist nature, which I am unable to endorse.'[23] Despite the clarity of his dissent, it was the attaché's rather than the ambassador's view that prevailed at the Foreign Office. Eyre Crowe, another senior clerk and a well-respected expert on Germany, was blunt:

> Colonel Trench expresses the view that if and when Germany considers her naval power equal to the occasion of defeating the British navy, whether by superior force or by concentrated attack on dispersed units, then Germany is likely to act by a surprise attack.

---

21 Minute by Villiers on Trench MA 119, 14 December 1908. TNA: FO 371/463, f. 555.

22 Minute by Spicer on Trench MA 25/09, 24 June 1909. TNA: FO 371/674, f. 416.

23 Lascelles to Grey, 1 May 1908, enclosing Trench MA 95, 27 April 1908.

Sir F[rank] Lascelles does not apparently share this view, but it is probably quite correct nevertheless.[24]

Was this view shared by the Army hierarchy? The total destruction of the original War Office files in which these documents were once contained has robbed us of the most obvious means of gauging the reaction of the General Staff to the information contained therein. For, with the pulping of these folders, the minute sheets containing the written response of the military hierarchy were destroyed for good as well; and unlike the reports themselves, these were not documents that were copied and distributed to other departments. They were literally irreplaceable. Thus, assessing how the army's top leadership regarded the information from its representatives in Berlin is highly problematic and, insofar as it can be done, it must necessarily be reconstructed by more tangential means.

On the face of it, one would have expected Trench's views on the likelihood of a German invasion – one of the most persistent themes of his reports – to have been extremely unwelcome to the General Staff. After all, at precisely the time when Trench was penning his various reports arguing that Germany was preparing to launch an unprovoked surprise attack on the British Isles should a suitable moment arrive, the War Office was resolutely maintaining before a special sub-committee of the Committee of Imperial Defence – the so-called Second Invasion Inquiry – that such an assault was out of the question. The Royal Navy's maritime supremacy, they confirmed, meant that it would be quite impossible for a full-scale invasion to be launched without warning and to succeed in reaching the British mainland, let alone disembarking a large army. A raid with fewer than 70,000 soldiers, although a difficult and hazardous undertaking, might just be feasible, but it could be contained by the armed forces protecting the country and stood no chance of achieving any meaningful results. Given this position, it is hardly to be wondered that in substantiating their views, the War Office submitted none of Trench's despatches as corroborating evidence. The contrast with the Admiralty, which buttressed its case partly by circulating reports that had been submitted to them by the British naval attaché in Berlin, Trench's colleague, Captain Philip Wylie Dumas, was extremely marked.[25]

---

24 Minute by Crowe, 4 May 1908. TNA: FO 371/459.

25 A copy of Dumas's report NA 7/08, 3 February 1908, in which the attaché reported that Tirpitz regarded a seaborne invasion of Britain by Germany as quite impossible, was submitted by the Admiralty to the Inquiry and is printed in the appendices to the Proceedings. TNA: CAB 16/3B, ff. 114–15.

So does the fact that Trench's writings were excluded from the 1907–8 invasion inquiry demonstrate that his views were not subject to the concurrence of the War Office? The answer is probably not. The reason for this is that the Army's unequivocal *public* position that an invasion was impossible did not accord with the *private* views of many of its leaders. One notable example was Colonel Gleichen, Trench's predecessor in Berlin. As head of the European Section of the Military Operations Directorate of the General Staff, he frequently put the Army's case that invasion was impossible to the Committee of Imperial Defence and also defended it robustly in questioning; yet privately he never doubted that an invasion was possible and that the German army was busily planning one. As he explained in a chapter that he wrote for the 1906 edition of the key (but internal) War Office publication *The Military Resources of the German Empire*:

> With all due deference to the 'Blue Water School', … an occasion might arise, perhaps before a declaration of war … when the British Fleet might be decoyed away, or split up owing to temporary necessities. In which case it is within the bounds of possibility that the German fleet might defeat ours … and, by masking its own object, elude it for sufficient time to carry out is plans of invasion.[26]

How is this discrepancy to be explained? The answer is politics. By the time of the invasion inquiry the British Army had undergone a major process of reform and restructuring. One consequence of this was that the bulk of the professional army had been consolidated into an expeditionary force capable of being deployed on the continent and fighting alongside a major land power. Concomitant with this development and intimately linked to it was the emergence of an expeditionary force strategy at the War Office: in the event of a continental conflict the General Staff wanted to send Britain's professional army to fight alongside our putative allies. As nothing was more likely to stand in the way of this desire than the need to keep major forces at home to block a hostile landing, the army leadership steadfastly supported the Navy's position that an invasion was not feasible and that only a raid on a scale which could be dealt with by territorial forces needed to be considered. Accordingly, this was what they told the invasion inquiry. But it was not what they said to each other either in 1907 or thereafter.

---

26   No copies of this publication are known to have survived. The quote comes from Gleichen's draft. See Gleichen, MA 34/05, 9 November 1905. TNA: CAB 17/61, f. 46.

A particularly strong indication of the British General Staff's real opinion, because it is expressed in a top secret War Office publication with limited circulation, is the view advanced in February 1912 in the volume *Special Military Resources of the German Empire*. Issued to a highly select readership, it advanced a quite different perspective to the one that the Army had put to the second invasion inquiry. To begin with, it assumed that, in a war with Britain, it would undoubtedly be the German goal, given their army's long tradition of going immediately on the offensive, to launch an immediate invasion. After all, 'only by invasion could Germany assume the offensive – a role entirely in consonance with her military tradition and policy'.[27] But was this desire, however rooted it may have been in Germany's known military culture, actually possible? While this was obviously a matter that could be debated, the book argued in no uncertain terms that it was considered a viable option by the Germans themselves. The invasion of Britain, it proclaimed, 'has for long received the attention of German experts, and ... it is not deemed by them to be nearly as impracticable as some English experts are apt to think'.[28] The reasons for their holding this view were many, but began with the belief that the obstacles to such an operation, while certainly not inconsiderable, could be surmounted by careful prior planning. As the text stated:

[While it was true that] over-sea invasions are very difficult enterprises ...; that the adversary is bound to receive warning...; and that, even if the sea were crossed in safety, a force invading Great Britain might eventually find its communications severed ... [such difficulties can] be largely overcome by careful forethought.[29]

Thinking through difficult military problems – that is, staff work – was, of course, an area in which the German army had an unparalleled reputation for excellence. The appraisal, thus, went on to observe that, in order to overcome the problems of an invasion, 'the highly efficient German General Staff may be relied upon to do everything possible', further adding:

The thoroughness and calculation with which both their military and naval staff, leaving nothing to chance, provide for every contingency, render it certain that, when the time comes, their plans will be well thought out and matured. ... What the German plans

27   General Staff, *Special Military Resources of the German Empire* (1912), p. 53. TNA: WO 33/579.
28   Ibid., p. 51
29   Ibid., p. 40.

will be it is, of course, impossible to forecast with exactitude; but it may be taken for granted that there will be several alternative ones, each dealing with broad issues and each worked out in comparative details.[30]

Although the above paragraph eschewed prophesies regarding the exact form of German plans, the volume did, in fact, make one clear prediction: their likely approach would be to attack suddenly and without warning. To the objection that such an act would incur international odium the reply was that this would certainly be no barrier. 'Sentiment,' the book proclaimed, 'has no place in Germany's *Welt-Politik* [*sic*].' The only consideration would be whether or not there was any likelihood of success. On this score, the manual noted that, however improbable this might appear, it could not be ruled out that 'a favourable opportunity might be seized by Germany ... to attack our fleets in home waters when temporarily separated for some purpose and so to attain a sufficient measure of superiority to justify her in attempting an invasion'.[31] Furthermore, there were important factors working in Germany's favour. It was assumed, for example, that any German invasion would be facilitated by a pre-prepared campaign of sabotage in Britain designed to support the operation. 'There is little doubt,' ran the argument, 'that a certain amount of hostile organisation already exists in our eastern and southern counties, and that preparations will have been made, if an invasion is seriously intended, to render the task of the invading forces easier by destroying bridges and communications in the interior.'[32] Finally, it was noted that, even if the invasion failed, 'the military strength of the German Empire would not be seriously diminished'.[33] In short, the losses that might result from failure were so low that they did not outweigh the tangible results of success – knocking Britain out of the war. Thus, for the Germans, it was a risk well worth taking.

All of these assumptions led to some simple conclusions: first, 'invasion has been considered by their General Staff'; second, 'preliminary measures have actually been taken by them, in England as well as Germany to carry out that invasion'; third, 'having regard to the perfect organization of the General Staff in Germany, and to its established practice of framing plans of campaign for all possible contingencies,

---

30   Ibid., pp. 40–1.
31   Ibid., p. 42.
32   Ibid., pp. 50–1.
33   Ibid., p. 41.

... if invasion be attempted at all, the attempt will ... be made in the very earliest stages of the war.[34] All of these conclusions, along with the logic behind them, would have been ones that Trench would have been very happy to endorse. Indeed, they were deductions about Germany's likely behaviour that had all featured many times in the reports he had written from Berlin. Thus, there seems every ground for believing, given the extent of the apparent commonality of their views, that the General Staff would have found his despatches entirely to their way of thinking. Whether Trench's reports about invasion merely demonstrate that there was a shared strategic outlook between the British General Staff and their man in Berlin – in which case Trench's reports would have reinforced views already held in the War Office – or show Trench actually leading the formation of opinion is impossible to determine in the absence of the original dockets in which his reports were contained. In favour of the later analysis, it should be said that Trench's reports predate the 1912 volume *Special Military Resources of the German Empire*, a volume which shows a remarkable degree of consistency with his known views. We also know that Trench provided the information on Germany for other printed War Office manuals from this period.[35] However, without specific documentary evidence covering this particular report, that is no proof of cause and effect.

There is, however, one link between the War Office view on invasion and Colonel Trench that it is possible to establish with documentary evidence. In 1909 Captain (later Colonel Sir) Vernon Kell was appointed as the Army's representative in the new Secret Service Bureau, working alongside Captain Mansfield Smith Cumming of the Royal Navy. This tandem structure quickly proved unwieldy and it was soon decided that Cumming would attend to the external gathering of intelligence information on foreign countries, while Kell would address the domestic aspects of the secret service problem. Traditionally, this has been understood to mean that Kell's organization, the forerunner of MI5, would be a counter-espionage body tracking down and apprehending the German spies operating in Britain.[36] Such counter-intelligence work did, of course, take place; however, as Nicholas Hiley has conclusively demonstrated, performing this function was not what Kell regarded

34 Ibid., p. 53.
35 In June 1908 the Foreign Office requested the authority for certain statements in the War Office *Report on German South-West Africa*. The reply, dated 1 July 1908, was 'our authority is Col. Trench'. TNA: FO 367/80.
36 For a recent iteration of this perspective see Christopher Andrew, *The Defence of the Realm: The Authorized History of MI5* (London, 2009).

22

as his main role.[37] The reason for this was Kell's analysis of the threat that Britain faced. Overall, he was less concerned by the dangers of German espionage than he was by the prospect of a successful German invasion – a potentially far more devastating blow for which the ultimate backstop was necessarily the army. What made him especially worried and also necessitated the active participation of his organization was his assessment of the form such an invasion would take. It was his belief that the German General Staff had placed an undercover army of reservists in Britain who would emerge from their civilian cover in the event of an Anglo-German conflict and commit acts of sabotage designed to disrupt the defence of the British Isles and so support the invasion that he was convinced that the German armed forces were planning, possibly in the form of an early or surprise attack.

From where did Kell acquire these views on the prospects and form of a German invasion? As with the War Office view detailed above, to say that they closely resemble Trench's ideas is not, of itself, proof of direct transmission. Moreover, it is always possible and, indeed, it has been suggested, that Kell was merely reflecting the popular prejudices of the time as reflected in contemporary invasion literature and the xenophobic commentaries of the gutter press.[38] However, for Kell, who employed a German governess to bring up his children, deep-rooted hostility to Germany does not appear to have been the determining issue.[39] Some other explanation is, therefore, required and intelligence from the military attaché in Berlin could be the answer. The reason for this is that we do know that at the outset of his stewardship of the fledgling secret service, Kell sought and received information from Trench.[40] In addition, at least one of the early surviving Secret Service Bureau files does contain copies of reports by Trench from Berlin.[41] There may have been more in MI5 files that are now missing, having been weeded many decades ago, but even if that were not the case, Kell, a former officer of the Military Operations Directorate – he served first in the European and then

---

37 Nicholas Hiley, 'Entering the Lists: MI5's Great Spy Round-up of August 1914', *Intelligence and National Security* 21 (2006), 46–76; idem, 'Re-entering the Lists: MI5's Authorized History and the August 1914 Arrests', *Intelligence and National Security* 25 (2010), 415–52. This analysis is also found in Thomas Boghardt, *Spies of the Kaiser: German Covert Operations in Great Britain during the First World War Era* (Basingstoke, 2004), p. 40.

38 Boghardt, *Spies of the Kaiser*, p. 38.

39 Andrew, *The Defence of the Realm*, p. 23.

40 See Kell's office diary for 29 August 1910. TNA: KV 1/10.

41 The reports in question are MA 120 of 15 December 1908 [document 39 in this volume], MA 23/09 of 24 June 1909, and MA 44/09 of 15 December 1909 [52]. The file is entitled 'Counter-Espionage Laws in Foreign Countries', although the reports are of a much broader nature than this title suggests, and can be found in TNA: KV 3/1.

FarEastern sections – would have had access to the original reports at the War Office. At the very least, therefore, Trench would have reinforced views that Kell already held; more probably, he helped to crystallize them in the first place.

As the example of Trench's reports clearly demonstrates, assessing the extent of the influence of the military attachés on the army hierarchy in respect of major policy questions is extremely difficult. The fact that the army publicly denied the possibility of invasion and made no use of Trench's reports at the Committee of Imperial Defence is belied by the fact that they privately shared his views and Vernon Kell, once installed as the chief of the domestic branch of the Secret Service Bureau, decisively acted upon them, either directly as a result of his contacts with Trench or indirectly through shared assumptions. Either way, it is clear that the reports from Berlin were not ignored. Their role in shaping and reinforcing perceptions of German hostile intent across various branches of the British government in the run-up to the First World War is, thus, evident.

Lieutenant Colonel Frederic Trench, pictured in 1904. From Lord Edward Gleichen, *A Guardsman's Memories* (London, 1932).

Part I

Lieutenant Colonel F. J. A. Trench

Despatches, 1906–1910

1906

I

An Interview with the German Emperor during an Inspection of Troops at Potsdam (Trench MA 1, 2 April 1906)

I have the honour to report that on Saturday last, the 31st March, in accordance with instructions from the Chief of the Military Cabinet,[1] I reported myself, on joining, to His Majesty the Emperor during the inspection, at Potsdam, of four companies of the 1st 'Garde Regiment zu Fuss'.

His Majesty, welcoming me, said he was glad to have a proper ('ordentlichen') Military Attaché, pointed out the desirability of having a safety valve ('scupape') and one that got on with people, and also indicated some errors to be avoided – doubtless for my guidance.[2]

He then said: 'What has come over your people? I cannot understand it at all! You make much of the Japanese in the streets, and go mad about them, and the women want to kiss them. It's not like the English – it's like the French. But you're making a great mistake and you will pay for it later: the Japanese are not doing it for *vos beaux yeux*. And then we are vilified in the press! I can't make it out! Something serious ought to be done to the journalists!'

His Majesty told me the last news received about the suppression of the revolt in German South West Africa[3] … 'A lot of Morenga's people

---

1   Dietrich Graf von Hülsen-Haeseler (1852–1908). Chief of the German Military Cabinet, 1901–8. The Military Cabinet was the branch of the army administration that advised the Kaiser on personnel and appointments and acted as a form of liaison between the Kaiser and the army.

2   This was a none-too-subtle swipe at Trench's predecessor, Lord Edward Gleichen (1863–1937), who had fallen out with the Kaiser and had had to be reassigned.

3   Starting in 1904 a number of indigenous peoples, most notably the Herero and Nama, took up arms against German colonial rule in South-West Africa (modern day Namibia). The resultant war lasted until 1907.

have fled over your border and are being dealt with by the Cape Police.' I assured him that they would certainly all be disarmed and ... 'Yes, but when you get Morenga you will probably give him a good staff appointment,' he cut in; and then asked about my own welfare, and a good deal about the doings and conduct of the troops during the operations.[4]

I conveyed to His Majesty General Grierson's[5] respectful duty: 'How is he? What's he doing? I suppose he's preparing a plan to invade us! Well tell him that I'm preparing a plan to beat him, and if he comes we'll throw him back into the sea', said the Emperor.

During the march past of the three regiments His Majesty again called me to his side and commented on, and gave me information about the various units as they passed. He spoke highly of the way Prince Albert of Schleswig-Holstein[6] – who was passing – carried out his duties, and said he was going to give him a year's leave to travel in Australia, &c.: 'I don't know what he's going to do – perhaps get a rich wife!'

The inspection of the four companies was most detailed and thorough – even to men marching past in file. The drill of the units, especially that of the 'Leib' Company, was very fine. The garrison marched past afterwards, and the 'Gardes du Corps' and 'Leib Garde' Hussars executed some movements on foot. Their Majesties left early in the afternoon for Wernigerode.

I have never seen the Emperor looking so ill, even at this time of year. His face was quite gray and puffy under the eyes which had little sparkle. I did not see him laugh at all during the two and a half hours which the parade lasted, although he became a little brighter at lunch. His mood could hardly have been due to the weather as the day was bright, tho' cold.

FO 371/77, f. 357

---

4   Jakob Morenga (c. 1875–1907). Also known as 'the Black Napoleon' on account of his considerable tactical acumen, Morenga was one of the leaders of the indigenous peoples opposing German colonial rule in South-West Africa. In May 1906 Morenga fled to British South Africa. Although at first imprisoned by the British authorities, he was released on parole, the condition being that he would refrain from re-entering German South-West Africa. Despite this he led a number of cross-border raids, as a result of which he was hunted down and killed by a combined British and German force.

5   Major General Sir James Moncrieff Grierson (1859–1914), Director of Military Operations, February 1904–August 1906. He had been Military Attaché in Berlin, 1896–1900.

6   Albert of Schleswig-Holstein (1869–1931), grandson of Queen Victoria and senior member of the House of Oldenburg. Ironically, given the Kaiser's comment, he never married.

2

Spring Parade at Potsdam
(Trench, MA 3, 1 June 1906)

I have the honour to report that at the Spring Parade of the Potsdam garrison on the 30th May His Majesty the Emperor was looking much better than at the parade held of the same troops two months previously: there was more colour in his face, more light in his eyes, more vivacity in his gestures. The weather was threatening and chilly for the time of year. This seems worth noting in conjunction with His Majesty's appearance and *état d'âme* and Dr Ilberg,[7] the Emperor's personal physician, to-day confirmed the view that many people carry away quite erroneous impressions of His Majesty's health because they leave the weather out of account.

The Emperor held a short *critique* after the parade, and on his way to the Schloss [palace] called me to him, halted his horse, shook hands with me, and said: 'Well, Trench, how did you like the parade? You've seen our people can fight, and now you've seen how they can turn out.'[8] He then kindly discussed several points about the march past, especially the condition of the horses, before riding on to lunch. I do not think he spoke to any of the other Attachés, except, of course, General von Tatischeff, who is attached to his person.[9]

After luncheon, to which all the Military Attachés were invited, I was presented to Her Majesty, who spoke to me for some time about South-West Africa, expressed much distress at the losses suffered last week by the troops operating against Morris, but said she was ready to let her 'own boys' go out if it was necessary, and did it not interfere with their responsibilities at home. I understood that one or two of the Princes had at one time suggested going.

The Emperor spoke a few words to Colonel von Michelson,[10] the Russian Attaché, had a chat with Major Klepsch Kloth von Roden,[11] the Austrian Attaché, and then came across to shake hands with me again and asked,

---

7   Dr Friedrich von Ilberg: he served as one of the court physicians.

8   This is a reference to Trench's service as British Military Attaché with the German forces in South-West Africa during the so-called Herero rebellion. Ironically, Trench had frequently been quite critical of the performance of the German Army when it came to colonial warfare.

9   General Ilya Leonidovich Tatishchev, Russian Military Plenipotentiary in Berlin in personal attendance on the German Kaiser.

10   Colonel Mikhelson, Russian Military Attaché in Berlin, 1906–11.

11   Alois Freiherr Klepsch-Kloth von Roden, Austro-Hungarian Military Attaché to Berlin 1902–8.

'Trench, what's the serial number of the Army Scheme you're busy with in England now? How can you have any organization,' he added, 'while the army is managed by civilians? Look at the state they are in in France! Saturated with *delation*! The Left reports the Right because they go to church, and the Right reports the Left because they don't go! And those are your allies! You make a difficult position. I send my greetings to my regiment on the anniversary of Waterloo, but with your *entente cordiale* I'm sure they are in a fix and don't know what to do.' The Emperor repeated to me a conversation I understood he had had with His Royal Highness the Duke of Connaught:[12] 'He tells me that Haldane[13] knows German well, and has studied the German army; but what good is that? One must see for one's self; he only knows what he reads and what he is told. I believe our army has a reputation for being well organized; he should write to his colleague here that he's coming over, and come and see the army for himself. We would be very glad to see him. Those were our new guns on parade to-day; I saw your French colleague eyeing them. You saw them?' On my answering that I had noticed they were there, but was hoping for an invitation to Jüterbog (the School of Gunnery), where I'd not been for twenty years, the Emperor said; 'Well, I shan't invite you – I shan't invite you,' but laughed so cheerily, I think he only half meant it.

The Emperor seemed very gratified to learn that His Majesty the King had inquired much after him, and had expressed pleasure at the visit of the Ober Bürgermeister and the welcome they had received. He added, 'I wonder what they thought of their appearance – your Lord Mayor is always so grand!' ... and then discussed the personality, looks, and nicknames of several of the German representatives.

Referring to the Red Eagle with Swords[14] which he had given me for the war in South-West Africa, the Emperor was gracious enough to say: 'You quite deserved it. You know, you are the only English officer living who has been attached to German head-quarters in war, except General Walker, who was with my father in 1870.'[15] General von Einem[16] then asked if the Emperor could spare time to sign some papers, but His Majesty expressed mistrust, and laughingly exacted an assurance that the signatures should not exceed five.

---

12 Prince Arthur, Duke of Connaught and Strathearn (1850–1942), third son of Queen Victoria.

13 Richard Burdon Haldane (1856–1928), Secretary of State for War, 1905–12.

14 The Order of the Red Eagle: Prussian order of chivalry, second only in precedence to the Order of the Black Eagle. The swords indicated that it had been awarded for service during wartime.

15 Sir Charles Beauchamp Walker, then a colonel, served as Britain's military observer attached to the Prussian forces during the Franco-Prussian War.

16 General Karl von Einem (1853–1934), Prussian Minister of War, 1903–9.

His Majesty seemed in excellent spirits, but among his *entourage* a good deal of disgust was expressed at the refusal of the Reichstag to vote the money for the Kubub–Keetmanshoop Railway in South-West Africa, and some heads were shaken over Colonel von Deimling's speech.[17] (This latter was present, however, at the banquet next day.)

The Emperor did not speak, as far as I could see, to any of the Attachés save the three noted. I have allowed myself to note the marked graciousness of his manner to me because I am convinced that it has nothing personal in it, and is entirely the expression of a desire to 'bury all unkindness' between the two nations.

At the Spring Parade of the Guards Corps on the Tempelhofer Feld yesterday His Majesty looked equally well, but appeared in sterner mood. The parade differed from the normal only in that the troops went past once only (in mass and at a trot), and that the 1st Dragoon Guards Regiment was absent owing, according to rumour, to the horses having some eye malady.

At the usual banquet to the Guards Corps in the Schloss an unfortunate mistake was made in the omission from the guests invited of the courteous and kindly French Naval Attaché, Admiral de Jonquières.[18]
FO 371/78, f. 111

3

Affairs in German South West Africa
(Trench MA 7, 3 July 1906)

[...]

According to a recent report from Governor von Lindequist,[19] from which the following notes are extracted, some satisfactory progress seems to be taking place in Damaraland.[20]

The Hereroes are still surrendering and coming in, although hostile bodies have attacked patrols.[21] The governor notes that some Hereroes are

---

17 Berthold von Deimling (1853–1944), German officer, who served as a regimental commander in South-West Africa 1904–7. He achieved notoriety for his belligerent and aggressive behaviour before the First World War, including his insensitive and inflammatory behaviour as a corps commander in Alsace, but became a committed pacifist once the conflict ended.

18 Marie-Pierre-Eugène de Fauque de Jonquières (1850–1919), French Naval Attaché in Berlin, 1906–8.

19 Friedrich von Lindequist (1862–1945), Governor of German South-West Africa, 1905–7.

20 Damaraland, a name given to the northern part of South-West Africa.

21 Herero: a pastoral people indigenous to South-West Africa. They were the first to take up arms against German colonial rule in 1904.

willing to fight against others, and he has sent out patrols composed of prisoners of war against the cattle thieves in the Onjati Mountains. The majority of the Hereroes that have come in have been so famished and emaciated that they could not be set to work for some time. The children all had bad coughs. The numbers that have surrendered in Omburo and Otjihaenana are 6,000 in round numbers.

The Hereroes have proved to be good workers. 'As great stress is laid on the war prisoners being justly treated and sufficiently clothed and fed it is not surprising that they prefer confinement to their previous life in the wilds.' Prisoners have only made their escape in isolated cases. After six months imprisonment the Hereroes receive a month's pay in cash – or earlier if they distinguish themselves by their industry and good behaviour. The Hottentots are also turning out better workers than expected.[22] The Witbois[23] are confined in Windhuk, and large numbers are employed there constructing roads and water channels.
[…]

With regard to the above report it is perhaps worth while noting that early in the year at Windhuk 'justly' meant 'without cruelty', 'sufficient clothing' meant a sack with three holes and that the month's pay was to be [3 Marks] or what a free Ovambo earned in a day in addition to his subsistence. It will also be remembered that the tribes referred to have mostly come in in accordance with proclamations – and are not prisoners of war in the strictest sense.
[…]

CO 417/430

4

South-west Africa
(Trench MA 9, 18 July 1906)

I have the honour to submit the following supplementary Report on the Operations in German South-west Africa.

---

22 Hottentots: a European term for the Khoikhoi people.

23 Witboi: presumably a reference to followers of Hendrik Witbooi (died 1905), one of the most important leaders of the Namaqua people, who joined the campaign against German oppression in October 1904. He died in battle in October 1905.

Sanitation, Hygiene and Medical Services

General

A high standard was to be expected owing to the strict discipline of the troops, the large proportion of medical officers – ten per thousand bayonets – and the fact that the force was furnished by one of the most scientific and painstaking of civilized nations.

The results were, nevertheless, far inferior to those obtained in the Zulu or Boer wars, and the reason is not far to seek. British troops serve a large part of their time in tropical and sub-tropical countries where the habits of the natives and the pollution of the rivers necessitate sanitation forming an important portion of the peace training of the soldier.

The German army – on the contrary – has, with the exception of a single expedition to China,[24] had no training, either in peace or war, outside temperate civilized countries, where an elaborate civil organization regulates the sanitation of the district, where, whether in barracks or in billets, the sanitation of the army proceeds automatically, and where special measures for the troops have to be evolved only on the rare occasions when they bivouac.

[…]

WO 106/269, f. 677

5

The Present International Conference on Wireless Telegraphy
(Trench MA 19, 7 October 1906)

I have the honour to draw the attention of Your Excellency to the frank admission of the *Berliner Tageblatt*,[25] a liberal journal with a wide circulation and not unfriendly to England, in its weekly Political Leader, in today's issue, that the convocation of the Wireless Telegraphy Conference now assembled in Berlin on the invitation of Germany,

---

24 Presumably a reference to the expedition led by Alfred von Waldersee in 1900 to suppress the Boxer Rebellion.

25 The *Berliner Tageblatt* was probably the most influential liberal newspaper. Throughout this period it was edited by Theodor Wolff and was frequently critical of the more extreme aspects of government policy.

is a step taken in conjunction with the intention to dispute England's command of the sea.[26]

The indiscretion of this early admission is perhaps explained by the report given further on in the same journal to the effect that, yesterday as on previous days, progress has been made, and the belief 'that the conference will lead to positive results'.

The following is a translation of the passage, which I also attach in the original:–

'A subject of still wider international interest is formed by the International Conference for Wireless Telegraphy which has also assembled in Berlin during the past week. Here, too, it is a question of adjusting antitheses, for, new as is the invention of wireless telegraphy, it has, nevertheless, already given rise to serious differences which must be set down chiefly to the monopoly held by the Marconi Company.[27]

'The invention, in itself so rich in blessing, thus threatens to become an apple of discord, separating the nations instead of uniting them. The difficulty of coming to an understanding with regard to the international control of wireless telegraphy lies clearly in the fact that England and the states which are well disposed to her recognise in it another means of maintaining the command of the sea. Precisely for this reason, however, the other naval powers have every reason to insist upon brushing aside the Marconi monopoly.

'We must patiently wait to see how far this will be achieved in the present conference, but it is quite obvious that, in the long run, a monopolisation by England of the realm of the air would be unbearable.'

FO 368/80

6

Supplementary Estimates
(Trench MA 22, 21 November 1906)

I have the honour to report that, since the reassembling of the Reichstag, a Supplementary Estimate of Imperial Expenditure for the Financial Year 1906 has been presented to it.

---

26 The conference ultimately led to the signing of the International Wireless Telegraphy Convention.

27 Marconi's Wireless Telegraphy Company, the business founded by the radio pioneer Guglielmo Marconi to exploit his patented inventions that made radio transmission and reception practical.

The Estimate is for £1,461,000 in connection with the native rebellion in the South-West African Protectorate, and will probably be discussed very shortly, in connection with a renewed demand for funds for the construction of the Kubub–Keetmanshoop railway and for compensation for farmers. [...]

I have had, during November, conversations with both the present and past Governors of South-West Africa, the officer who succeeded Gen. v. Trotha[28] in command of the troops and a number of junior officers recently home from the protectorate and old acquaintances of mine, and a summary of the information gained may be of interest, although, for obvious reasons, it does not seem desirable to give the authorities for each item.

[...]

There seems little likelihood that the Bondelzwarts[29] will surrender at discretion, though they would most probably do so if they could be sure of being given their cattle, enough land to pasture it on, and their personal liberty. This last point, however, is the great difficulty as they were not prepared to trust the Germans. The Witbois were promised their freedom when they surrendered, and (as I reported at the time from Windhuk) this was explained to the Home Authorities as meaning only freedom to build their shelters as they liked, but not where they liked – still less to dispose as they liked of their time and persons. From the south they were moved to Windhuk, etc, and after six months, – several of them having run away – they were moved to Shark Island at Lüderitz Bay.[30] I have already – from Lüderitz Bay – reported on the exposure and lack of sanitation obtaining there; if they still exist, it is not easy to avoid the impression that the extinction of the tribe would be welcomed by the authorities. The hardness of their fate (anglice, harshness of their treatment) excited even the sympathy of two officers who had known them, and who reminded me that they had never murdered or ill-treated civilians or prisoners, but had waged war without cruelty, and proved useful allies against the Hereroes. The case of the hundred men disarmed and exiled in Togoland, where nearly all soon died, will be remembered

28 Lothar von Trotha (1848–1920), Commander of German forces in South-West Africa, June 1904–November 1905. He has achieved notoriety for issuing the now infamous 'extermination order' against the Herero people, thereby heralding the twentieth century's first genocide.

29 Bondelzwarts: a Nama-speaking community that lived north of the Orange River. Many fled to British South Africa following their defeat by the Germans.

30 Shark Island was the most notorious of the concentration camps set up in South-West Africa. Lying off the port of Lüderitz in the south Atlantic, its exposed position meant that the people incarcerated there were exposed to bitter, cold and fierce winds from which they had little or no shelter. Combined with their poor diet, this proved lethal for several thousand prisoners.

in this connection. I have observed, however, that a quarter of a century of colonial Empire has not sufficed to teach the fact that a black man is a human being, and also entitled to having faith kept with him.

[...]

If I read correctly between the lines, the following are the principles accepted for the present and future administration of the protectorate: The Native rising is to be exploited to the utmost in order to obtain from the Reichstag votes for public works, etc. The Hottentots are to be 'permitted' to die out, but the Hereros and Damaras, who are good labourers and herdsmen, are to be retained, in a semi-servile state, as farm labourers, etc. Steps are to be taken, however, to make the country a white man's country and above all an all-German one. (Steps are already being taken to control immigration from British South Africa.)

The fiction that England assisted coloured people in a struggle against white people is to be maintained – possibly for future use as justification.
CO 417/430, ff. 703–14

1907

7

Official Army List
(Trench, MA 32, 31 January 1907)

I have the honour, with reference to the sixth anniversary of the appointment of H.M. the German Emperor as Field Marshal in the British Army, which, as Your Excellency is aware, occurred this week, very respectfully to submit that it would, without doubt, please the Emperor, who has on several occasions, in conversation with me, referred to his position as Field Marshal in our Army, to receive, each year a suitably bound copy of *The Official Army List* which is published every year during the last week in January.

Should this suggestion be approved, it would be easy for the Emperor to receive the copy at one of his minor dismounted inspections, to which the military attachés are invited, as I have known him do a copy of the French Army List, which I am given to understand, is offered to him periodically.

FO 244/682

8

German Views of the Channel Tunnel
(Trench, MA 33, 4 February 1907)

I have the honour to report that during the past month the proposal to make a Channel Tunnel has been a good deal commented on in the German press.

I attach a translation of what seems the most interesting of the contributions, not only because it appeared in a liberal organ over the signature of one of the ablest of the military journalists whose contributions are not anonymous, but also because the views expressed agree with those of the most large-minded of the officers with whom I have discussed the question.

The opinions expressed by Colonel Gaedke[31] that there is no necessity for a war to be preceded by a declaration or a period of strained diplomatic relations, and that the English army is not in a position to defend the native soil against invasion are especially interesting, and, to the best of my belief, they are held very generally by the officers of the German Army, and above all, by the Great General Staff.

FO 371/252

9

Walfish Bay
(Trench MA 34, 6 February 1907)

I have the honour to report that since the dissolution of the Reichstag, there have been from time to time, in the German press, references to a harbour for Swakopmund, which seem to have a certain method in their connection.[32]

The official recognition of the importance of a coaling station in South West Africa and the mission of certain naval officers to investigate were first reported. Then came the announcement of arrangements that were being made with private firms for the construction, at their own risk, of harbour works, on a large scale, at Swakopmund. This was followed by the statement that these works would make Walfish Bay[33] – which had, up to this, been only casually referred to from time to time as a sort of pedal note – absolutely worthless. Finally, a project was announced on the authority of an English radical paper, for the exchange of Walfish Bay against a strip of the German coast of Lake Tanganika and the press reported yesterday that Hr Dernburg[34] had, at Darmstadt on the 4th

---

31 Colonel Richard Gädke, military correspondent of the liberal newspaper, the *Berliner Tageblatt.*

32 Swakopmund, despite a tendency to silt up, was probably the best German-controlled harbour in South-West Africa.

33 Walvis Bay, the best deep-water harbour in south-west Africa, was a British possession, entirely cut off from Britain's other possessions in the region and completely surrounded on all its landward sides by the German South-West African Protectorate. The fact that this vital strategic enclave was in British hands was a constant irritation to the German authorities.

34 Bernhard Dernburg, former banker, Director of the Colonial Division of the German Foreign Office, 1906–7; subsequently Colonial Secretary, 1907–10.

instant in reply to the question as to whether he proposed exchanging a portion of German East Africa for Walfish Bay, stated that he was not thinking of doing anything of the kind. ('Aber das faellt mir ja gar nicht ein! Meine Herren, was denken Sie Denn von mir?').

The South West African Protectorate is now playing an important role in German politics, both 'Welt' and internal, and this deprecation of Walfish Bay, with great schemes for a port at Swakopmund suggests that the German Government realizes the fact that in retaining Walfish Bay, the British have kept what is practically the key to the protectorate.

That the acquisition, sooner or later, of Walfish Bay is of the greatest importance to Germany, not only if she wishes to develop the colony but also if she desires to establish a coaling station in those waters, is evident from a consideration of the seaboard in question.

Along the 900 miles of the coast-line of the Protectorate, and indeed along several hundred [*sic*] of miles both to the north and south of it, there are only two good harbours: Luderitzbucht and Walfish Bay.

The former is good enough in its way, but is of limited size and has a rocky bottom, only moderately deep water and the great drawback of having no drinking water, whatever, in the vicinity. (A year ago the water required here was all condensed or imported and cost over £1,000 a week.) Moreover, it is situated in the southern, and sterile part of the country, and separated from it by a desert belt a hundred miles wide.

The geographical position of Swakopmund and Walfish Bay* is, however, an admirable one. They are situated in the centre of the seaboard of the colony, four hundred miles from the northern, eastern and southern frontiers, opposite the fertile Damara country, where the capital, Windhuk, is situated, and just at the point where the desert belt is narrowest and the State and Otavi Mines Railways reach the coast ... only Walfish Bay is a British Possession and Swakopmund has nothing but open beach.

Walfish Bay has an area of about twenty-five square miles good holding ground and deep water, is sheltered from the prevailing south-westerly gales and could easily be fortified.

The so-called harbour of Swakopmund consists of an open roadstead where, when there is any sea on, ships have to lie two miles out from the shore, an open sandy beach exposed to frequent south-westerly gales especially from April to September. The surf gets up very rapidly and is worst at full moon.

A northerly current sweeps the sand up the coast, and a mole, some four hundred yards long, built at a cost of over £150,000 has been completely sanded up, in spite of the efforts of two dredgers and a 25 hp steam pump. A year ago one dredger just managed to keep itself afloat alongside but could not get away. The second dredger worked at a bar which was nearly awash at low water and it generally took refuge at Walfish Bay whenever the sea got up, by all accounts.

One-third of the stores &c., used to be landed on the open beach in surf boats manned by Krooboys, the remainder being landed at a wooden pier built by the troops. Everyone has to be cleared off the pier when there is a big sea on, and the piles are reported to have been attacked by the bore-worm. The 'Palatia'[35] took longer to land her troops and horses than she took coming out from Hamburg, and freight ships have at times taken months before they could get their cargo ashore. The rails for the Otavi line had to be unloaded at Walfish Bay on account of the swell, and tugs, dredgers, &c., used to go there to fit up or repair their machinery. Launches and tugs have been wrecked, and even Krooboys drowned in bad weather.

To sum up, there seems little doubt that the construction of a good harbour at Swakopmund itself is practically out of the question save at a prohibitive cost and the acquisition of Walfish Bay is of great importance for Germany, whether for the development of the South-West African Protectorate or for the establishment of a naval base in the South Atlantic. Its value should therefore increase as time goes on, and with not only every mile of railway built and well sunk in the colony but with every addition to the German navy.

*They are only 22 miles apart, and the surface of the ground admits of an easy and inexpensive extension of the railways.

ADM 1/7974

10

German Military Budget for 1907
(Trench MA 35, 20 February 1907)

I have the honour to attach a translation of an article, on the German Military Budget for 1907, which was published in the *Berliner Tageblatt* of the 17th inst. and which seems of interest as it sums up tersely the proposed expenditure on the armed forces of Germany during 1907.

---

35   SS *Palatia*, Hamburg America Line steamer launched in 1894.

The German Budget gives, however, for purposes of comparison with other nations, an erroneous idea of the total useful effort made each year, for purposes of offence and defence by the German Empire, firstly because obligatory service fills the ranks with the pick of the nation who train for war at a nominal wage, and, secondly, because the whole social and political organization of the state is so arranged that the military authorities obtain a great deal of the most valuable labour in the way of preparation for war, – at low pressure from those not belonging to the active army, and at high pressure from those still serving in it – in return for rewards of various kinds which are very highly prized although they are not of a nature to be expressed in pounds, shillings and pence.

FO 244/682

II

Rising in German S.W. Africa (Trench MA 37, 26 February 1907)

I have the honour to forward herewith a 'Memorandum on the Course of the Rising in South-West Africa' (No. 107 of 22/2/07) prepared by the General Staff and issued to the Reichstag by the Imperial Chancellor.

The paper contains the proposals of the government with regard to the troops and the natives in the colony, a description of the present state of affairs in justification of the plans, a narrative of the negotiations with the Bondelzwarts during October, November and December, and half-a-dozen reminders that the English helped the natives.[36]

The extension of the railway at Keetmanshoop is apparently urgently needed for military reasons. The liberation of the prisoners is to be postponed, and the majority employed as labourers under military supervision. Continuous drives are to be undertaken to disarm the natives (presumably the Rehobeth Bastards and the Berseba Hottentots who during the war have given such loyal help to the troops). Finally, it is proposed to reduce the number of troops to 7,400 by the end of the financial year. This number is stated to be the minimum below which they cannot with safety (*sic*) be reduced until the colonization of the country has made some progress, the natives have become reconciled to

---

36 This was a common German complaint. In fact, despite some sympathy in certain quarters for their plight, the British authorities were loath to do anything that might undermine European colonial rule in Africa.

labour and the country has been further opened up by the construction of railways.

The account of the present state of affairs in the colony, given on page 4, will surprise all those who have been following the progress of events and who believe Damaraland to have been quite pacified since the beginning of 1906, the Omaheke Desert to be tenanted only by the bones of the Hereros who died of thirst in their flight eastward after the Waterberg,[37] the Witbois to be 'dying like flies' in confinement on Shark Island, the whole of the Bondelzwarts to have made their submission, and Lambert and Fielding to have never been anything more than the leaders of small robber bands now entirely dispersed.

It is hard to avoid the conclusion that the account of the state of affairs has been based on the plans for the future, and that the General Staff is desirous of maintaining a large force in South West Africa for use against an enemy other than the natives lately in revolt.

FO 367/41

12

Conversation with the Emperor (Trench MA 38, 3 March 1907)

At the dinner given yesterday by the Emperor to the Ambassadors, His Majesty, who wore naval mess dress, appeared in excellent spirits and fairly good health.

He at once, after greeting me, referred to Mr. Haldane's scheme for the reorganization of the territorial army, and suggested its similarity, if not partial indebtedness, to a Memorandum drawn up a few years ago by the Emperor himself. 'My proposals were based on the organization of the Hungarian Landwehr, only Mr. Haldane has included the Volunteers, too,' said the Emperor.

I suggested that Mr Haldane had no doubt found the conferences in Berlin with the War Minister and the Chief of the General Staff, to which the Emperor had invited him, most informing. 'I should think so;

---

37   Battle of the Waterberg (11 August 1904). This was the key engagement between the German forces and the Herero. Following their defeat many Herero were forced, as a deliberate result of von Trotha's policy of extermination, to flee into the desert, where lack of water quickly caused their deaths.

we told him more than anyone had ever been told before,' exclaimed the Emperor; and he really seemed to believe it.

His Majesty, who had referred in fun to the high serial number reached by our recent army reform schemes, added with a twinkle: 'Now I suppose you're ready to fall on us?' On my protesting that the scheme was only meant to meet invasion, the Emperor returned: 'Oh, we won't come,' and proceeded to ask what I thought of the proposals.

In the intervals during the concert after dinner, the Emperor several times called me to where he was sitting, and made me take part in his conversation with Prince Bülow,[38] who also was most kind and friendly, and said to me how pleased he (Prince Bülow) was that 'the King had been able to send me to Berlin'.

On the departure of the Ambassadors and German Ministers, the Military and Naval Attachés were invited to the Emperor's smoking room. Here His Majesty talked for two full hours to Admiral de Jonquieres (the French Attaché) and myself. The subjects touched on were very wide, and included visits to Gibraltar and the Riviera, the recent storms in the North Sea, submarine signalling, the recent wireless signalling between the *Caronia*[39] in the Mediterranean and the *Kaiser Wilhelm II* off the Dutch coast, the expedition in the Middle Ages of the English Crusaders against the Prussian pagans, and the Battle of Königsberg, the Emperor's private pottery works, his interest in naval history shown by his having read James' history, in his youth, from cover to cover.

He described at some length the dangers of the mouth of the Elbe after wintry weather, when the ice alters the shape and position of the sand-banks, and he said how pleased he was that the other day two of his cruisers were able to help a distressed British merchant-vessel in those waters.

The conversation was carried on in English and French, but mainly in the former language, in which the Emperor seems more at home in technical terms. His Majesty did not speak at all to the other Attachés in the smoking room, beyond saying 'good night' to them when we all left at a quarter to 1 o'clock; and he seemed to be desirous of laying special stress on his friendly feeling for France and Great Britain.

FO 371/259, f. 34

---

38   Bernhard von Bülow (1849–1929), Imperial Chancellor, 1900–9.

39   RMS *Caronia*: British ocean liner, launched 1904. It was owned and operated by the Cunard company.

13

Views of the German Press on Mr Haldane's Army Scheme
(Trench, MA 46, 9 April 1907)

I have the honour to submit a summary of the criticisms which have appeared in the German Press of the plans of the War Office for the reorganization of the Field Force and the formation of a Territorial Army as well as of the opinions on the same which seem to be held by the officers of the Army, as far as I have been able to ascertain them.

To deal first with the press, approximately 50% of the newspapers that mention Mr Haldane's schemes content themselves with either bald statements of the plans, or gave summaries of the comments of the English press, without the addition of any further remarks of their own.

Of those that criticise the proposals, half lay stress on the great difficulties with which a British War Minister has to contend, while eight journals express the conviction that this is a last effort to produce an efficient army with voluntary service – if this fails there will be no avoiding the adoption of obligatory service for home defence.

Five journals find fault with the proposals for the Field Army, and ten with those for the Territorial Army although both General v. Janson and Colonel Gaedke insist on the necessity of special organizations to meet special circumstances.

Nearly all the papers fully appreciate the great difficulties with which Mr Haldane has had to contend, and praise the way in which he has tackled them.

To take the views expressed, now in detail, the view of the *Berliner Lokal Anzeiger* is that Mr Haldane has simply and clearly solved the two problems of forming reserves of both officers and men and of organizing the Militia and volunteers into formations for war. It also has great hopes of the good effect to be produced by the healthy rivalry of counties.

The *Frankfurter Zeitung* makes fun of the previous attempts at reorganization as well of the miniature rifle clubs, but is of the opinion that Mr Haldane's work will prove a lasting memorial; it finds the Field Force organization especially good.[40]

Among the journals that consider the proposals the best that could be made under the circumstances, but are doubtful if Mr Haldane be

---

40   The *Frankfurter Zeitung* was an influential liberal newspaper.

not too optimistic, the *Vossische Zeitung*[41] doubts 300,000 young men enlisting voluntarily for the defence of their country, and the *Borsen Zeitung* thinks that the reforms will in all probability be wrecked on the same obstacles as their predecessors ('Mr Haldane has also to make bricks without straw').

The *Neues Tageblatt* praises the reforms already introduced, especially the formation of the General Staff and the abolition of petticoat influence (*sic*) but fears that it may be found very difficult to secure the renunciation of many old-world privileges and to bring under military discipline tens of thousands of men who have till now played at soldiers in the volunteers.

The *Hamburger Nachrichten* says Mr Haldane has one of the hardest and most thankless tasks that can fall to the lot of a British statesman: on the one hand he has to do what none of his predecessors have succeeded in doing and organise the army for defence, and on the other he has to reduce its cost.

The *Kolnische Zeitung* says that the English War Minister is in a thankless position, but that if the task be at all possible, it can only be on Mr Haldane's lines.

Among the papers that think no adequate and efficient organization is possible under the circumstances, the *Weser Zeitung* says that only two views are tenable: either invasion is impossible and troops are not needed to defend the mother country, or it is possible, and the troops must be good enough to meet trained continental soldiers – but no minister holding these views could remain in office for a day. The *Vossische Zeitung* says, however, that it is evident that Mr Haldane is moving in the direction of obligatory service.

The opinion of the *Tag* is that Mr Haldane has an unenviable task with a couple of fetters from which nothing in the world will free him: he must reduce expenditure but must not touch the sacred doctrine of voluntary service. The result is – as Mr H. well knows – that he cannot produce an organization that would bring strength and glory to his country, but must produce what patchwork he can within the limits laid down. The germ of his scheme is the raising of the Auxiliary forces to the standard of a real reserve.

The *Tageblatt* says that something had to be done to produce a more efficient force for service abroad and to increase the preparations for home defence; Mr Haldane's scheme is the only possible alternative to obligatory service.

---

41 The *Vossische Zeitung* (colloquially known as 'Auntie Voss') was a noted liberal newspaper.

Among the objectors to the proposed organization of the Field Force, the *Hannoversche Courier* says that the whole of the trains and columns are still 'en l'air', yet the readiness for active operations depends on these very columns.

The *Berliner Borsen Zeitung* thinks it doubtful whether men to make up the field army will be forthcoming, and the *Tageblatt* doubts whether the Field Force would be ready within three months of the commencement of hostilities.

The view is general that the proposed Territorial Army is a great improvement on the present heterogeneous collection of auxiliaries, but very few of the critics believe that it would be equal to the task of tackling trained continental soldiers.

The *Hannoversche Courier* says that it will be many years in all probability before the Territorial Army will be a factor that continental armies will have to take into account, and the *Neues Tageblatt* draws attention to the way, in the auxiliaries, the officers give notice in dozens and the men in hundreds 'if they are hustled or their sacred traditions touched, as Messrs Brodrick[42] and Arnold Forster[43] found to their cost' and doubts if the strength of the Territorial Army will not fall very short of the 300,000 required.

The *Militarisch-Politische Korrespondenz*, in an article which has been reproduced in extenso in several other journals, finds the difficulty in training officers and technical troops the great drawback of the scheme; the strongest criticisms came however from three recognised authorities. Thus in the *Tageblatt* Gaedke doubts whether, with the greater demands made upon them, the requisite number of volunteers will present themselves, and finds incomprehensible the optimism which anticipates having six months to train the men when once the country is really attacked 'England will, in all probability, if she ever has to defend herself from an attack made on her coast, have to do so in the first days of a war.'

The *Kreuz Zeitung*[44] thinks the scheme for the reserve of officers will produce people trained only superficially and theoretically; and General v. Janson, in the *Militär Wochenblatt* doubts if the numbers required will be forthcoming for either the Territorial Army or the reserve of the Field Army, and points out the injustice of expecting one man to leave his work to defend his country while his comrade continues his trade. Writing

---

42 William St John Fremantle Brodrick, 1st Earl of Midleton (1856–1942), British Secretary of State for War, 1900–3.

43 Hugh Oakeley Arnold-Forster (1855–1909), British Secretary of State for War, 1903–5.

44 The *Neue Preußische Zeitung*, generally known as the *Kreuzzeitung*, because of the cross emblem that adorned its top banner, was the mouthpiece of the German Conservative Party.

from the point of view of continental armies, he finds the schemes lacking in fixed principles and commenced without distinct aims ('ohne sichere Grundlage und ohne festes Ziel') but adds that England can afford herself the luxury of an experiment as long as she retains her command of the sea with even approximately her present superiority.

I respectfully submit that the value of much of the hostile portions of the above criticisms is probably in great measure discounted by the fact that the majority of the writers are, most likely, not sufficiently acquainted with the difficulties of the problem to be good judges of the best way of solving it. One point, however, has struck me as standing out clearly and distinctly both in newspaper comments and in the opinions expressed to me verbally by officers, and that is that should we ever have occasion to use either the Field Force or the Territorial Army it will be with a few days notice and not a few months. If this be the opinion in Germany, it is probably for excellent reasons which should be more within German knowledge than ours.

The opinions held in the army have not been so easy to find out, and those whose views were the most valuable were not the most communicative; I think, though, that the following summary is correct.

The greater number of the officers who have interested themselves in the proposals have, apparently, considered them from their own strictly Prussian point of view, and the schemes, being based on voluntary service, have been condemned forthwith.

The small proportion who have studied the question with interest, and are acquainted and sympathise with the peculiarities of English life, and character, seem to me to be of opinion that the proposed organization is the most promising – compulsory service being out of the question – that has so far been suggested. It has apparently, however, in their opinion, two weak points which may possibly wreck the whole scheme. The first and chief point is the postponement of the six months training till war is imminent – the second and minor point, is the difficulty of getting 300,000 volunteers to accept more onerous conditions of service than those which have previously obtained.

The most important views of all, those of the Great General Staff, I can only judge from those expressed to me by a couple of senior officers whose bona fides I think I can rely on (the remarks of several others have been eliminated), but the training and teaching of the Great General Staff is so homogeneous and thorough that I think the opinion of these few may be taken as giving a very fair clue to the opinions of the whole. They were briefly these: the territorial troops proposed would be quite unfit to oppose to trained continental troops, but as long as England maintains her present overwhelming superiority at sea the question of home defence is one of relatively minor importance.

It must not, however, be inferred from this statement of the views probably held by the Great General Staff that there is, for the present, any cessation of the unhasting yet unresting work of preparation for possible operations over the water. I believe that, on the contrary, in addition to constant improvements in the organization of the troops and, above all, of communications in the country, a very systematic and thorough study is being made of the possible terrain of operations in the United Kingdom, not only by persons domiciled in the country, but by numbers of officers who, every year, combine special facilities for leave with the useful employment of much of their time with topographical and other studies.

FO 371/259, f. 261

14

Changes in German Army in 1906
(Trench MA 49, 20 April 1907)

I have the honour with reference to my No. 31 of the 7th January 1907, to submit some supplementary notes on changes, etc which took place in the German Army during 1906.

[…]

Miscellaneous

An order forbidding operations to be held on Sundays or Church Festivals has been issued. Troops may only march on Sundays when this will bring them to their own garrison or to their standing camp.

Owing to the increase in the price of food, the compensation to be paid in billets when full rations are supplied has been raised from ten pence to fifteen pence.

FO 244/682

15

Social Democracy and Military Service
(Trench, MA 55, 9 May 1907)

Owing to many statements to that effect having been made during the debates in the Reichstag by Members belonging to the Centre and Right, as well as elsewhere by prominent personages on various occasions, it has seemed possible that the conclusion might be come to that the Social Democrats in Germany are opposed to military service on principle, and that, were hostilities imminent, the decisive action of Germany would, possibly, be impeded by some practical expression of anti-militarist views on the part of the social democracy.[45]

I am convinced that such a conclusion would be far from being correct, in spite of the fact that this party is generally satisfied with Germany's present 'place in the sun,' and would prefer that the Government should devote itself more to improving the condition of the working classes and less to *Weltpolitik*.[46] I have, moreover, no doubt whatever that, were war with a European Power to break out, the social democracy of Germany would evince the same patriotism as the rest of the nation.

A most interesting statement of the views of the German Social Democratic party was, a few days ago, made in writing by Herr Bebel,[47] the leader of the party in the Reichstag, regarding military service, to the representative of a French newspaper, in connection with the anti-militarist propaganda in France, of M. Hervé and others.[48] This statement was as follows:–

---

45 The German Social Democratic Party (SPD) was a growing force in German electoral politics in the Wilhelmine era and in 1912 would become the largest party in the Reichstag. They presented themselves as a revolutionary Marxist organization emphatically opposed to the existing social and political order. The reality, as would be shown in 1919 when they took power, was that they were more wedded to liberal constitutionalism than their rhetoric made out. Despite their ostentatious pre-war anti-militarism, in 1914 the majority of them supported the German war effort much as Trench predicted.

46 *Weltpolitik* or 'world policy' was the programme of German overseas expansionism launched in 1897 with a view to gaining Germany her 'place in the sun'. Arguably, its main purpose was to buttress the conservative monarchical regime at home through the acquisition of prestige overseas. However, lacking any clear objectives and implemented in an extraordinarily clumsy manner, it was regarded suspiciously by most other powers, who ensured, sometimes collectively, sometimes individually, that it achieved very little.

47 August Bebel (1840–1913), leader of the German Social Democrat Party.

48 Gustave Hervé (1871–1944), French history professor and politician. Although later attracted to ultranationalist doctrines, at this point he was an ardent pacifist and socialist and espoused a fervent anti-militarism.

'The anti-militarist ideas and propaganda of Hervé are impossible in the German social democracy. German social democracy is the acknowledged opponent of the present military system, but it is of opinion that some military organization will be necessary in those States which are now in existence as long as all civilized nations do not establish Conventions and institutions to put an end to war once and for all.

'As long as the danger exists and that war is possible, every nation must possess a military organization sufficiently powerful to meet an aggressive war, and to protect its territory against invasion.

'Although German social democracy supports all loyal endeavours to avoid war and to secure peace, such as, for example, the organization of international tribunals for settling differences between different States, it considers a military organization of some kind to be indispensable as long as the danger of war still exists.

'This is the reason that German social democracy inserts on its programme: (1) An education which will fit all citizens for military service; (2) the substitution of Militias for standing armies.

'Consequently, were a member of the German Social Democratic party to spread ideas and make claims like those defended by Hervé, the programme of the Socialist party would justify the question: does this member still belong to the party? The party cannot permit a propaganda which is in opposition to its programme, which would do great harm to the party and which makes claims which, given the present state of affairs, cannot be realized, because they are contrary to the interest of our native land.'

May I here record the fact that it is the opinion of many thoughtful officers in Europe that the military system of the future is universal service on a militia basis (such as at present obtains in Switzerland), and that most European nations will adopt it (for service in Europe) before the end of this century.

Such a system is, however, suitable for defence only. Any nation bent on enlarging its 'place in the sun' by the method, 'Und bist du nicht willig, so brauch ich Gewalt',[49] will retain conscription until its object is attained or abandoned.

FO 371/260, f. 117

---

49 The quote comes from Goethe's poem 'Der Erlkönig' and translates as 'if you are unwilling, then I will use force'.

16

The Pacification of South West Africa
(Trench MA 56, 11 May 1907)

[…]

During the recent discussion of the Estimates in the Reichstag, the Government was questioned respecting the fate of the Hottentots. Hr Dernburg explained that, in July last, there were 1700 Hottentots in a kraal at Windhuk, and the question was raised as to where they should be sent, East Africa, the South Seas, Togo and Cameroons being proposed one after the other. During this discussion, the natives learnt that they were going to be deported and (incorrectly) that the chiefs were to be hanged, and some of them made their escape. They were therefore moved to Lüderitzbucht and confined on Shark Island.

In support of the contention that the great mortality was not the result of their confinement on Shark Island, Hr Dernburg stated that 'after the Boer War was over and the Boers in concentration camps, in a climate they were accustomed to, and people able to help themselves, the mortality 264 per mil and among children, 433 per mil.'

He added that it was to be regretted that 1200 had died on Shark Island, but that the Commander of the Troops was aware of the mortality but had declared that he could not finish the war if he took them away. Hr Dernburg did not add that the majority, probably, of the prisoners confined on Shark Island had surrendered on the condition of giving up their cattle and lands, but retaining their freedom.

I received a few days ago a letter from a reliable German who has been many years in South West Africa. He writes:– 'Of the 1800 that were sent (to Shark Island) in September, 1000 are dead, including Cornelius … the greater number will never leave it … when I was there, three months ago, they were dying at the rate of 12 to 18 a day.'

WO 106/268, ff. 549–51

17

Conversation with the Emperor
(Trench MA 59, 22 May 1907)

On the 20th instant I attended, with the other Military and Naval Attachés the celebration at the New Palace at Potsdam, of the Anniversary of the

Infantry Instructional Battalion. The Birthday of the Czar of Russia having occurred on the previous day, all the members of the Russian Embassy were also invited, and the Ambassador sat at lunch, on the right of Prince von Bülow, who sat opposite the Emperor.

During luncheon, the Emperor proposed the health of the Czar, and afterwards during the 'Cercle', conversed a good deal with the Russian Ambassador.

Both on parade and after lunch, His Majesty had long conversations with Major-General v. Deimling who reported himself on return from German South West Africa. These latter conversations were very animated on the part of the Emperor, who seemed in good health and spirits. During the men's dinners the Emperor had a few minutes conversation with the American Military and Naval Attachés. During lunch, his remarks were almost exclusively addressed to the Imperial Chancellor and the Russian Ambassador.

After the march past of the battalion, the Emperor called me to him, and asked on what day the deputation from the Duke of Cambridge's regiment was to go to London to attend the unveiling 'because I'll send Hanke on the same day'. His Majesty told me that he proposed sending the commanding officer, a major, a captain, a lieutenant and a second lieutenant. On my telling His Majesty the dates (communicated in writing to the Military Cabinet on the 13th) he issued orders for Field Marshal v Hanke to go also on the fourteenth. The Chief of the Military Cabinet told me that the Field Marshal would travel with the deputation, which he would introduce, and that one of the officers would act as his aide-de-camp.

I received, to-day, a letter from the Chief of the Military Cabinet informing me that the Emperor has appointed General Field Marshal v Hahnke,[50] Commander in Chief in the Marken and Governor of Berlin to represent His Majesty on Saturday the 15th of June at the Ceremony of the unveiling of the monument of His Late Royal Highness the Duke of Cambridge.[51] The letter also stated that the Emperor had ordered a deputation from the Infantry Regiment von Goeben (2. Rheinischen) Nr. 28, composed of the commanding officer a major, a captain, a lieutenant and a second-lieutenant, to attend the ceremony of the unveiling of the monument of the late Chief of the Regiment.

50   Wilhelm von Hahnke (1833–1912), Chief of the Military Cabinet, 1888–1901.
51   George, Duke of Cambridge (1819–1904), Commander-in-Chief of the British Army, 1856–95. An equestrian statue of him, erected in 1907, is located in Whitehall, London, opposite the old War Office.

The due communication of the above will be made to the Government of His Majesty by the German Imperial Embassy in London. A list of the names of the officers composing the deputation is also promised
FO 371/259, f. 429

18

Imperial Manoeuvres 1907
(Trench MA 67, 24 September 1907)

I have the honour to submit the attached report on the German imperial Manoeuvres of 1907.
[…]

Report on the Imperial Manoeuvres by Colonel F. J. A. Trench, CVO, DSO, Military Attaché, Berlin.

These manoeuvres took place on the 9th, 10th, and 11th of September in Eastern Westphalia and were carried out by the Seventh and Tenth Army Corps, to which the 'A' and 'B' Cavalry Divisions were attached.
[…]

Artillery

The fire tactics of the Q.F. field artillery have, so far as could be seen, not been far modified since the introduction of the new gun-recoil mounting. Indirect laying is very rare and is not encouraged; even the regulations say that the advantages of covered positions must almost always be sacrificed if decisive effect is to be obtained. On the only occasions on which I saw aiming rods used, or rather out, the batteries were no longer using them. In one of the cases, standing corn had interfered with the line of sight.

The flash of the guns was seen at ranges estimated at nearly 5000 yards. It is much more conspicuous than that of the English Q.F. field guns.

The field artillery seemed to entrench only when occupying a defensive position, and no gun pits were seen on the 9th and 10th. The pits on the 11th were generally irregular shaped holes suited to a line of fire over a fairly wide arc of fire. No attempt was made to hide newly thrown up earth, or guns, or wagons, with branches as is done so effectively in Switzerland.

Theoretically, German field artillery comes into action simultaneously, and in large numbers, early in the fight, so as to form the framework on which the infantry attack is developed. It is supposed to change position rarely, and manoeuvre mainly by its fire. As a matter of fact, at these Imperial manoeuvres (except in the case of the guns of the Seventh Corps on the 11th of Sept. which were used as position artillery) the field artillery generally came into action piecemeal – often by single guns – and changed position frequently, the light howitzers being generally used exactly like other guns. If I may venture a comparison, I think that the average English 'Gunner' has a much better eye for country than his German colleague.

[…]

FO 371/262, f. 335

19

Walfisch Bay
(Trench MA 68, 11 November 1907)

I have the honour to report an apparent revival of the agitation for obtaining the transfer of Walfisch Bay to Germany.

A similar movement – reported on in my No. 34 of the 6th of February – occurred early in the year, but apparently came to nothing. That the present time has been selected for a fresh endeavour to obtain possession of this harbour, the key of German South West Africa, is probably due to two causes:– (1) the increase in the cordiality of Anglo-German relations and (2) the growing conviction of the German government that it is impossible to make Swakopmund a port.

In connection with this latter point two interesting papers have appeared within the last three weeks:– 'Why Swakopmund is not a harbour' from the pen of Captain Hutter,[52] the author of an interesting work on the Kameroons and who is now in South-West Africa, and a semi-official reply to the above by Dr. Paul Rohrbach,[53] the Imperial Emigration Commissioner for German South West Africa.

Captain Hutter, who, in a previous paper, has drawn attention to the futility of the mole at Swakopmund, describes, in the one under report,

---

52 Franz Karl Hutter (1865–1924), author of *Wanderungen und Forschungen im Nord-Hinterland von Kamerun* (Braunschweig, 1902).

53 Karl Albert Paul Rohrbach (1869–1956), German author and journalist. He served as Settlement Commissioner to South-West Africa.1903–6.

the action, more especially during the past year, of the boreworm and the surf on the wooden pier. He says: 'The *pièce de résistance* of the opponents of the pier is the boreworm, the existence and destructive effects of which are fully admitted by the builders of the pier' but claims that those of the piles which can be saturated and cased with iron will resist for another eight or ten years. He admits, however, that at Luderitzbucht, the destruction of the pier by the boreworm has made such progress that it is not expected to last another couple of years, and continues: 'the Swakopmund pier is and will always be, a makeshift ... The heavy seas and surf which roll up irresistibly from the South-West will prevent Swakopmund ever having a real harbour, piers and moles notwithstanding. It is true that there are, on the average, 250 days in the year on which stores can be landed, and these would allow a considerable amount of unloading to be done, if only they could be foreseen, but it often happens that a heavy surf, which makes all communication between ships and the shore impossible for days, gets up so suddenly that lighters which have lain in calm water alongside the ships, are unable to reach the pier. The sudden and unexpected way in which these heavy seas get up has been of great commercial disadvantage, and could, under certain circumstances, have military and political results which it is impossible to foresee.' 'These unfavourable conditions,' he goes on to say, 'can be removed by neither piers nor shelters for the lighters. Not only will Swakopmund never have a harbour but it does not even afford the facilities which one has a right to expect from a roadstead.' [...]

Such outspoken criticism has naturally been followed by a semi-official dementi but Dr. Rohrbach's defence is far from being a strong one. He admits that, without the pier, the question of the supply of war and other material would, during the recent operations, have presented serious difficulties, but he points out that the landing facilities afforded by, even an improved and enlarged pier, would be far from adequate for the economic development of the colony.

[...]

These two papers may, I think, be taken as an indication that the experience of 1907 strongly supports the opinion expressed in my No. 34 that the construction of a harbour at Swakopmund itself is out of the question, save at a prohibitive cost, and the acquisition of Walfisch Bay is of the greatest importance for Germany. With a closer acquaintance of the plans of Herren Dernburg and v. Lindequist for the development of the colony, I should like, to-day, to express the belief that the future of German South-West Africa depends very largely on the acquisition of

Walfisch Bay, and that Germany will be, ultimately, willing to pay a very big price for it.
ADM 1/7974

20

German Opinion on the Boer War
(Trench MA 69, 15 November 1907)

I have the honour to draw attention to a review which recently appeared in No. 125 of the *Militär-Wochenblatt* of the Official *History of the War in South Africa, 1899–1902* and to forward herewith (Appendices A and B) a copy of the article and a translation of it which has appeared in the *Daily Telegraph*.

The article, of which the source is undoubtedly official, is most friendly in tone, and forms a satisfactory 'amende honorable' from Germany 'where (as the critic admits) the bounds of justifiable criticism have not infrequently been overstepped'.

The writer, while gracefully giving credit for the more correct views which now obtain, frankly admits that the operations in German South West Africa have helped not a little to the adoption of a more generous point of view: ('Ein ähniche Erfahrung hat auch die deutsche Truppenfuhrung bei Beginn des Aufstandes in Südwestafrika machen müssen').

It would be a mistake, however, to infer from this article that a complete change has recently taken place in German opinion regarding the Boer War. The official German account published by the Great General Staff and translated by Brig. General Waters,[54] contains much which is, I believe, accepted by English soldiers generally as justifiable and not unfriendly criticism, while, on the other hand, even now after the experiences of the Herero and Hottentot wars, there are not a few journals in this country that still find appreciation of the British soldier unacceptable.

The *Germania*, for example, in referring to the review in the *Militär-Wochenblatt* under report, heads its article 'English Tactlessness' and takes exception to a portion of the English press having compared the more appreciative views of the British Army now expressed with 'the attacks made upon the same army during the Boer War'. Many of the

---

54   Wallscourt Hely-Hutchinson Waters (1855–1945), British Military Attaché in Berlin 1900–3.

papers content themselves with the publication of a few extracts from the *Militär-Wochenblatt* and offer no comments of any kind.

FO 371/263, ff. 282–3

21

Count Zeppelin's Balloon
(Trench MA 72, 29 November 1907)

In the Imperial Estimates for 1908 under the Home Office Vote, appears the following item of proposed expenditure:– To reimburse General Count Zeppelin[55] & to acquire the two balloons built by him – £107,500. [...]

In consideration of these payments by the state, it is intended, should the necessity arise, to make a special agreement for the supply of other balloons at a reduced price.

FO 371/263, f. 347

22

Demand for Obsolescent Firearms
(Trench, MA 75, 13 December 1907)

I have the honour to draw attention to the large demand which appears to exist in the trade in Germany for large quantities of rifles, carbines, Maxims, etc. of obsolescent patterns. This demand is apparently in excess of the supply available locally as I have, recently, had several applications for assistance in the purchase of Martini Henrys etc. which the British Government was believed to be desirous to dispose of. One firm talked of buying 300,000 rifles and another even enquired about field guns of Ehrhardt make.[56]

These purchases which it is desired to make may not be unconnected with the visit to Germany in August of a mission from Abyssinia [...] especially as the persons composing it not only visited Messrs Krupps

---

55   Ferdinand Graf von Zeppelin (1838–1917), German soldier, best known for the rigid airships he invented and which bear his name.

56   Ehrhardt: a common way of referring to the armaments company Rheinische Metallwaren- und Maschinenfabrik Aktiengesellschaft (also known as 'Rheinmetall'), founded by the industrial engineer Heinrich Ehrhardt in 1889.

works at Essen and the practice ground at Halensee but showed considerable technical knowledge of fire-arms. In any case, they are most likely intended for sale in that portion of Africa in which Germany does not lay stress on the principle of White solidarity so frequently referred to in connection with the operations in South West Africa.

FO 371/263, f. 519

23

Reconnaissance Duties
(Trench, MA 76, 15 December 1907)

I have the honour to draw attention to the apparently systematic visits paid by considerable numbers of German officers to the United Kingdom, etc., under circumstances which leave little doubt that their objective is reconnaissance duty.

Definite and early information about these visits is difficult to obtain, firstly, because German newspapers similar to the *Army and Navy Gazette* and the *Broad Arrow*, and giving chatty news of the doings of individual officers, do not exist, and, secondly, because the German system of universal police control does not obtain in England, and foreign officers are free to come, go and do exactly as they like.

The information obtained is thus less precise than is perhaps desirable, but I have no doubt whatever that numbers of officers do go to England on duty of a confidential nature.

The following facts may not be without interest in this connection. Major-General Scholtz,[57] 'Oberquartiermeister' and chief of a section of the Great General Staff, a most hard-working officer who seems to take no interest in anything save his work, spent two or three weeks in Scotland last summer; he seems to know all about the neighbourhood of Edinburgh, Glasgow and the Clyde, but as far as I could make out, has not been to any of the places usually visited by tourists. [...]

FO 371/263, f. 528

---

57   Friedrich von Scholtz (1851–1927).

24

The Military Character of the German Navy League (Trench, MA 77, 20 December 1907)

I have the honour to draw attention to the military aspect of the German *Flotten Verein*.[58]

Formed ten years ago to persuade the electorate, and through it the Reichstag, to vote the enormous sums needed for the provision of a fleet which should dispute the command of the sea with England, it has quite outgrown its comparatively modest original purpose and now forms not only the most powerful organised body in the state outside the army and navy, but one of the most important wheels in the machinery of mobilization for war of the German nation.

It boasts of nearly a million members, 4000 branches and an annual income of about £50,000 and has, up to this week, been the one corporate body in Germany of which the members belonged to every religion, every class in society, every party in politics and every state in the Empire. Its organization is complete and most efficient, its office-holders are the most distinguished princes, generals and government officials in the country. Prince Henry is its principal patron and the Emperor and Chancellor give it their support and encouragement on every occasion.[59] It is intimately connected with the Pan-Germanic League,[60] with which it holds, occasionally, joint meetings, and its anti-English feeling is so marked that even the *Berliner Tageblatt* referred this morning to its 'ewigen Treibereien die uns … gans (sic) besonders … mit England zu verfeinden drohten' [never-ending intrigues which threaten to embroil us most especially with England] and its 'anti-englischen Hetzerieen' [anti-English agitation].

The *Verein* with its complete organization reaching to all classes in society and to every town and village in the Empire can influence and create a popular movement with marvellous rapidity and it is the very

---

58 *Flotten Verein*: the German Navy League was the largest nationalist pressure group in Wilhelmine Germany. It was well funded by Germany's major naval armaments firms and, after some early independent behaviour had been suppressed, tended to work in cooperation with Tirpitz and the Imperial Navy Office in promoting those naval expansion plans desired by the government.

59 Prinz Albert Wilhelm Heinrich von Preussen (1862–1929), better known as Prince Henry of Prussia, was the Kaiser's younger brother. He was a career naval officer and, while certainly aided in his promotions by his status and connections, rose to become Commander-in-Chief of the High Sea Fleet between 1906 and 1909.

60 The Pan-German League was a small but influential militant right-wing pressure group with, as its name implies, a strongly nationalistic agenda. It campaigned actively for the promotion of an idea of Germandom that was ethnic (racial) in character and global in its reach.

obedient servant of the government, absolutely at its disposal for any business of which the object is an increase of the greatness of Germany.

It is this intimate relation with the ruling power combined with its popular organization which would make it so useful in the event of hostilities. It has been stated that a war with Germany would certainly be preceded by a period of diplomatic tension especially in the case of a life-and-death struggle when every force of the Empire would have to be brought into play, but if I judge the *Flotten Verein* it would render such period quite unnecessary. The usual preliminary campaign in the public press would be superfluous, the *Flotten Verein* would – when the authorities thought that the moment was appropriate for an appeal to the *ultima ratio regis* – be entrusted with the suitable preparation of public opinion, and (on the sudden outbreak of hostilities) there would be but one mind in Germany.

FO 371/260, f. 201

1908

25

Annual Changes Report on German Army
(Trench, MA 78, 6 January 1908)

I have the honour to submit, herewith, my annual report on the changes which have taken place in the German Army during the year 1907.
[…]

XX. Machine-guns.

Machine-gun companies were formed during last summer […]. Each company consists of six guns (each drawn by two horses), three ammunition wagons, 4 officers and 83 men. The horses have been taken one from each battery of artillery, temporarily replaced by casters and now by remounts although the batteries still keep the casters.

All references to these companies in the press have suddenly ceased owing possibly to a notice which had the appearance of an official communiqué and which was to the effect that the publication of information concerning these companies was not desirable for patriotic reasons. […]

FO 371/457, f. 262

26

The Visit of the Prince of Wales to Cologne
(Trench, MA 83, 26 February 1908)

I had the honour of being received yesterday by the Emperor, who was graciously pleased to accept a copy of the *Army List* for 1908, offered to him on the anniversary of his appointment as Field Marshal in the British Army.

On my communicating to him the wish of H.R.H. the Prince of Wales to inspect, on the 26th of March, the Von Gesseler Cuirassier Regiment of which he is Colonel-in-Chief, His Majesty expressed his approval several times, seemed very pleased and gave me instructions as to my communicating with the Military Cabinet in order that His Majesty might give the requisite orders. This I have done.

Your Excellency has also communicated the wish of His Royal Highness to the German Foreign Office.

FO 371/458

27

Power Traction at Posen Manoeuvres
(Trench, MA 92, 16 April 1908)

The following notes on the Power-traction experiments at the big fortress manoeuvres which took place last autumn at Posen in the presence of the Emperor have been published in the *Grenzboten.*[61]

The vehicles experimented on were 21 wagons and 39 trucks (to hook on) formed in two columns.

The light column consisted of 4 benzine wagons each with three trucks, 3 benzine wagons each with two trucks, a benzine wagon with one truck and 2 steam-propelled wagons with a truck each – and included the new Daimler train as also a Bussing omnibus intended mainly for the use of the office staff.

The heavy column consisted of a N.A.G. wagon with two trucks, a Siemens-Schuckert wagon with five trucks, a road locomotive with two trucks and one with one truck.

It was hoped that the light column would be able to cover 100, 80 or 60 kilometres a day according as the country was (flat) hilly or mountainous, the heavy column doing 60, 46 or 30 kms in similar circumstances. The results are said to have exceeded the expectations.

Hand in hand with experiments with power traction, the army administration is making endeavours to secure the use of a sufficient quantity of private vehicles in case of mobilization, and with this view

---

61   The *Grenzboten* was a prominent National-Liberal newspaper.

the War Ministry is offering premiums – not only for the purchase but also for the maintenance of vehicles on the condition that the owners undertake to keep their wagons efficient for war, that they allow the authorities a certain right of inspection and that they place the vehicles at their disposal whenever they need them.

Practical experience leads to vehicles of from 24 to 45 horse-power being preferred as they permit of a truck being hooked on when the roads are good. It is proposed that Benzine shall be used as it is a German product.

FO 371/459, f. 390

28

Training of Reserves, etc., 1908
(Trench, MA 93, 20 April 1908)

The Instructions for the Training of the Reserves and Landwehr (*Beurlaubenstand*) during 1908 have been published and are contained, for Prussia in No. 6 of the *Armee-Verordnungsblatt*, and for Bavaria in No. 9 of the *Verordnungsblatt*. Those for the Saxon and Wurtemberg army corps are not available but they are sure to be practically the same as those for the Prussian army corps.

[…]

General Remarks. The following points seem not unworthy of notice in connection with the Instructions under report. The number of officers and men of the *Beurlaubenstand* called up each autumn for training is being increased every year by about ten per cent and, for 1908, it equals more than three quarters of the establishment of the standing army. The existing peace units are thus, each autumn brought up to a strength so closely approximating to war strength that they could without actual mobilization be effectively used against a country with a small army were it desired to avoid a preliminary mobilization in order to gain the advantage of surprise. The decentralized procedure followed in calling up men would in conjunction with the custom of training a large number with other corps than their own permit probably, of, say, four or five army corps being got ready within a night's journey of the transports, with very little movement that would strike outsiders and without any notice or comment whatever in the public press.

CAB 17/61, ff. 135–8

29

Should Warning Precede Hostilities?
(Trench MA 95, 27 April 1908)

From the speeches of prominent persons and the actual and proposed organization of the defence forces, both regular and other, as well as the freedom given to foreign officers to acquire local military information in the United Kingdom, there seems good reason to suppose that the belief generally held there is that, should war unfortunately break out between England and Germany, hostilities would be preceded by a period of diplomatic tension and at least three days – or possibly even three months – warning could be counted on.

This view (if it be held) is, I think, quite erroneous, and I respectfully submit my belief that, when Germany comes to the conclusion that her navy is strong enough, or the British fleet sufficiently scattered or otherwise occupied, for there to be a reasonable prospect of success and, for other reasons, the occasion to be a suitable one to contest England's naval supremacy, the first move will be made without any warning whatever except such as are being given every day by such unmistakeable action as the yearly increase by two or three million pounds of the army expenditure, the rapid augmentation of the navy and the strategic enlarging of the Kiel Canal to say nothing of the hopes and views freely expressed in political and patriotic speeches and publications of all kinds.[62]

I am aware that it is desirable that expression should not be given to so serious an opinion without the production of a certain amount of proof in support, but I submit that the very nature of the case makes this almost impossible to procure.

In the first place, various episodes that played a not unimportant role in the rapid rise of Prussia to wealth and power have so convinced the nation that carefully prepared surprise brings success and that success will always bring pardon for any act no matter how lacking in scruples, that these views have become axiomatic and such matters of common conviction that their expression is superfluous and rare. In the second, the very nature of surprise makes it a *sine quâ non* that the intention should

---

62   As originally built, the Kiel Canal was not large enough to allow for the passage of Dreadnought battleships. Following the Dreadnought revolution and the German decision to build warships of this class, it became necessary for the canal to be widened and deepened if Germany's fleet was to be able to pass from the Baltic to the North Sea without going round Denmark. The enlargement of the canal was completed in the summer of 1914.

be kept a secret. That anything at all is allowed to leak out here can only be put down to a conviction on the part of the Great General Staff that nothing will persuade the English nation to forsake the procedure so often followed in the past of postponing its preparations for war·until hostilities have practically commenced.

As far as I can judge, there is a good deal of resentment in this country that Germany's present naval inferiority forces her to accept for the moment hindrances which she encounters in that world expansion which she considers her right and her duty, and this resentment is intimately bound up with a fixed determination to put up with these hindrances no longer than is absolutely necessary, to strain every nerve in every sphere of national and international activity to provide the necessary means and conditions for their removal and to employ these latter in the most profitable way. Exaggerated punctiliousness is not a Prussian characteristic, when there is nothing to be gained by it, and I can see, as a soldier, nothing in the results of the Hague Conference to prevent 'a reasoned declaration of war' being handed in in the Wilhelmstrasse[63] (or in London) *after* the High Sea Fleet with its convoy of transports had passed the Forth Bridge or the Nore Light Ship.

I have already reported the semi official but only half officially acknowledged role, played by the *Flotten Verein* in the 'Imperial' and/or anglophobe education of the people, and, as an example either of the progress the education has made or of the means adopted for carrying it out, beg to attach a copy of a typical publication entitled 'The Offensive Invasion of England' which is now on sale. The pamphlet is, of course, quite valueless either as a strategical study or as an expression of intention, but it is one of the numerous straws which show the direction of the wind. It is typical of the manner in which the public is being continually reminded that England would, but for certain difficulties at home and abroad, assume the offensive exactly in the same way that Germany hopes herself to be in a position to do before long and it gives an idea of the general knowledge of (but hardly kindly interest in) the British army, navy and colonies which now exists in Germany.

After some suggestions of the inefficiency of the English staff and of coming difficulties in the colonies and India, the writer describes a surprise attack on some British dockyards, the landing of an expeditionary force and a naval struggle ending more or less in a stalemate and his moral is as follows: 'If the Reichstag, which always places party bargaining

---

63   The Wilhelmstrasse was the street on which the German Foreign Office was located and was a common way of referring to that office.

before patriotism, had approved of a more rapid construction of the German fleet one would have been better equipped. Unusual measures had to be adopted to equalize the balance.' Although the booklet itself has no value whatever some extracts I attach in an appendix have some interest as being an expression of views and hopes which I believe to be those of no small number of persons.

FO 371/459, f. 358

30

The Rhine–Herne Canal
(Trench, MA 101, 20 May 1908)

[...]

As Your Excellency is aware, the Rhine–Herne Canal is the final portion of a costly canal connecting the Rhine with the North Sea at Emden and intended to divert from the Dutch reaches of the Rhine the traffic which now passes through Rotterdam.

It is understood that the ultimate object of this great outlay is to bring such pressure to bear on the Netherlands as will induce that country to enter the German customs union.

[...]

According to the last annual report published of the Society for Mining Interests in the 'Oberbergamts' District of Dortmund ... it is expected that the canal will be completed in the year 1913. It is interesting to note that a number of plans of the German Government, not unconnected with facilities for bringing pressure of various kinds to bear on neighbouring and competing powers, seem to have been so made that they shall be completed more or less about the year 1915.

The Naval Intelligence Department might perhaps like to see this report.

FO 371/460, f. 133

31

German Finances
(Trench MA 103, 7 June 1908)

I have the honour to draw attention to a work entitled *Die Finanzen der Grossmächte* recently published by Dr Friedrich Zahn,[64] the Head of the Royal Statistical Bureau in Munich. My ignorance of Finance does not permit me to offer any criticisms on this work – of which I herewith forward a copy as well as a review of it which appeared in the *Spectator* – but, although Dr Zahn states in his preface that the monograph is purely private in character and has no connection with his present official position – I think that it may very reasonably be accepted as an exposition of the financial views of the German Government, which lead it to raise large loans for military objects while leaning only very gently on certain sources of revenue on which far heavier burdens are laid in other countries.

I suggest that the 'moral' of Dr Zahn's work is to be found on pages 17 and 18, in the following passages:–

'From the development of national finances here related, stands out in bold relief the enormous effect which wars, and above all disastrous wars, have on them … Timely financial precautions in view of the occurrence of international complications, in the shape of suitable organisation and adequate timely armament – in a word such a state of preparedness for war as will ensure victory – are not only absolutely necessary for the successful conduct of the operations but the truest economy. The exhaustion of the national finances caused by a war undertaken without due preparation is far and away greater and more serious than that caused by the greatest existing military budgets.'

These views may, without very great exaggeration, I think, be summed up as follows:– Preparation for war is the safest and most productive form of national expenditure.

FO 368/194

---

64   Dr Friedrich Wilhelm Karl Theodor Zahn (1869–1946), a leading German statistician.

32

Public Feeling in Germany
(Trench, MA 107, 17 August 1908)

I have the honour to draw attention to the very remarkable present state of tension of national feeling in Germany and to the strong current of irritation which has characterized it during the last few weeks.

This feeling not only finds expression in chauvinistic journals, as well as in those which are believed to frequently receive official inspiration, but it is, as far as I can judge, very general throughout the country. I have been able, during several weeks' leave of absence spent in central and southern Germany, to get into touch with very varied classes of people in a way that is not possible at my post in Berlin, and I must admit that the result has not borne out my previous belief, and hope that detestation of England was more or less limited to the northern States.

The strong patriotic feeling so much *en évidence* at present is very different to that which has existed since the great disappointment caused by the result of the Boer War. I mean the conviction that Germany has a high mission to carry out with the right to Colonies for the expansion of its growing population and the hegemony of the world's trade, as well as – if the people be willing to make the pecuniary sacrifices necessary to build a sufficient navy – the command of the sea. These views have been held for the last ten years, indeed, many leading men, notably among the officials and the professors, resent strongly that the possession of a formidable army, a high state of culture and a patriotic population has not enabled Germany to carry out, in a couple of decades, that for which other nations have required a couple of centuries. Beyond and above all this, there seems to have been recently an awakening to the conviction that things are not going as well as had been hoped and expected, that it is not quite sure after all that the sacrifices which are being made will enable Germany, in the near future, to fulfil her high destiny, and the result is, in the opinion of many observers, a state of nervous excitement so great that the like of it has not been seen since the summer of 1870.

Two large manufacturers, one of them a Rhinelander and a Catholic and the other a Dresden Protestant, assured me of this in so many words when narrating their experiences in that campaign. Professor Delbrück[65] asked last month, in the *Preussische Jahrbücher*, 'are these merely moves

---

65 Professor Hans Delbrück (1848–1929), a leading German military historian and editor of the influential periodical the *Preussische Jahrbücher*.

in the diplomatic game or do they herald another 1870?' General von Liebert,[66] in the *Tag*, has stated that many people say that the situation resembles that in 1870, and wonder whether they should leave their homes, although, in his opinion, Germany has no cause for apprehension (not because neither France, Russia, or England dream of going to war, but because the Russian army has no terrors, England can only block the coast, and the German army is more than equal to tackling the French army). A Professor of Leipzig told 10,000 workmen, in a recent lecture, that the next few years would be very critical, with the position of the country in the world at stake; and even the pastors of the Lutheran Church, in their organ, the *Reichsbote*, express their conviction that the nation is only waiting for energetic leadership, and will advance boldly behind whoever manfully holds up the national flag.

This nervous irritation does not, moreover, seem to be the state of mind of only irresponsible persons in inconspicuous walks in life, it would seem to have not left entirely untouched even those whose influence and position are all powerful. I had the honour of reporting last week (in my No. 106) observation of what I believe to have been due to something similar during a conversation with which I was honoured, and surely the remarkable manner in which (so I understand) the Naval Attachés were treated at Kiel during the Regatta week[67] can only be set down to intense preoccupation or vexation.[68]

To turn now to the causes responsible for this general state of nervous tension, there seems little doubt that they are the shocks received by German foreign policy in the last few months, especially the meeting of the King and the Czar at Reval, the Panslavonic Congress, and finally the constitutional movement in Turkey, with its accompanying manifestations of national friendship for England. This latter event must, I take it, have seriously upset German war plans, as it would be in all probability quite unsafe now to trust to Austria–Hungary and Turkey to neutralize the Russian army, so that it would be no longer possible to hurl practically the whole of the German army on France.

In addition to these serious disappointments in the domain of *Weltpolitik* there are some minor matters nearer home which tend to

---

66 Eduard Wilhelm Hans von Liebert (1850–1934). A soldier and colonial administrator – he was Governor of German East Africa, 1896–1900 – he subsequently became a member of the Reichstag where he loudly advocated a far-right political agenda.

67 The Kieler Woche was an annual yachting regatta held in the port of Kiel. During the 1908 Kiel Week the foreign naval attachés were deliberately snubbed by a number of high officials and personages.

68 Trench's report no.106 of 12 August 1908 recorded a conversation he had had with the Kaiser.

increase the general sense of dissatisfaction. Unless I greatly mistake the temper and feelings of the large body of the officers of the army, there is a growing weariness of the endless dreary routine of training soldiers only to pass them to the reserve, rewarded only by an occasional decoration or tardy promotion. An implicit belief in the high state of training and valour of the army, together with its unquestioned superiority to any possible foe, is combined with an intense desire to reap the harvest so carefully and patiently sown in its preparation for war. In the south there is, I believe, considerable irritation at the use to which the *Flottenverein* has been put. That, in addition to its original purpose of assisting in the provision of a fleet worthy of Germany's great future, it should serve to assist in the dissemination of views and feelings on patrio-political points which the Government desired should be spread was right enough; but to these has been added not only the work of opposing the political parties hostile to the Imperial Chancellor's policy, but also (so I am assured) that of helping on the Prussianization of the southern States. This is, naturally enough, strongly resented, especially in Bavaria, and is, so I am told, at the bottom of the split in the *Flottenverein*, although the point is not referred to in public.

Perhaps one of the most striking effects of this nervous state of excitement has been the enormous enthusiasm all over Germany for the Zeppelin balloon, which held out hopes of German superiority in even a third element. About the time of its long journeys into Switzerland and down the Rhine (both to the strains of 'Deutschland, Deutschland über Alles') nothing else seemed talked or thought about, and in the south the smallest villages had telegrams posted several times a-day indicating the plans of the Count or his progress. Finally, when the balloon was destroyed by a storm (as had been the French and British balloons), the provision of one or more successors was felt to be a national matter, and the large sums which Princes, municipalities, houses of business, and individuals spontaneously contributed in all parts of the country afforded a proof of Germany's practical patriotism and determination to let nothing stand in the way of the realization of its hopes and plans. A straw which shows, perhaps, their bellicose nature is the fact that these dirigible balloons are now called in German 'air cruisers' (*Luftkreuzer*).

I have, I fear, in this Report touched on matters somewhat outside my province, but I felt it my duty to draw attention to the fact that, as far as mental preparation for war goes, this country is mobilized, so that, should it be determined to appeal to arms at any time before a relaxation of the tension takes place, all that will be necessary will be to give the word to start. I do not write 'mobilize', as, although mobilization would undoubtedly take place more or less at the same time, I do not believe that the troops employed against England would be previously mobilized; the formations would be special (and with a minimum of horses and vehicles) and the units would embark with only such augmentations of their peace strength as the presence of reservists up for training permitted. The order for the general mobilization would, in all probability, not be issued until the transports were well on their way across the North Sea. I do not for a moment think that anything of the kind is going to take place at present, but I greatly fear that the actual feeling in the country is such that, were the foreign policy of Germany, or the schemes which she has carefully built up to provide herself with active support in the case of war, to receive without some preparation, another serious blow such as – to take most improbable eventualities – were the United Kingdom to become a protectionist State or Austria–Hungary a Slav monarchy, patient discretion would prove unbearable, and Germany would strike without awaiting the completion of a good deal of work of preparation now in course of being carried out, and most of which seem to have been so organized that, as the year 1815 saw the final overthrow by Germany of her arch enemy Napoleon, so its centenary shall offer the surest prospect of the overwhelming of her 'world-enemy' England.

FO 371/461, f. 463

33

Reduction of Armaments: German Views
(Trench MA 108, 25 August 1908)

I have the honour to draw attention to an attempt which has apparently been made by the press to make the public here believe that England, having failed at The Hague to induce Germany to accept some limitation of her armaments, is still pursuing the same object but in a more insidious way. It has even been hinted that this object was at the bottom of the visits of both His Majesty to Cronberg and of Mr Lloyd-George[69] to Berlin, and it was remarkable (especially considering the general state of excitement at the time) how the press accounts of the King's visit

---

69   David Lloyd George (1863–1945), Chancellor of the Exchequer, 1908–15.

to Germany were well damped down, big head-lines and details being avoided and no satisfaction or hopes being expressed.

There seems to have been a general feeling of irritation that England should continue to interfere in matters which, it is thought, concern Germany alone, and especially that she sh[oul]d attempt to check the growth of the German navy while overlooking that of the American and assisting in that of the Spanish and Japanese fleets. The best expression, however, of the general opinion held here in uninspired circles will be found perhaps in the views of Colonel Gaedke – the military editor-correspondent of the radical *Berliner Tageblatt* – as stated in an interview given a few days ago to the representative of the *Matin*.[70] These views are all the more interesting as Colonel Gaedke is strongly opposed to the constant increase which is going on, in this country, of the burden imposed by modern armaments and frequently contributes carefully reasoned articles urging its reduction.

'I consider,' said Colonel Gaedke, 'that the question of the reduction of naval armaments is not only a difficult one to solve but also a dangerous one. Its mere discussion may give rise to controversies which not only set matters back to where they were in the beginning but may cause fresh tension in the relations between the two countries. I think, however, that the chief reason for the suggestion lies in parliamentary needs and that England would be satisfied if Germany made a few trivial concessions, say, for example, if she gave as assurance that a fresh law for the augmentation of the fleet would not be voted. I must add, however, that such a suggestion has no practical value when one considers that America has increased her fleet in far greater proportions than Germany, and that other nations, Italy and Japan among them, are working hard at the development of their respective fleets.'

The remarks recently made to me by a distinguished Prussian lieutenant-general, on this subject of involuntary limitation of armaments, are perhaps not without interest. He said: 'How can you make a rich and patriotic nation like Germany forego the defensive measures which she considers necessary for her present safety and future welfare and progress? If a rival or a competitor tries to persuade her she naturally becomes suspicious and redoubles her efforts! Look at the teaching of history! In 1806, Napoleon had Prussia absolutely at his mercy and imposed upon her the limitation of her armaments. What has been the result? The most formidable army the world has ever seen, with four

---

70   *Le Matin*: prominent French daily newspaper.

million men fully trained and organised, and a partially trained reserve of four million more.'
FO 371/462, f. 4

34

New Armament for German Infantry
(Trench, MA 109, 31 August 1908)

I have the honour to report that, according to reliable information, the arming of German Infantry with Machine-guns is proceeding rapidly but with great secrecy and no information about it is allowed to appear in the press.

Five hundred guns have been delivered and issued to the Guard Corps and the Corps in North and West Prussia and in the Reichsland.[71] Five hundred more are contracted for and are to be delivered approximately during the present financial year. The pattern contracted for is Maxim, but there seems some prospect of the next contract being given for Schwartzlose guns.[72]

Each regiment of the field troops is ultimately to have a company – No. 13 – armed with six of these guns which are expected to be very useful in enclosed country or when the proportion of field guns available is small.

The introduction of these Maxim companies is taking place within the establishment of the army and at present only a small number have been formed with spare men and cast horses from the artillery to act as schools of instruction to which officers and men are sent for courses from the other regiments of the army corps. The number of these – so called 'experimental' companies – is, so far, only acknowledged to be fourteen but two fresh units are to be formed on the 1st October by the 58th Regt at Glogau and the 155th Regt at Ostrovo (both V. Corps) and their gunsheds and stables being already completed. Courses of instruction for officers and men in the mechanism and repairs of machine-guns are being held at Spandau.

The 13th (machine gun) companies are not to be added to the peace establishment until the new organisation of 1910, but there seems no doubt that every regiment of the field army would mobilize a Maxim

---

71 Reichsland: Alsace-Lorraine.
72 Andreas Wilhelm Schwarzlose (1867–1936), German gun designer, best known for a distinctive pistol. His machine-gun – the O seven twelve – was adopted by the Austro-Hungarian army.

company were mobilisation to take place any time after next spring; at present it seems probable that only about eighty regiments would be able to do so. These Maxim companies have no connexion with the Maxim batteries ('Abteilungen') of which 16 are on the peace establishment and which are intended for the cavalry divisions.

[…]

FO 371/462, f. 68

35

Object of German Motor Balloon Society (Trench MA 112, 8 October 1908)

Last night was held in Berlin the first public meeting of the newly formed 'German Society for Motor Balloon Travel', and the President, Regierungsrat Rudolf Martin, delivered to an audience which, drawn apparently from all classes of society, overflowed the auditorium and frequently expressed its concurrence, an opening address which lasted nearly an hour and a half on 'The Political, Military and Economic Importance for Germany of Motor Balloon Travel' in which he declared that the chief task of M.B.T. was for the continental powers to build a large number of balloons of the Zeppelin type, man them with a score of men apiece, station them on the coast and, when opportunity offered, attack and capture England. This gentleman has written several works on balloons, etc., and is a senior official of the Imperial Statistical Office, but his suggestions seemed intended to appeal more to the general public than the scientific mind.

The foundation of this society (with the statement made by the President as to its objective, in the first public meeting) is indicative, I think, of the patrio-aggressive nature of the national enthusiasm about the success of the Zeppelin balloon. Either the Society has been founded with the aim to assist the German Government in the provision of offensive weapons for use against England, or its founders believe that a suggestion of this nature is the best means of enlisting public support and sympathy.

FO 371/462 f. 298

36

New Machine-Gun Companies
(Trench, MA 114, 23 October 1908)

I have the honour, with reference to my No. 109 of the 31st August, to report that the silence 'for patriotic reasons' which the press has been enjoined to keep, during the past year, upon all points connected with the formation, equipment and training of Machine-gun Companies, has been, this week, so far relaxed that the *Frankfurter Zeitung* has been permitted to announce that 'a considerable augmentation of the German army (Wehrkraft), less in numbers than in technical efficiency, has been carried out this autumn in that, to the 17 machine-gum companies formed in October 1907, one in each Prussian army corps, thirty-three new companies have just been added'. 'Thus in the majority of the 21 German corps, although not in all, this has been attained that the brigades – the largest formations consisting solely of infantry – have each been provided with six machine-guns intended for use with infantry only.'

It would appear from this communication, combined with others previously received, that the authorities propose now acknowledging the six hundred infantry machine-guns (believed to be actually in possession) and providing forthwith for their accommodation in the way of gunsheds and stables: also that the four hundred other machine-guns to be delivered (as is believed) during the present financial year will be handed over as they are received to the second regiments of each brigade, the officers and men to man them on mobilization being meanwhile trained with their sister units.

The recently-built government machine-gun workshops at Spandau had their machinery fitted up during the summer and were to have started work this month with workpeople drawn, for the remainder of the financial year, from the other workshops at Spandau which employ, it is believed, some eleven thousand hands.

It is also reported that the new Infantry Construction Board (Büro) will forthwith be formed at Spandau with a staff of one field officer, 2 captains and 2 administration officers. It is intended to relieve the General Construction Board of some of its duties which have become very onerous, especially since so much importance has been attached to power-traction.

With reference to the apparent discrepancy in the figures of the *Frankfurter Zeitung*, it is perhaps desirable to note that – owing doubtless to the peculiar relations of the four German War Offices, one of which leads while the others conform – the North German press not infrequently makes general statements about the German army and supports or follows the with [*sic*] details which refer only to Prussian troops. Thus, in the case in point, the 17 and 33 no doubt point to three companies per *Prussian* army corps, (in the immediate future) no count being taken of those in the other army corps, as far as figures go.

FO 371/462, f. 438

37

The Feeling in Germany
(Trench, MA 116, 4 December 1908)

I have the honour to report that quite recently while discussing with a staff officer I know extremely well and with whom I have formerly talked much about South and South West Africa, I expressed my inability to comprehend why people in Germany had been so vexed with the *Daily Telegraph* interview.[73] My friend replied: 'I will tell you quite frankly … it was that while all our sympathies and interests were with the Boers, the Emperor should have sent a plan to help the English!' 'There were of course many things that they were annoyed about, but this was a climax!'

I have, personally, felt it difficult to find any other reason for this sudden outburst of ingratitude against the Emperor on account of this publication; but this admission by an experienced staff officer that there is a feeling deep down in their hearts, strong enough at a pinch to come into conflict with their ingrained sense of loyalty and discipline, seems to be yet another indication of the existence of a wide-spread conviction that a conflict with England is not only inevitable but desirable.

FO 371/463, f. 446

---

73   In August 1908 the Kaiser and Colonel Edward Montagu-Stuart-Wortley, a British officer eager to promote better Anglo-German relations, had conceived the idea of publishing an article in a British newspaper demonstrating the friendly feelings held by Wilhelm for Britain. The article was eventually published in the *Daily Telegraph* in the form of an interview between Wilhelm and Stuart-Wortley. It failed spectacularly in its intended purpose. In Britain, the Kaiser's words aroused no more than mild amusement, but failed to convince anyone that Germany was anything other than a rival power. In Germany, the Kaiser's claims to have helped Britain aroused a storm of indignation and anger that at one point threatened to undermine the credibility of Wilhelm's regime.

38

The German Landing in England
(Trench, MA 119, 14 December 1908)

I have the honour to report that last Thursday I attended a public meeting of the German Society for Motor-balloon Travel, at which a lecture was given by the President on 'the German Landing in England'. There were between 300 and 400 people present, including officers in uniform and a few ladies. The lecture, which, with the discussion that followed it, lasted an hour and a-half, had for its subtitle: 'The Military and Political Importance of Motor-balloon Travel,' and consisted of:–

1. A brief study and comparison of the landings in England proposed or carried out by Julius Caesar, William the Conqueror, and Napoleon;

2. A consideration of the great future which the recent successes of Zeppelin, Gross,[74] Parseval,[75] and the Wrights[76] assured Germany; and

3. A discussion as to which was the best way to carry out this landing.

The lecturer and his audience (with one exception) seemed to take it for granted that they were all of one mind, that the event to which they all looked forward and, which was one of the great aims of the Verein, was the invasion of England – the only question was, How best to do it? It is true that the lecturer once (*pro forma*) and one of the speakers, at the end of his remarks, said that no one wanted a war with England, but on both occasions the observation was received in silence. When, however, the lecturer said both in the course of his lecture and in his reply, that the insular position, which had up to now enabled England to impose her will upon the world, was a thing of the past, and that the invention of motor-balloons and aeroplanes, together with her central European position, would enable Germany in future to impose her will on the world, the applause was very hearty. It was still more so when Herr Martin said that

---

74 An important type of semi-rigid dirigible favoured by the German army. It was designed by Major Hans von Gross and Nikolas Basenach.

75 Company founded by Major August von Parseval, Germany's leading developer of non-rigid airships.

76 The Wright brothers (Orville and Wilbur) were aviation pioneers. They are generally credited with achieving the world's first powered heavier-than-air flight in December 1903.

Germany did not want India or Egypt, out of which England would be 'chucked' (herausgeschmissen) before long, but they wanted a free hand in those lands where there was an opening for them, and they intended to have it.

The most interesting feature of the lecture, &c., was its tone, so indicative of the frame of mind of many people in Germany, and so suggestive of the distance which separates the English and German standpoints and the difference between the two meanings of the same phrases when used by the two nations. There was no excitement, 'highfalutin' sentiment, or big phrases – but only the thorough conviction that might is right and that Germany has both. These have (with history to justify the conviction) become so bone of the Prussian bone that nobody here ever thinks it necessary to express such truisms, or believes that, even in England, any sensible people ever really doubts [*sic*] the right, nay duty, of Germany to take everything she can get. I have been aware of this conviction for some years now, but the thoroughness and simplicity with which it is held continue to impress me.

The recent debate in the House of Lords was dismissed by the speaker with the remark that everyone did not agree with Lord Roberts[77] – General von Blume, for example – but then General von Blume was perhaps not infallible.[78]

The account of the measures taken by Napoleon included an anecdote of how his failure had been perhaps partly due to his refusal to adopt Fulton's suggested gunboats moved by steam, with the comment that a century later history had repeated itself and placed other marvellous inventions – motor-balloons and aeroplanes – in the hands of Germany; this time the inventions would be utilized! Stress was also laid on the elaborate foresight and preparations of Napoleon, and the speaker was of opinion that the next invasion would also prove to have been carefully thought out beforehand. The more technical part of the lecture consisted mainly of a comparison of the relative advantages of balloons and aeroplanes and their strategical use. A milliard marks would produce either 1,000 Zeppelin balloons or 50,000 aeroplanes; the latter could take 100,000 men, while the former (in three trips) could take only half that number. Lecturer was in favour of aeroplanes, but laid stress on the Belgian (or French) coast being used as a point of

---

77   Field Marshall Frederick Sleigh Roberts, 1st Earl of Kandahar. After a very long and successful military career, he became an active campaigner for the cause of conscription.

78   Wilhelm Carl Hermann von Blume (1835–1919), a retired Prussian general and author of a number of important books on military affairs and strategy.

departure. It was not a question of coast; landing could be effected anywhere. London was the best objective. Fog or night should be chosen; there was no need to take supplies – the country was full of all kinds. No cause to be scrupulous – England had always been 'sehr rücksichtslos' [very ruthless] with weaker nations. Cavalry and artillery were not necessary: aeroplanes could reconnoitre much better than cavalry. Mr Wright, who was coming to Berlin in May, was going to put a Maxim on his machine. *Verein* had bought an aeroplane from him which was being made in America.

The lecturer seemed to think that the best way to employ the German aeroplane fleet would be for it to attack our navy with high-explosive grenades (aeroplanes were not very vulnerable, and Sheerness[79] was very near), and then, when the ships were sunk, the troops could go over in ordinary steamers. The lecturer indicated the necessity that England should be made to feel the power of Germany, and the audience seemed much pleased with the hopes he dangled before it.

FO 371/463, f. 555

39

Laws and Regulations Protecting Military Information
(Trench MA 120, 15 December 1908)

I have the honour to draw attention to some of the precautions taken in Germany to prevent the collection in peace time, of military information – called reconnaissance by soldiers and spying by civilians. The list is not complete owing, in great measure to the care taken in this country to keep these precautions as confidential as can be. That this is done is doubtless due to the fear that England should take a leaf out of the German book, and also take precautions, as an invasion of Germany by French or English troops is believed here to be out of the question and, since the campaign of 1870–1, the French nation is well aware of the precautions that need to be taken.

It is hardly necessary to note here that (in these days of armies millions strong and of rapid transit and communication) intelligence concerning permanent fortifications, &c. has lost much of its value, whilst detailed

---

79 Sheerness in Kent was where the Nore naval command was based. At this point, a significant proportion of the Home Fleet was stationed there.

information concerning the topographical features of a country, its means of communication, supply resources, etc. has become all important.

These precautions consist of:–

1. The 'Act against the Betrayal of Military Secrets'.

2. Special provisions in the Penal Code of the Empire.

3. The police regulations affecting foreign 'military persons' travelling in Germany.

4. The constant police control of all persons moving in the country.

5. The indirect communication to the population of a knowledge of the nature, and an interest in the prevention of the collection, of any military information. These are the result of universal military service and the patriotic efforts of such organizations (at least semi-official) as the Flotten Verein, the Pan-German League and their numerous branches.

The 'Act against the Betrayal of Military Secrets' ('Gesetz gegen den Verrath Militärischer Geheimnisse') is dated 3 July 1893, and was published in the *Reichs-Gesetzblatt* of the 14th July 1893. A translation is attached to this report. The useful effect of Section 8 will be apparent when it is remembered that practically every drill and manoeuvre ground in this country is protected by such a notice.

The Penal code of the German Empire (of the 15th May 1871) applies (v. Sect 3) both to natives and foreigners. The section which deals with the subject under report is section 92, of which the provisions are as follows:–

'Whosoever intentionally
1. Communicates to another Government or publishes state secrets or plans of fortresses or any documents (Urkunden), papers (Aktenstucke) or information (Nachrichten) which he knows that the welfare of the German Empire or of an allied state demands should be kept secret from that Government,

2.   Prejudices the rights of the German Empire or of an allied state in relation to another Government by the destruction, falsification or suppression of documents or proofs relating to these rights, or

3.   Carries out a state duty entrusted to him by the German Empire or an allied state in such a manner with another government as to prejudice his employer

shall be punished with not less than two years penal servitude. In the case of mitigating circumstances, not less than six months imprisonment in a fortress may be inflicted.'

To the above law is, in the *Guttentagsche* Edition of the Laws of Prussia and the German Empire, 22nd edition, appended the following note:– 'The offence may in Germany be committed by either a German or a foreigner.' Subsection 1: It is necessary that the information should not be known to the foreign Government and that therefore there was a possibility of keeping it secret from it; it is immaterial that it is not a secret in Germany (dass sie im Inland nicht Geheim ist, unerheblich).

I beg to draw especial attention to the inclusion of information in general in paragraph 3 and to the comment that the law in Germany does not consider it material that the information was a matter of common knowledge. The law would apply, therefore, (for example) to a communication that the new railway bridge at Spandau on the Berlin–Hamburg line has three bays or that the last lock on the Rhine–Herne Canal is 33 ft wide. The desirability of secrecy is considered in Germany to apply much more universally than in England and I was informed in the Prussian War Office that more than half of even the printed matter it issued is either secret or confidential and is printed by the confidential Imperial Press.

Regulations for foreign 'military persons' travelling in Germany are contained in the enclosure to Sir Frank Lascelles' Despatch No. 421 of the 20th Sept. 1908.[80] They were communicated only after two requests and a delay of six months. They make constant reports obligatory in the provinces adjoining the Russian and French frontiers. Passports are asked for locally.

With regard to the permanent police control of the movements of all persons in Germany, I understand from the police that everywhere in

---

80   Sir Frank Cavendish Lascelles (1841–1920), British Ambassador to the German Empire, 1895–1908.

Germany a foreigner (or his host) must report his arrival in any new police district, within four days in the case of an open town and from four to eight hours in the case of a fortress. I hear also that persons making visits of any duration have, this year, even in large towns such as Berlin and Dresden, had their passports asked for by the police. Foreigners crossing the frontier in autocars are obliged to have white *circular* number boards so that the police may everywhere recognise foreigners and keep an eye on them. (Natives have *square* number boards.)

Finally, while the law provides for the punishment of almost every possible form of collection or betrayal of valuable military information and the police keep a careful watch on the movements of all persons having any connection with foreign combatant services of any kind, universal military or naval service and the patriotic societies convert the whole male population into intelligent and watchful auxiliaries of the police eager to prevent or detect in Germany the collection of military information which Germans collect with so much system and foresight in less careful countries.

KV 3/1

1909

40

The Emperor's Speech to his Generals
(Trench, MA 2/09, 8 January 1909)

I have the honour to draw attention to the views said to have been expressed by His Majesty the Emperor last Saturday on the occasion of his annual reception of the General Officers commanding army corps.

An account of what took place was originally published by the Nationalist *Tägliche Rundschau*, and although its indiscretion has been blamed by some papers, there has been a general outburst of criticism of the action of the Emperor. What happened appears to have been somewhat as follows (I omit details which have been denied): The Emperor, after dinner, discussed, with maps and in considerable detail, the operations at the manoeuvres of the XVth, XVIth, XVIIth and Ist Army Corps at which he had been present during the autumn and then read to the Generals either the whole or part of an article which had just appeared in the *Deutsche Revue* for January, entitled 'War in the Present' and which His Majesty said was by General Count Schlieffen,[81] General v. Moltke's predecessor as Chief of the Great General Staff. The Emperor appears to have said that there was no need for him to express his opinions regarding the military position of Germany at the commencement of the new year as his views entirely coincided with those expressed in the article. The manner of the Emperor is reported to have strongly impressed his generals and is described as 'hoheitsvoll, selbstbewuszt, schlicht und von vornehmster ruhiger Bestimmtheit' (dignified, self-conscious simple, and determined).

---

81   Alfred Graf von Schlieffen (1833–1913), Chief of the German General Staff, 1891–1905.

This article, of which I attach a copy in German with a summary of the first portion and a translation of the final political part, consists of eleven pages of which eight or nine are devoted to an account of the improvements in modern fire arms and their effect on tactics. The last two or three pages of the article are entirely political and describe Germany as standing isolated in the centre of Europe 'opposed to a zealous endeavour to unite all the forces round her in a common attack on the centre'. With the exception of the *Berliner Tageblatt* which gives some extracts from the military portion of the article, the press generally ignores the first part of the article and refers only to the political part which many of them quote in extenso.

From the views on tactics which I have had the honour of hearing the Emperor express it seems most likely that it was mainly on account of the military views contained in the first part of the article that he read it to his generals and indeed it is possible that he did not read aloud the last two pages at all. May I, very respectfully, remark however, that I have no reason to suppose that His Majesty disagrees with the political views expressed in them – rather the contrary.

To turn now to the press comments on the episode, the readiness with which the organs of nearly all parties grasp the opportunity of blaming the sovereign is remarkable, and all the more so when one remembers how intimately all but the most independent journals are connected with the Press Bureau in the Foreign Office.

The *Frankfurter Zeitung* describes the Emperor as 'endeavouring to describe the political situation of Germany between the people of Europe by reading aloud from beginning to end an article … and declaring his concurrence with the views of the author'. The journal goes on to say that 'enemies all round' is the pith of this part of the article and it (the *FZ*) is not surprised to learn that the Emperor substantially shares the views of the author for this is the motto of many a speech he has made. While the journal thinks that the tendency of the military mind is to anticipate situations which will call for the use of the sword, it admits that the description of the military situation is accurate. It compares the expression of Count Schlieffen's views with that of those of Lord Roberts and says that what is uncomfortable is that the Emperor has said that he agrees with them.

The semi-official *Kölnische Zeitung* makes no better defence than the statement that the Emperor's views were not meant for publication and that for this reason there can be no question of a storm like the one in November.

The *Rheinisch-Westfälische Zeitung* declares that it thoroughly agrees with the contents of the article but regrets very deeply that the Emperor should have declared that they were his views. 'What are the views of the Emperor? In the most unfortunate interview he declared himself England's best friend who has always done and will always do what he can to maintain friendly relations. In this article he points to England as the "Implacable enemy". It is doubtful that King Edward will look upon this as welcoming his visit. What answer will Italy, France and Russia give to the Emperor? William II took over the German Empire as the most powerful state in Europe … now he admits that there is a coalition which forms a standing menace … that is the captain's statement of the results of the new course.'

The conservative *Post* alone expresses entire approval and says that the German people agree with Count Schlieffen. It adds that, while the Emperor considers the maintenance of peace a sacred duty, he will always hold the honour of Germany to be most precious.

FO 371/671, f. 56

41

General Count Schlieffen's Essay
(Trench, MA 4/09, 16 January 1909)

I have the honour to report that, in spite of the official statement in the *Reichsanzeiger* that the Emperor's remarks to the Army Corps Commanders on the 2nd inst. contained no reference to the political views expressed by General Count Schlieffen, the press has continued to discuss the episode, and the Pan-German *Täglische Rundschau* has been a good deal blamed by the press – the *Kreuz Zeitung*, the *Kölnische Volkszeitung* and the *Berliner Tageblatt* amongst other journals – for its 'Mangel an patriotischem Empfinden' [want of patriotic sensitivity].

With regard to the attribution of blame for the communication to the public of the Emperor's views as expressed to his Generals, it is very difficult to believe that any one of two dozen officers, the pick of the German nation and who have had half a century's training under the strictest military discipline that exists, should have been either so unwise or so disloyal as to repeat to the world a confidential communication made to them on an official occasion by the sovereign and commander-in-chief. There seems little doubt that the leak was political, especially as a large portion of the press so readily seized upon the episode in order to find fault with the Emperor.

With regard to the expression of concurrence, on the part of a large portion of the press, in the views expressed by General Count Schlieffen, I think that there can be little doubt as to whether this agreement is with his military opinions or with his political views:–

The first portion of the essay states that, owing to the improvements which have taken place in firearms, battles will in the future be fought in very thin lines and taking every advantage of cover. This tactical lesson was learnt by the British army in South Africa but Germany has been unwilling to accept it and the first Imperial Manoeuvres where one saw anything of the kind were those held last autumn. It is most unlikely that these are the views acclaimed by the press.

Concurrence in the historical fact that, as artillery became more powerful, more extensive fortifications were raised to oppose it and so along various frontiers chains of works were erected – is not worth expression.

There remain, therefore, only the last two – political – pages of the essay and I have little doubt that it [is] with their contents that the agreement is meant.

General Count Schlieffen is reported, in last Saturday's *Berliner Allgemeiner Zeitung* to have stated to a representative of that journal the previous day: 'In any case the political situation is so serious that we Germans have every reason to sink our differences and familiarise ourselves with the possibility that we may be compelled in the not very distant future notwithstanding the undoubted and oft-proved love of peace of our rulers to defend our country and our position in the world.' I have little doubt that this opinion is also very generally held.

FO 371/ 670, ff. 310–11

42

Dirigeable Balloons
(Trench, MA 6/09, 30 January 1909)

I have the honour to report that there seems to be little or no doubt that there are now in Germany, built and building, twelve dirigeable [*sic*] balloons designed for use in war.

[…]

FO 371/672, f. 4

43

Dirigeable Balloons
(Trench, MA 7/09, 3 February 1909)

[…]

For some little time the German press has shown a good of [*sic*] discretion about their dirigeables, and while fairly full accounts have been given of the successful trips, details of a technical nature (especially about the motors) have been excluded. It is said that the War Minister,[82] Count Zeppelin and Major v Parseval have laid great stress on this point, and even that the Emperor was asked to give an order inculcating secrecy. It is also worth noticing that the serial numbers by which the balloons are referred to have been changed: those now generally used are the serial numbers of the balloons taken over for service by the War Office – not the inventors' numbers.

FO 371/672, f. 12

44

Dirigeable Balloons
(Trench, MA 8/09, 12 February 1909)

I have the honour to report as follows:–

I learn from a reliable source that the Great General Staff and the Admiralty Staff are desirous of establishing an intimate connection between the balloon and torpedo-boat services, and that, with the stationing of a *Zeppelin* at Wilhelmshafen and possibly another balloon at Heligoland, it is proposed to practise the two services in the combined performance of the duties with which they would be entrusted immediately before or after the outbreak of hostilities.

[…]

It is stated that the formation of army dirigeable stations at Strasburg, Mayence and Cologne is in contemplation.

[…]

FO 371/672, f. 19

---

82   Karl von Einem.

45

Army Organization
(Trench, MA 13/09, 25 March 1909)

I have the honour to submit what I believe to be an approximately correct general statement of the plan for mobilization of the German Army should it have to conduct operations on three frontiers. The information has been obtained from very different, but I believe on the whole reliable sources; on some points – though not all – the information has been confirmed from other sources.

Including active, reserve and Landwehr formations, 125 infantry divisions will be mobilized. The 23 active army corps will be at once made up to three divisions each, and seven reserve army corps will be formed. These thirty army corps are for operations on the Western and Eastern frontiers; the reserve corps are believed to be intended to mask or invest fortresses – at least in the earlier stages.

The thirty army corps will be formed in seven armies, the composition of which agrees generally with that of the 'army inspections'. Exceptionally, the Fourth Army will consist of the Guard, IIIrd and IVth Army Corps with one reserve army corps – the whole under Field Marshal von Hahnke. Each army will also include two or three 'mobile Landwehr divisions'. There seems a certain amount of doubt as to whether Prince Friedrich Leopold of Prussia will command the army corps that he now inspects, also whether, if hostilities do not take place for several years, Prince Leopold of Bavaria[83] would not be succeeded by Prince Rupprecht.[84] It is believed that the chiefs-of-staff of the armies will be four of the Prussian general and chief quartermasters, the chief staff officer of the Guard Army Corps & the Bavarian & Saxon Chiefs-of-Staff.

No active formations are allotted to the northern (coast) frontier. The formations told off to it are: 3 reserve divisions and 7 mobile Landwehr divisions.

The cavalry units will be mobilized on the second day. The infantry divisions of the standing army will be mobilized on the third day. The new third divisions of the majority of army corps will move to the front

---

83 Prince Leopold of Bavaria (1846–1930). A career army officer, Prince Leopold retired in 1913. However, he was recalled to the colours when the First World War began and served with distinction on the eastern front, eventually becoming the Commander-in-Chief of German forces there.

84 Prince Rupprecht, Crown Prince of Bavaria (1869–1955). He commanded the Sixth Army at the start of the First World War and continued to serve on the western front for much of the war.

immediately behind the rest of their corps; in the case of six corps, however, a delay is expected and the new third divisions may not be up on the frontier for three weeks. The reserve army corps and the three reserve divisions for the northern frontier will be mobilized on the tenth day. The majority of the mobile Landwehr divisions will be mobilized on the tenth day – some however not till the twelfth day.

The 23 active army corps, the cavalry divisions and the 3 reserve divisions for the northern frontier will be made up by the addition of reservists and ersatz reservists only. All the reserve formations are organized in peace time and, as far as possible, the men of the 'Beurlaubtenstand' are, when they come up for training, exercised under the officers they will be under when mobilized.

Counting the divisions as averaging 58,000 each, this Plan gives a Field Force of two-and-a-quarter million men, of which one-and-a-half million in first line and three-quarter million in second line. About one-quarter million will probably be mobilized for garrisons, lines of communication and to meet waste. I have no information as to how the remaining one-and-three-quarter million trained men will be disposed of.

FO 371/673, f. 41

46

General von der Goltz's Appointment to Reorganise the Turkish Army
(Trench, MA 22/09, 15 June 1909)

I have the honour to report, with reference to recent rumours that the reorganization of the Turkish army was to be entrusted to General von der Goltz,[85] that the *Berliner Tageblatt* published yesterday an interview in which Gabriel Noradienghian,[86] Turkish Minister for Commerce, Trade and Public Works, and one of the special mission to announce the accession of Mohamet V,[87] made the following statements to representatives of the paper:–

'This appointment was notified to Baron von der Goltz by the Turkish Ambassador about a week ago, after the Turkish Government had, four

---

85 Colmar von der Goltz (1843–1916). A prominent Prussian officer and military writer, he was sent on a mission to modernize the Ottoman army.

86 Gabriel Noradounghian: Ottoman Minister of Commerce, Trade and Public Works, 1908–12.

87 Mehmed V, Ottoman Sultan, 27 April 1909–3 July 1918.

weeks previously, at the request of the whole army, decided to entrust the well-known Prussian General with the reorganisation of the army. Baron von der Goltz had accepted the appointment, much to our satisfaction, and will shortly start for Turkey with several German officers who will act as instructors. Moreover a large number of Turkish officers will be detailed for duty with the German Army. General von der Goltz will remain a Prussian officer for the present, and spend only four or five months each year with us; we hope that it will be possible later on to win the general definitely for the Turkish army.'

There would appear, therefore, to be no doubt that this appointment has been made, and with the approval of the Emperor. Turkish officers have also already commenced to arrive for duty with German regiments, and fourteen German instructors for the Turkish army have been selected. Three of these latter are senior officers, one is a very capable artillery specialist, and the other ten are instructors in various branches.

The importance of this appointment is evident when the past career and present position of General von der Goltz in the Prussian army are considered. [...]

General von der Goltz is very East Prussian in many respects and is believed to sympathise in great measure with most of the political views which his able compatriot Professor Schiemann,[88] on whom has fallen the mantle of Trietschke,[89] inculcates at the Kriegs-Akademie and in the *Kreuz-Zeitung*, and in all probability on board the *Hohenzollern*. When General von Schlieffen retired several years ago from the position of Chief of the Great General Staff it was thought that Von der Goltz would be his successor, and there is said to have been a good deal of disappointment in the army at his not having been chosen.[90] Von der Goltz has, however, a great deal of independence of character, and not long ago, having strongly criticised in print some views of the Emperor's, fell into such disgrace that it is said he was on the verge of being retired from the army. He strongly dislikes England and the English. He appears to have an excellent physique and strong constitution.

---

88   Theodor Schiemann (1847–1921). A Baltic German and native of Estonia, he left his homeland in 1887 because of Russian pressure. On reaching Germany, he secured an appointment at the Kriegsakademie and used this position and subsequent appointments in Berlin to advance German nationalist causes, especially in regard to the Baltic, and to promote hostility towards Russia. In addition to his academic career, he was an active publicist, writing numerous newspaper articles on anti-Russian themes.

89   Heinrich von Treitschke (1834–96), a highly influential German historian who propounded a strongly nationalistic ideology in his writings and lectures.

90   Von der Goltz was certainly in the running, but his selection appears to have been opposed by Schlieffen.

The present Chief of the Great General Staff has systematically diminished the facilities for acquiring military information granted to those nations that do not give a satisfactory *quid pro quo*, either in the shape of orders for materiel or of political support, and it seems most unlikely that the services of one of the ablest of the German generals would be again put at the disposal of Turkey unless that country could be trusted to render substantial assistance to Germany in return. (This is even less likely if, as is believed to be the case, General von der Goltz is the officer who will command the Sixth German Army on the Polish frontier on mobilization.)

There is reason to believe that, in the event of a war between the Triple and the Dual Alliances, Germany counted on the Turkish army (under the old regime) assisting the Austro-Hungarian Army to neutralize the Russian forces, so that practically the whole of the German troops could be directed against France. Is it possible that the Young Turks, taught by recent events the weight that the big battalions of the Triplice carry even at peace negotiations, has put its sympathies in its pocket and also given guarantees?[91]

FO 881/9543, ff. 209–10

47

Measures Protecting Military Information (Trench, MA 25/09, 24 June 1909)

I had the honour, in my No. 120 of the 15th Dec. 1908, to draw attention to some of the precautions taken in Germany to prevent the collection in peace time of information of military value. This report was almost entirely confined to laws, police regulations, etc. and had reference to information concerning *matériel*, i.e., in the first place, fortifications and fixed armaments and, in the second, permanent means of communication such as railways, canals, roads, bridges, etc., which modern science has made of equal if not greater military importance. The precautions referred to are directed equally against all classes of persons.

I beg in this present report to draw attention to the systematic measures taken since the appointment of General v. Moltke[92] as chief

---

91   Possibly a reference to the Bosnian annexation crisis, in which German pressure forced Russia to acknowledge Austria–Hungary's annexation of Bosnia.

92   General Helmuth Johannes Ludwig von Moltke, the younger (1848–1916), Chief of the German General Staff 1906–14.

of the Great General Staff to prepare the protection on information concerning *personnel* and mobile means of transport, such as rolling stock, vehicles and vessels. These steps are almost entirely directed against persons with technical military training, and especially officers, and consist of a diminution, every year of the facilities allowed to attachés and other officers whose presence is announced and of whose object no secret is made, and of an increasing power of tabooing, for strangers, any district in which troop movements are taking place which it is desired to keep secret. The various steps were duly reported as they were taken, but it will probably not be without interest to recall them and to note their close connection.

The first move was made in 1906 and consisted of a marked diminution of the number of permits granted to British officers to attend manoeuvres in plain clothes. Fourteen passes having been requested for the Imperial Manoeuvres for officers in plain clothes, only three were granted. This reduction from the thirteen granted in the previous year was explained by H.M. the Emperor who said that 'such nasty things' had been written and that the officers had forgotten that they were guests and had not behaved as guests. General v. Moltke said that disparaging comparisons had been made with the French Army at a critical time and that was the reason, while General v. Wachs,[93] the chief of the Central Department of the Prussian War Office, informed me officially that permits were superfluous when officers spoke German and that there was no objection to foreign officers doing what the remainder of the public did and looking on with everybody else. Yet three weeks later General v. Moltke spoke to me with a good deal of warmth about a British cavalry officer who had spent a day at manoeuvres in plain clothes (although he had reported himself at once to the general officer in command). The above facts would seem to indicate that, while a decision was come to to diminish the number of passes granted (and, possibly, to ultimately abolish them altogether) a clear understanding as to what reason was to be given was overlooked.

I understand that in 1906 it was also found necessary, for the first time to obtain from the German Government passes for the Staff College students visiting the 1870 battlefields in Alsace-Lorraine.

1907. In June, 1907, the Prussian War Ministry informed that the decision had been come to to give in future no plain-clothes manoeuvre passes whatever to officers of any nation. General v. Wachs however again laid stress at length and very much in the same words as he had used

---

93   Rudolf von Wachs (died 1916), Director of the Central Department of the Prussian Ministry of War, 1903–13.

the previous year, on officers being quite free in Germany as in England to watch the manoeuvres with the remainder of the public and without needing passes to show to the police.

He also communicated to me an arrangement which I understood had been come to that the British and German Governments should mutually communicate to each other the names of officers given leave by their superiors to go to foreign manoeuvres (in plain clothes). I have already reported how one-sided such an arrangement would be owing to the differences in the conditions under which German officers live in England and English officers live in Germany.

The same year the German Government laid down the rule that in future all applications for facilities for officers must come through the Imperial Foreign Office instead of going as formerly direct to the Prussian War Office. The new course suffers not only from the delay due to a longer channel of communication but also from the fact that the Chiefs of the Great General Staff and the Imperial Military Cabinet – who are in such matters practically independent of the Prussian War Minister, although legally his subordinates, – are far less sympathetic to England than is General v. Einem.

In August, 1907, in a communication based, no doubt, on General v. Wachs' repeated statements that there was no objection whatever to officers in plain clothes looking on with the remainder of the crowd, the Imperial Foreign Office was informed, as an act of courtesy, that two officers who were on leave proposed attending the Imperial manoeuvres as spectators with the remainder of the general public. The communication was met with the statement that the German Government could not grant permission for any officers to attend manoeuvres in plain clothes. On it being pointed out that no permits or passes were required a further communication was made that the Emperor was personally very much opposed to officers attending in plain clothes. (The officers were instructed not to attend.)

As an offset probably to these measures 6 officers were allowed to attend minor manoeuvres and 5 were invited to the Imperial Manoeuvres. At the minor manoeuvres facilities were given, but the German officer who was placed in charge of the British officers at the Imperial Manoeuvres took great pains, and sacrificed even courtesy, to prevent them obtaining anything but the minimum of information. (See my No. 73 of 4/10/07.)

During this year strict regulations were introduced affecting the movements of foreign officers in the four eastern provinces of Prussia and resembling those which had been in force for some time in Alsace-Lorraine (see No. 81 of 6/2/08). These regulations were not communicated to this Embassy or the British Government till September of the following year, and then after two requests.

1908. In 1908 the number of days on which the attachés were allowed to be present at the inspection of the Guard Cavalry Division at Doeberitz was reduced from three or four which it had been on previous years to only one, and they were not permitted to be present at the parade of any of the army corps taking part in the Imperial manoeuvres, as formerly. During the three days at the manoeuvres they, with other foreign officers, were very strictly shepherded by the five German officers detailed for the purpose, and kept as much as was possible from obtaining any information of any value or even interest. One day we were hurried from the terrain before the troops had got into contact, and on the others were kept as much as possible from going near the units, especially those with interesting equipment. To such an extent was this carried that once, encountering a telegraph company on the march, we were asked to trot – till we had passed it.

The treatment of other persons at these manoeuvres was even more interesting. German journalists not representing Government organs, but provided with passes, complain that they were worried by plain clothes detectives and it is stated, and not contradicted, that the troops were given orders to give no information of any kind to even German retired army officers. A French M.P., in spite of his being in possession of and producing, a communication from the German ambassador in Paris to the effect that there was no objection to his going to the manoeuvres was (according to the French press) arrested and escorted to the frontier because he had not a military pass. An English officer paying a visit in the vicinity was twice stopped, although he had been informed through the German military attaché that there was no objection to his looking on at the manoeuvres, and a complaint was made to me about him by the G.O.C. Imperial Hd. Quarters.

1909. It is too early yet to say what turn will be given to the screw during the current year, but already the military attachés (the Austrian excepted) were not permitted to be present at the Guards Cavalry Division Inspection on even one day nor were they bidden to the Emperor's annual inspection of the recruits at Potsdam; I understand also that they are not to be allowed to attend the *parades* of the Army Corps taking part in the Imperial Manoeuvres although they will probably be shown something of the operations. Permission for two British officers to attend the cavalry exercises at Doeberitz of the Guards Cav. Division was refused.

So far the successive measures have resulted as follows:–

1. Passes for officers in mufti are abolished.

2. Military Persons are not allowed in the vicinity of (Imperial?) Manoeuvres without passes.

3. The facilities granted to attachés, etc. are being systematically diminished, and those given are more apparent than real.

4. The movement of strangers are more closely watched by the police both at and away from manoeuvres than has previously been the case (No. 120, 18/12/08).

There seems little doubt that all of these measures are part and parcel of a general scheme of which, each year, further developments may be expected. That it does not extend to the military officers only is, I think, shown by the way the Naval Attachés were made to feel that they were unwelcome during the 'Kiel Week' last year.

I respectfully submit that the ultimate object aimed at is the power of practically excluding military persons at any particular time, on the plea that manoeuvres are taking place, from any area in which it is desired to assemble and move in secrecy as far as the outside world was concerned an unusual amount of troops or warlike *matériel*; in other words, these measures are part of the preparation for war without warning.
[Postscript]
Note. The institution of special cavalry exercises on a large scale and the introduction of the practice of holding a second set of 'Imperial manoeuvres' (East Prussia, 1906 – Saxony, 1909) would make it very easy to give a plausible reason for putting any desired district out of bounds, so to speak.
KV 3/1

48

National Military Service Bill
(Trench MA 28/09, 20 July 1909)

I have the honour to report that the debate, last week, in the House of Lords on the National Service Bill does not seem to have excited much interest in the German press – and a large majority of the newspapers content themselves with a summary, varying in length from ten to a hundred lines, of the chief arguments of the advocates and the opponents of the bill, and make no comments. In only one journal with any military authority – the *Militaer Wochenblatt* – are the principles and provisions of the bill discussed and that in an article published before the debates took place.

The semi-official *Koelnische Zeitung* refers to the Territorial Army as a sort of Landwehr and describes Lord Roberts' scheme as a watered form of universal service 'to the tune of wash my skin but don't make me wet' and continues: 'Whether, however, this new militia would be able to hold its own against thoroughly trained troops is another question as to the answer to which no one with the slightest idea of the elementary facts of warfare would have the slightest doubt.' It considers that Lord Lansdowne put his finger on the weak point of the scheme, and that its adoption would not set the fleet free to leave home waters.

The Nuremberg, moderate-radical, *Frankische Kurier* is of the same opinion and agrees with the *Daily News* that 'it would be madness to think that amateur officers and soldiers that had served only four months could oppose an invading army composed of men who had served two years and led by professional soldiers'. It thinks, however, that this proposal is only the thin end of the wedge.

The chauvinistic *Deutsche Warte* says the chief objection to the scheme seems to be the cost, but it cannot understand why universal service should be so unpopular in England, where apparently the same views obtain as did in Hanover in the year 1866.

The *Schwaebische Merkur* the organ of the Evangelischer Bund, says that little has been done to reorganize the British Army during the last ten years and that it will welcome the adoption of the principle of universal service on account of the pacific tendencies it creates. It thinks any changes unlikely, however, as long as the soldier is despised as he is at present.

The *Hamburger Correspondent*, which plays in a minor way in Hamburg the same role that the *Koelnische Zeitung* does in the Rhine province, also points to the difficulties that will have to be overcome in the way of class prejudice, quotes Lord Crewe[94] at some length and hints that although the scheme was nominally to protect the country against invasion it was in reality intended to facilitate the formation of a larger striking force.

---

94 Robert Offley Ashburton Crewe-Milnes, Earl of Crewe (Marquis from 1911) (1858–1945), Secretary of State for Colonial Affairs, 1908–10.

The chauvinistic *Tag* heads its summary: 'Lord Roberts' last inflammatory speech'.

The conservative *Neue Preussische (Kreuz) Zeitung*, the organ of the Prussian officers and landowners, thinks that the introduction of universal service in England is only a question of time although there are still great difficulties to be overcome, and welcomes Lord Roberts' proposals 'with sincere pleasure and sympathy and best wishes for its success.['] It thinks that its acceptance would cause people in England to look upon a war between two great states far more seriously than formerly because all classes of society would be directly affected. In a second article it adds that the playing with thoughts of war which goes on almost as a form of sport in a part of the British public and press would encounter far more opposition from the great mass of the people from the moment that universal service became law, as from that time on every layer of society would be affected by the inevitable consequences of a war. 'It is only from the time that a whole nation is called upon to pay with the flower of its sons the cost of a war brought on with a light heart by sensation-loving and interested politicians that a speedy end is put to the irresponsible activity of these people and a constant element of unrest is excluded from international politics. This is the teaching of history in all countries in which universal service has been introduced.'

The article in the *Militaer Wochenblatt* – the organ of the General Staff – is by Lt-General v Janson, the author of a number of works on combined naval and military operations and in it the writer, as above indicated, comments on Lord Roberts' draft law and not on the speeches made in the House of Lords. He considers that 'it is a thoroughly practical idea for an island kingdom with extensive colonial possessions to have existing alongside one another a militia for home defence and trained in accordance with legal obligatory service, and an army constantly ready for war and composed of professional soldiers. Its realisation would greatly increase the strength of England's armed forces and, above all, its power of taking the offensive and make it independent of the mood and temper of the populace which is not the case with the present system. For the present, however, a considerable portion of the English nation sees in the obligation to perform any military service an attack upon the liberty of the subject. Moreover, there is fear of the great expense especially as the financial situation is already unsatisfactory and promises to become still more so on account of the feverish endeavours to augment the already exceptionally large fleet.[']

The general proceeds to discuss in detail and with commendation the somewhat similar but rather more comprehensive proposals made by Mr Spenser Wilkinson[95] in the *Morning Post* of the 22nd/27th May. He agrees especially with the opinion that a short period of training demands excellent and well-trained officers and holds that 'everyone will recognize that if Great Britain is to maintain her position and do her duty the change must be carried out. War comes like a thief in the night and there is no hiding the fact that the country is not ready.' His general observations, which apparently apply to both the systems proposed, are as follows: 'It is impossible to express an opinion as to when, if ever, so radical a change will be carried out; one thing only is certain, that the introduction of universal service in some form or other would be sure to have a great effect on the English mode of thought which now looks upon the army as consisting more or less of a lot of mercenaries and which leaves to a number of idealists the duty of gratuitously undertaking the defence of the mother country. When every mother's son has to fight – it is no question here of half-civilized races – one takes care not to play with fire (in the shape of war).'

FO 371/675, f. 115

49

Press Comments on Imperial Defence
(Trench, MA 29/09, 30 July 1909)

I have the honour to draw attention to the unfriendly tone of the German press with regard to the steps now being taken to impart some organisation to the defence forces of the British Empire. Owing to the extreme sensitiveness which is shown to any foreign mention of Germany, in spite of the great freedom with which the affairs of other countries are criticised here, it was perhaps not surprising that references in parliament to German programmes should have been taken amiss, but the comments which are being made about the Imperial General Staff and the Imperial Defence Conference suggest the existence of a hope that the steps now being taken will prove abortive. What this tone is, a few quotations will perhaps suffice to indicate.

---

95 Henry Spenser Wilkinson (1853–1937), British military thinker and author. He was leader writer for the *Morning Post* until 1909 when he was elected Chichele Professor of Military History at the University of Oxford.

The *Vossische Zeitung* says: 'The British soldiery has shown itself thoroughly useless (*untauglich*) as a modern army. The men lack discipline and the officers scientific military training. This is especially the case in the badly organised colonial militia. It is now hoped to make up for this with a general staff; trained English officers are to be sent to the colonies. … Further, each part of the Empire will provide for its own defence; second, it will help in the common defence of the Empire. … These are, no doubt, great plans, but they will be very difficult to carry out, and it is the task of the Imperial Defence Conference to test their practicality. Above all things, the question of national (allgemeinen) service will be earnestly discussed.

Although it is gaining favour in England, most of the [?] refuse to accept it' (and the writer proceeds to prove at great length that local conditions make it impossible at present in Canada, Australia and New Zealand.)

The *Kreuz Zeitung* gives an outline of the General Staff scheme and concludes: 'One must certainly agree … that these intentions are all very fine, but they will be of no use till all portions of the Empire are agreed about the introduction of national service (allgemeine Wehrpflicht).'

The *Königsberger Zeitung* says: 'England has not an army capable of defending the Island Kingdom and its great colonial possessions including India.'

The *Tägliche Rundschau* reports: 'The Imperial Conference was opened today at the Foreign Office. The Premier Asquith[96] greeted the representatives of the colonies. The discussions are strictly secret; Asquith is reported to have briefly set forth the proposals of the Imperial Government. We are anxious to learn what attitude the colonies – which have a strong German element – will maintain towards the programme as far as it refers to pressure to take their share when England attacks or is attacked.' (It will be remembered that 'German' as used above means 'of Germanic race' and includes the 'Low-German' Boers.)

The attitude which it is desired that 'the strong German element' should assume is clearly indicated in the *Deutsche Tages Zeitung* (which I do not quote as my naval colleague is reporting its views[97]). It is true that the *D.T.Z.* has been taken to task by some of the other journals – not, however, for its advocacy of disloyalty in friendly and hospitable dominions – but for its tactlessness.

FO 371/675, ff. 184–5

---

96   Herbert Henry Asquith (1852–1928), British Prime Minister, 1908–16.
97   The British Naval Attaché was Captain Herbert Leopold Heath.

50

Change of Prussian War Minister
(Trench MA 35/09, 12 August 1909)

I have the honour to report that the Prussian War Minister, General von Einem, has, at his own request, been relieved of his duties as minister and appointed to the temporary command of the Seventh Army Corps in the place of General von Bernhardi[98] who is on leave.

The retirement of General von Einem from the post which he has held for six years has come as a general surprise, and only surmises are made as to the reasons for his going, among them being – friction with the Military Cabinet of the Emperor, discontent with the more rapid promotion of naval officers then military officers, quarrels with Count Zeppelin, pecuniary difficulties and indifferent health. Perhaps the most likely cause is a desire to exchange office work and parliamentary disputes for the active work and very independent position of a commander in chief. Indeed the *National Zeitung* states that the vacancy at the head of the Seventh Corps, to which the general is attached, led him, when recently the guest of the Emperor at his shooting box, to ask to be appointed to its command.

The articles in the press are generally complimentary to the outgoing minister to whom they give credit for much solid progress – especially in the introduction of scientific warlike appliances – if for no brilliant measures of reform. He has maintained the rights of the army and diminished the ill-treatment of soldiers by their superiors. As might be expected, he is blamed for first trying to screen and then treating with culpable leniency the highly-placed officers who a couple of years ago were accused of unnatural crime.

The officer who has been appointed to succeed General von Einem as War Minister is General of Infantry von Heeringen,[99] commanding the Second Army Corps. He is 59 years old, belongs to a Hessian family which has held many positions at court and he was badly wounded at Woerth. He held appointments at the War Office from '87 to '90 and from '98 to '03. He commanded the 22nd Division from '03 to '06 and from then till now the Second Army Corps. He is believed to have been in the Emperor's good graces for a number of years and he and

---

98   Friedrich von Bernhardi (1849–1930), Prussian general and military writer, best known for his polemical work *Germany and the Next War*.

99   Josias von Heeringen (1850–1926), Prussian Minister of War, 1909–13.

his family are popular in Stettin where they try to bridge over the gulf between the officers and the civilians and take an active interest in works of charity.

The new commander of the Second Corps is Lt-General von Linsingen[100] who was born in Hanover 59 years ago, served with distinction in 70/71 and commanded the 27th (Wurtemberg) Division from 1905 to 1908. He is a big man with a strong character, a kindly manner and a quick temper. He is very clear-headed and has modern views about military matters; he is not a staff college graduate.

I hope to send photographs of these two officers shortly.

FO 371/675, f. 277

51

Landing Operations at Manoeuvres
(Trench, MA 36/09, 13 August 1909)

I have the honour to a report [*sic*] that there are going to be landing operations practised on a large scale from the 6th to the 10th September, after the Naval Manoeuvres. It is possible that only the navy will take part in these, but it seems more than likely that at least a portion of the Ninth Army Corps (the Brigade manoeuvres of which take place from the 6th to the 10th Sept. near the Mecklenburg coast) will also practise embarking and landing.

The 33rd Brigade, quartered in Bremenstade and Hamburg goes to Rostock for its manoeuvres, the 35th Bde goes from Schleswig, Hadersleben, Flensburg and Sonderburg to Bützow and the 36 Bde from Altona, Rendsburg and Kiel to Wismar, i.e. from ports to ports (save Bützow which is a day's march inland). The Training Ground of the Ninth Army Corps, Lockstadt, is only sixteen miles from the Kiel Canal of which one of the objects of the enlarging is believed to be to prepare it for embarkations on ocean liners.

It is stated in the press that during the manoeuvres of the Ninth Corps cyclists will be trained in small formed bodies – a novelty here – with machine-guns attached, also that motorcyclists will be employed to replace cavalry for reconnaissance duties. As the Ninth Corps will probably have some sixteen thousand reservists, &c up for training in

---

100 Alexander Adolf August Karl von Linsingen (1850–1935), Commander of the Second Corps 1909–15.

1909 it is not impossible that any units which practise embarking and landing will do so at war strength.

FO 371/675, f. 282

52

Protection of Military Information
(Trench, MA 44/09, 15 December 1909)

I had the honour, in my reports No. 120 of the 15th December 1908[101] and No. 25 of the 24th June 1909, to draw attention to the far-reaching measures taken in Germany, not only to prevent the acquisition of information concerning fortifications, fixed armaments, topography and permanent means of communication, but also systematically to increase the restrictions placed on the movements of even those foreign officers who are present in the country with the permission of the German authorities.

It is naturally almost impossible to ascertain the administrative steps taken to carry out the undoubted intentions of the authorities, especially as British officers are very careful while in the country to avoid even the suspicion of offence, and the officers of the Prussian War Office and General Staff protest again and again that foreign officers are, in Germany, as free in their movements as foreigners are in England. That effective steps are taken to prevent anything of the kind being the case is, I think, shown by the following incident.

Last summer, two military attachés, interested in the purchase of ammunition from the Ehrhardt Company, were invited by its representative to attend some tests at the Company's ground at Unterlüss near Hanover. One of them, for convenience of trains, slept the previous night at Hanover but during his absence from Berlin did not go near any troops or military works.

Very shortly afterwards, a description of him, with appearance, gait, attire, manner of speaking German, &c. came out in orders in the Tenth Army Corps, together with instructions that if he was seen he was to be reported, as were any questions that he asked, but that no answers were to be given him. I understand that notices to the same effect were also posted in barracks and that one which is believed to have been to the same effect was also seen on a police notice board.

---

101 Document 39 in this volume.

The stricture [*sic*] of this procedure is all the more remarkable as the officer belongs to a transatlantic republic with which Germany is most desirous to be on the best of terms and the soldiers of which are perhaps the least likely of all ever to land in Germany; he had moreover recently taken up his duties. He has heard nothing officially about the matter, and I cannot think of any way in which he could have offended. Perhaps the procedure is normal. I, personally, think it wise whenever I sleep away from Berlin to report myself to the local military authorities; and, indeed, eighteen months ago, on my mentioning at the Prussian War Office that my doctor had recommended me to go to the seaside for a fortnight's 'aftercure', I was asked to report myself to the military authorities wherever I went.

KV3/1

Lieutenant Colonel Alick Russell pictured in 1918. IWM Q11458. Reproduced by permission of the Imperial War Museum.

Part II

Lieutenant Colonel A. V. F. V. Russell

Despatches, 1910–1914

1910

53

Reception by the Emperor
(Russell MA 11/10, 24 March 1910)

I have the honour to inform you that on Friday 18th instant, in accordance with instructions from the Chief of the Military Cabinet, I reported myself to His Majesty the Emperor on the occasion of the inspection of four companies [of] the 1st Foot Guard Regiment at Potsdam.

His Majesty welcomed me very graciously and referred in cordial terms to the fact of my having lived here previously in the days when my father was British Ambassador in Berlin.[1] His Majesty enquired after my relations and finally expressed a hope that I might be as 'comfortable' here as my predecessor.

The Emperor's manner towards Col. Trench was marked by great cordiality and both in bidding my predecessor farewell and in several previous conversations His Majesty gave evidence of being animated towards him by sentiments of much friendliness and esteem. His Majesty presented Col. Trench with a signed photograph of himself in the uniform of a British Field Marshal.

His Majesty appeared to be in good health and spirits.

The inspection of the four companies and of the Body Guard Hussars was carried out as usual and calls for no special comment. The drill was very fine.

I am anxious to take this opportunity of testifying to the very admirable and complete manner in which Col. Trench has handed over to me the records of his office.

FO 371/904, f. 163

---

1   Lord Odo Russell (later Lord Ampthill) (1829–84): was British Ambassador in Berlin, 1871–84.

54

General von Bernhardi's Work on Infantry Problems (Russell, MA 13/10, 12 April 1910)

I have the honour to draw Your Excellency's attention to an important work which has recently appeared from the pen of General von Bernhardi. The publications of this eminent military authority have been hitherto chiefly confined to the domain of cavalry, which is the arm to which the General belongs. In a striking work, however, entitled 'Taktik und Ausbildung der Infanterie' [The Tactics and Training of the Infantry], the General of cavalry now deals with certain burning infantry problems.

The author himself states in his preface that he does not affect to teach, but only to rouse his comrades to reflect more and more deeply over these important military questions.

One great interest of the work lies in the fact that it is a criticism of the existing infantry drill regulations – this criticism is moderate but incisive; it is not only destructive but constructive also, since the author does not omit to state what he himself considers the wording of the regulations should be. That the whole subject matter is closely reasoned and admirably clear will be admitted even by those who cannot agree with all the arguments put forward. If it were possible to point out one portion of the text as being of special interest, I would select that in which the author discusses the question of the attainment of superiority of fire. The general very justly affirms that there is a certain contradiction in two passages in the regulations: one states that the attackers must gain superiority of fire before they can expect success, and another says that the attackers must advance on the enemy, cost what it may.

The author further states that the assailants can never expect to gain a superiority of fire over a defending force of even approximately equal strength.

For infantry on the defensive, however, the maintenance of superiority of fire is a *sine qua non* for success.

It is held on the other hand by many authorities in our own country and elsewhere that superiority of fire must be attained by the attackers before the final assault is made, and that it was due to the failure to realize this principle that our want of success in the early stages of the late Boer War must mainly be attributed.

General von Bernhardi wishes to rule out of the regulations that the attacking infantry must gain a superiority of fire and emphasize[s] all the more the necessity for maintaining it in the case of the defending infantry. He asserts that the notion that this superiority of fire is essential for the attackers, sets up undesirable excuses for delay. The defenders, as a rule, have cover available, the attackers on the other hand should realize that only in a successful assault is safety to be attained, and that with each step backwards double destruction awaits the soldier. He does not omit to urge the necessity for artillery support and affirms that the attacking artillery must confine themselves almost entirely to firing on the defending infantry.

It is interesting to note that the author warns his readers against overestimating the military skill of the Japanese; 'When at last again the trumpet of war calls us' says the General, 'let us at all events hope that we shall carry on the campaign in a different spirit to that in which the Japanese did; not to say anything of course about the Russians.' The author maintains, with perfect right indeed, that it is not by the multiplications of orders through technical means – and here he no doubt has the Japanese in mind – but through educating the troops in self-reliance that success must be sought for.

The author's remarks at the commencement of the book on infantry reconnaissance are, I consider, admirably thought out.

In the concluding chapter in which the author refers to the relation of the people to the army, the necessity for realizing that peace at any price is not a desirable doctrine, the importance of educating the children in military virtues and other kindred subjects, the General affirms that a time may come in the immediate future, not unlike the days of Frederick the Great, when the combined cabinets of Europe planned to crush the rising Prussia.[2]

I regret that it is impossible within the compass of this despatch to do more than indicate a few isolated points in this admirable work. I attach, however, a valuable criticism by the well-known General Gädke, which appeared in the *Berliner Tageblatt* of the 7th instant.

General von Bernhardi's latest work will doubtless be of special interest to the Directorate of Military Training at the War Office.

FO 371/904, f. 234

---

2 Frederick II (1712–86). He became King of Prussia in 1740 and promptly provoked a series of wars by seizing the Habsburg territory of Silesia.

55

Russell to Sir Frederick Ponsonby[3]
(23 April 1910)

I was dining with General von Löwenfeld[4] (Commander of the Guard Corps) the other night and the Crown Prince was present.[5]

During the course of a long conversation with H.R.H, it became evident to me that one of the Crown Prince's dearest wishes was to belong to an English regiment, or rather a Scottish one. I think H.R.H would particularly like to wear a kilt!

Do you think the question could possibly be raised? I presume that he could hardly be made a Colonel-in-Chief, but perhaps he might be made an Honorary Colonel in some Highland regiment, as the King of Norway is in the Norfolk Yeomanry.

I wish you would be so very good as to use your unerring discretion in this matter and refer it to the King, if you think it desirable to do so.

The Crown Prince is, I think, animated by the friendliest sentiments towards England and everything English and an arrangement of this kind might assist in further cementing these feelings. I do not think the Emperor would mind if his permission were first asked.

[...]

RA: VIC/X 23/31

56

Aviation and the German Press
(Russell, MA 17/10, 6 May 1910)

Recent aeronautical events and particular the disaster to Zeppelin II[6] have naturally furnished the German press during the last days with abundant opportunities for purveying comment, criticism and counsel.

The general effect of the destruction of Zeppelin II will, I am convinced, be to advance the cause of aviation, paradoxical as it may appear to say so.

---

3   Sir Frederick Ponsonby (1867–1935), Assistant Private Secretary to the British monarch.

4   Alfred von Löwenfeld (1848–1927), Adjutant-general to the Kaiser.

5   Friedrich Wilhelm Victor Augustus Ernest of Hohenzollern (1882–1951), eldest son of Kaiser Wilhelm II and Crown Prince of Prussia.

6   *Luftschiff Zeppelin 5* or *LZ5* (known to the military as Zeppelin II or Z.II) was destroyed on 25 March 1910 when it was carried by the wind from its moorings and wrecked.

The catastrophe has indeed given rise to a feeling throughout Germany that further and more energetic steps must be taken to reduce the chances of disasters to airships and many proposals which are now being out forward in the press, will no doubt be adopted to the great benefit of aviation in this country.

The most important of these suggestions are as follows:–

(1) *Meteorology is not sufficiently studied in connection with aviation.* The German press and the whole German nation are the first to admit that loss of material and even danger to life must be risked when preparation for war demands it, but it is now urged that greater care must be taken to observe conditions of wind and weather, and that in peace time needless risks must not be incurred.

(2) *When an airship is anchored in the open, an adequate guard must be left with it.* It is pointed out that, had an adequate guard been left with Zeppelin II, it might have been possible to have got the airship under control when it broke loose, and eventually to have effected a safe landing elsewhere.

In bad weather and in case of unsatisfactory anchoring ground, it is further urged that the motors ought to be held in readiness for almost immediate use. It is maintained that regulations to this effect should be at once laid down.

(3) *The erection of a number of airship sheds at suitable points* is very generally recommended. Accidents and advent of bad weather must constantly cause airships to seek refuge at the nearest possible point, and it is clear that a number of such harbours would be of great assistance in reducing the chances of disaster. These airship sheds must moreover be connected with each other and with the nearest meteorological offices by telephone and wireless.

Another and less expensive proposal which is put forward by the *Deutsche Tageszeitung* is that heavy stones or blocks of cement should be firmly set up in a large number of suitable anchoring places all over Germany. To these stones, or blocks, rings would be attached to which a piece of heavy iron chain ending in a steel hawser would be fixed. Airships could then, when they desired to anchor, make fast their own anchoring cables to the ends of these steel hawsers. The weight of the chain would furnish the elasticity which is required, if a steel hawser is not to break when a sudden and specially heavy strain is put upon it. Lists of these anchoring places would have to be made out and the places themselves marked on all maps.

(4) *Airships and airship sheds*, it is urged, *must be subsidized by the state* in the same way that motor wagons have been. It is important from a military point of view that airship sheds built by private enterprise should be suitable for military airships, and similarly that privately constructed airships should to a certain extent fulfil military requirements. The advantage of such conditions in time of war is obvious.

A preliminary step in this direction has already been taken some time ago by the military authorities in the case of the 'Leichlinger Haller' of the 'Rheinisch-westfälischen Motorluftschiffgesellschaft', which has been heavily subsidized.

The Berlin paper *Die Post*, in an article urging the construction of more and more airship sheds, argues that a proper strategical distribution of such sheds is also desirable.

* * *

We have it on the authority of Lt. Gen. Frhr.von Lyncker, the Inspector of Transmission Troops, that any idea of repairing the shattered Zeppelin is quite out of the question. It appears, however, likely that Zeppelin III now will be bought by the state.

Recent aeronautical achievements in England have not been commented on with much enthusiasm by the German press, but the people here do not take the same interest in the heavier-than-air machines, having 'put their money on the other horse'.

FO 371/905, f. 66

57

Law for the Systematic Increase of the Army
(Russell, MA 20/10, 16 June 1910)

The *Friedenspräsenzstarke* Law of the 30 March 1905, which provided for the systematic increase of the army during a period of five years, will have to be renewed at the end of the financial year of 1910, i.e. by the 31 March 1911.[7]

The desirability of such a law is apparent; it may also be said to be necessary. The number of men who annually become eligible for service in the German army increases each year; there are thus only two alternatives possible, either to undermine the principle of universal service, or at stated intervals to enlarge the army by the creation of new formations and by the increase of the number of appointments of officers and non-commissioned officers.[8]

The German press has already commenced to indulge in a certain amount of speculation as to possible impending changes and such papers as *Der Vorwärts*[9] to utter complain[t] with regard to the probable heavy cost of increased establishments. The corresponding Naval Law, although not due for renewal till 1912, has equally of late received its share of notice in the press.

In the early days of this month currency was given to a report with regard to the army, to which, we imagine little credence can have been attached by the general public. It was to the effect that at the impending conclusion of the current period of five years a standstill in the development of the German army was to take place. It was even stated that a decision in this sense had already been arrived at, when the present Chancellor took office.[10] In order to throw a veil over the failure to reform the finances of the Empire, it was intended, so the report ran, to affect economies at the expense of the army. A Hamburg paper on the 10th

---

7 As part of the compromise that led to the founding of the German Empire, the law regulating the size of the army was not passed annually, but every five years (originally every seven years). This nominally gave the legislature some say in military matters, but avoided the kind of scrutiny that was anathema to the army and had been at the heart of the Prussian constitutional crisis of the early 1860s.

8 It was the practice of the Prussian Ministry of War to emphasize quality over quantity. Quality was partly determined by physique and fitness, but was also assessed on reliability. The Prussian military authorities wished to avoid conscripting those who were hostile to the regime and might be reluctant to enforce monarchical rule at home in the event of a confrontation between the regime and the populace.

9 *Vorwärts* was the principal newspaper of the German Social Democratic Party.

10 Theobald von Bethmann-Hollweg (1856–1921), Imperial Chancellor, 1909–17.

of this month even stated that it was able to confirm the fact that the present Imperial Chancellor, when accepting office had indeed made it a condition that at the end of the current period of five years any larger demands for the army should not be made. This condition was, however, to be kept dark; it was besides possible, according to the Hamburg paper, to take refuge behind the subterfuge that no special Bill was necessary in 1911, as it was possible to increase the army without one.

These reports have now been silenced by a semi-official statement in the *Norddeutsche Allgemeine Zeitung* which, after repeating the reports given above, continued:–

'We wish to state definitely that all such reports, including the alleged power of economy demanded by the Imperial Chancellor, are pure invention. There is nothing to be concealed with regard to impending new demands for the army. These are being prepared for the next five years in full agreement between the Chancellor and the military authorities and completely in the sense of the statements already issued on the subject, nor will these demands omit anything which, in the opinion of competent authority, is necessary in the interest of the efficiency of the army.'

It would be interesting to learn whether the rumours under discussion were purposely circulated, and if so, whether they were intended to serve any other purpose than that of testing public opinion. The affair is perhaps part of the usual practice of preparing the ground beforehand.

FO 371/905, f. 284

58

Trials with Military Aeroplanes
(Russell, MA 23/10, 21 October 1910)

I have the honour to bring the following facts to Your Excellency's notice:–

On Tuesday 18 October at 7 p.m. I received a telegram from the Secretary of State for War, which read as follows:–

'2262. Reported that trials with military aeroplanes take place tomorrow Döberitz.[11] Please endeavour to attend and send report. Attendance to be open and official if possible.'

---

11   Döberitz: a village and area to the west of Berlin. It was requisitioned by the army in 1895 as a training ground. In 1901 a balloon squadron was stationed there and in 1910 it became the home of an air training school.

As the Prussian War Office was shut at the hour at which I received the telegram, I telephoned to the private residence of the Director of the Central department of the War Office (Lieutenant-General von Wachs). The General replied at once through the telephone that he had no knowledge of any trials of this nature.

On the following morning (Wednesday) I proceeded to the Prussian War Office, ostensibly with the object of apologizing to the General for having troubled him unnecessarily, but also in the hopes of obtaining further information on this subject, and having the statement, made to me through the telephone, confirmed at a personal interview. The General again assured me that he knew nothing whatever of any trials with military aeroplanes.

On Thursday morning I read in the German newspapers that trials had taken place the previous day and that these trials had been conducted under the auspices of the Prussian War Office. I repaired, therefore, once more to the *Leipzigerstrasse* and enquired of General von Wachs whether, in view of what he had told me, I was to disbelieve the statements in the newspapers with regard to this matter. The General was visibly embarrassed, particularly when I produced the cutting giving an account of the trials, and protested that, as German officers had taken part in the flights, the matter could not be quite without the sanction and cognisance of the War Office. He was as courteous as ever and assured me once more that nothing was known at the War Office of any such trials. He promised, however, to give me an official answer to my enquiries in due course.

In the circumstances I considered it inadvisable, until this matter was cleared up, for me to attempt to attend the trials at Döberitz, which I gathered from the newspapers would again take place that afternoon.

This morning (Friday) I again visited General von Wachs, having received a telephone message from him inviting me to do so. The General began at once by saying that he wished to clear himself of any impression he may unintentionally have given me of not having spoken the truth. He then proceeded to maintain that these trials with aeroplanes had been conducted entirely without the knowledge of the War Office, and that, in fact, the Minister for War had only been informed of them this very morning. The trials had been held under the superintendence of General von Lyncker, the Inspector of Transmission Troops, who was president of a committee for making experiments with aeroplanes, which committee had been formed for some time. I naturally accepted the General's explanation without further question, though I must admit that I was surprised that the Minister for War and the Director of the Central Department at the War

Office should have been in ignorance of a matter of this nature, which had, moreover, been referred to repeatedly in the public press during the last few days. I could not, however, refrain from asking before I left, whether, if it had been known at the Prussian War Office that these trials were taking place, I might have been given permission to witness them. The General replied that permission could not have been given, in view of the fact that the matter was still in the experimental stage and was therefore being conducted secretly. It is to be regretted that an answer somewhat to this effect could not have been given me on Tuesday evening.

It has thus been impossible for me to attend the trials with aeroplanes which took place at Doberitz on Wednesday and Thursday last, in accordance with the instructions of the Secretary of State for War.

FO 371/907, ff. 132–3 and 275

59

Henry Wilson[12] to Russell, 7 November 1910

On page 17 of your report on the recent manoeuvres you say as follows:–
It would appear that the cavalry have resigned themselves to the inevitable, and have accepted the new principles under which they are expected to fight with whole hearted zest. To the men the dismounted combat is interesting from its novelty, and the manner in which they crawled, crouched, and took every advantage of every accident of ground …

What exactly does this mean? What are the new principles under which the cavalry are expected to fight in the future? Have the Germans gone so far as to consider that the rifle is stronger than the sword or the lance, and are they prepared, if they have come to that decision, to carry out the training to its logical conclusion and insist on the cavalry being riflemen first and shock soldiers second[?]

WO 106/59, f. 69

---

12 Sir Henry Hughes Wilson (1884–1922), Director of Military Operations, 1910–14.

60

Military Defences on the German North Sea Coast (Russell, MA 29/10, 7 December 1910)

Some of the military defences on the German North Sea Coast are in a stage of evolution and it is interesting to note by means of certain minor indications the gradual course of this development.

It is probable that in the scheme for the defence of the German North Sea littoral against a foreign blockade, fortified torpedo boat bases at Borkum, Heligoland and Sylt are intended to play an important role.[13] I desire to draw attention to certain facts which are of no great importance in themselves, but which do assist to a small degree in substantiating this theory and also point to a future gradual accession of military strength along this portion of the German coast line.

Heligoland is already fortified and money has been voted in the current Naval Estimates for the improvement of the torpedo boat harbour at that place.

Frequent statements have appeared in the German Press during the last few years to the effect that a torpedo boat base is to be established at Sylt. The landing experiments which were carried out with some secrecy earlier this year on the island would appear to lend colour to this report. It may no doubt be assumed that these operations were not conducted without some desire to test the strategical and tactical value of the island, and may at all events be taken as indicating that the question of constructing a fortified harbour at Sylt is still under consideration.

The report of the building of barracks at Heide (Schleswig-Holstein) would appear to point to a future military accession of strength at that place.

At Borkum some 4 or even 5 forts are in existence (according to a press report there are '4 shore and 5 inland batteries') and 3 batteries from the 2nd FOOT Artillery Regiment were transferred from Danzig in April this year to garrison the island. It was given out at the time that these three batteries were to be accommodated at Borkum until the 1 April 1911, by which date the new barracks at Emden would be ready to receive them. One battery however, it was said, would always be quartered at

---

13 Britain's naval war plans up to 1912 envisaged an observational blockade (watching for signs of enemy movements) of the German coasts by destroyers. Maintaining such a watch would have been greatly facilitated by capturing an advanced base and, at various points, both Borkum and Sylt had been considered for this purpose. The fortification of these islands was one of the factors that prompted the Admiralty to reconsider its strategy of closely watching the German coasts.

Borkum, being periodically relieved from Borkum. With only one battery at Borkum, however, the guard duties, already heavy and no doubt still more so now, since certain regrettable incidents of recent date, would not admit of time for the proper training of troops. The barracks moreover at Borkum are large enough to accommodate 700 men and those at Emden at least 1,000. It appears, therefore, more probable that a whole regiment will be detailed to garrison these two places and that three batteries will be retained at Borkum.

The creation of a new foot artillery regiment is demanded in the current Military Estimates and the three batteries now at Borkum are to be employed in making up new formations. It seems, therefore, not improbable that this new regiment, which is to be designated No. 16 and to which no destination has as yet been assigned, will have its head-quarters at Emden and will furnish a detachment of not less than three batteries at Borkum.

It seems doubtful whether one foot artillery regiment will long be considered an adequate garrison for this part of the coast. It is stated in the press that fortifications are to be undertaken at Knock, a supporting point between Emden and Borkum, and it is known that defensive works are in the process of construction on the island of Wangeroog. These works will in time require troops to occupy them.

A further consideration is whether the huge wireless station at Nörddeich is adequately protected from hostile attack by the batteries at Borkum. It is stated in the newspapers that this wireless station is to be largely increased in the near future. It may, therefore, later on be considered to be desirable to fortify Nordeney as well.

There can thus be little doubt that a further increase of military strength in this portion of the German coast is inevitable. I think it may also be inferred from the indications given above that Borkum, Heligoland and Sylt are destined as supporting points for the German fleet in the case of a foreign blockade.

[Postscript] **Note**. The islands of Sylt and Borkum were both popular watering places, the resort of numberless tourists in the summer months. Sylt still retains this character, but Borkum has now passed completely under military control.

FO 371/907, f. 323

61

The Resources of Germany and France in the Matter of Trained Soldiers
(Russell, MA 30/10, 15 December 1910)

I have the honour to call your attention to the accompanying articles by the well known Colonel Gädke, which appeared in yesterday's issue of the *Berliner Tageblatt*.

Colonel Gädke's chief preoccupation – not for the first time – is to combat the suggestion which has been put forward from various quarters, that France has no object in increasing her army, as the available supply of trained men in that country is distinctly greater than that in Germany. Colonel Gädke singles out for special refutation that article of a certain Herr Kolbe, who has written in the *Reichsbote* and is apparently the most recent exponent of this doctrine. Herr Kolbe's main contention is that Germany can only oppose 3,800,000 trained men to the 5,500,000 which France can put in the field.

Colonel Gädke then produces figures which he has taken from a number of annual volumes of *The Statistical Yearbook for the German Empire* (*Statischtisches Jahrbuch für das Deutsche Reich*), which he claims as an unimpeachable authority and as one which is accessible to everybody. The figures referred to in the Statistical Yearbook are taken from the Annual Official Recruiting Statistics. Colonel Gädke has been obliged to strike an average, which he believes to be a low one, for the years 1909 and 1910, as the figures for these years are not yet available.

The number of men who have passed through the school of the army according to Colonel Gädke is as follows:–

> In the 12 latest yearly contingents from 1899 to 1910 of the Line, the Reserve and the 1st Ban of the *Landwehr*, i.e. the existing Standing Army with its Depot formations:–

> 3,182,000 men.

> In the 7 yearly contingents from 1892 to 1898 of the 2nd Ban of the *Landwehr* in round numbers:–

> 1,763,700 men.

In the 6 yearly contingents from 1881 to 1891 of the 2nd
Ban of the *Landsturm*:–

1,119,000 men.

Thus the number of men who have received a military training in
Germany during the last 25 years, i.e. since 1866, are in round numbers
as follows:–

In 12 yearly contingents	3,182,000
" 7 " "	1,763,000
" 6 " "	1,119,000
Total	6,064,000

Colonel Gädke admits that this large figure does not by any means
represent the actual number of men who would be available at the
present moment in case of war, because allowances must be made for
numerous casualties of every kind. The same deductions, he urges,
must however be made from the 5½ million trained men alleged to be
available in France. Colonel Gädke then endeavours to demonstrate
that the comparison given by the figures 6,064,000 trained Germans
and 5,250,000 (this figure is reduced by 250,000 for reasons not yet
stated by the author) puts the case in much too unfavourable a light for
Germany. The French, he urges, must fill up their numerous Depot
battalions, which are not destined for work in the first line, from this
number of trained men, as owing to their small birthrate, there is no
further supply of men available. In Germany, however, there are 1½
million men in the *Ersatz* Reserve (or after the necessary deductions
for casualties something over 1 million men) of whom, Colonel Gädke
claims, some 400,000 could be immediately called up. The 5¼ million
Frenchmen are not, so Colonel Gädke continues, in reality all trained
men and considerable numbers would only be suitable for services in
rear of the fighting troops. For such duties which these men would
perform and which would be the only ones they could perform, there is
available in Germany, besides the remainder of the *Ersatz* Reserve, the

countless number of men who are passed each year into the 1st Ban of the *Landsturm*.

The French theoretical 5¼ million men must, moreover, become less each year owing to the falling birthrate, whereas the German total – without any enlargement of the establishment of the army – must increase.

Colonel Gädke considers that this state of affairs, which is an eminently favourable one for Germany, is in great measure due to the reduction of the period of service with the colours (except in the case of the cavalry and horse artillery) to two years. It is evident, he continues, what advantage Germany has gained by this means in the event of an armed encounter and with what confidence, from the numerical point of view, the nation may regard the possibility of such a conflict.

Colonel Gädke sums up with the assertion that never now should demands for an increase of the army be made on the score of Germany's inferiority to her western neighbour. He states in conclusion his wish that every man who is physically fit without exception pass through the ranks, but he looks forward at the same time to a further diminution in the period of service with the colours.

It is interesting to note in this connection that the number of men who perform military service in Germany at the present time is less than 1 per cent of the population. (Prussia: .843%, Bavaria: .875%, Saxony: .863%, Wurttemberg: .879%).

FO 371/907, f. 383

1911

62

Russell to Major H. H. Wade (MO2c)[14]
(4 February 1911)

You may be amused to hear of a remark which the Emperor made to me the other day at Potsdam after his inspection of the recruits of the 'I Garde Regiment zu Fuss' at which I was present in company with the remainder of my military colleagues. The remark was rather exquisitely characteristic! We had a long talk and His Majesty seemed in the best of spirits. He was very pleased at the way the parade had gone off, so I ventured to say that it was very remarkable how much the recruits had learnt in the short time which had elapsed since they joined the colours in early October, and what fine looking men they were. The Emperor seemed very pleased at this and with immense vigour ejaculated 'Yes, with fellows like that one feels as if one could smash up (*sic*) anyone!' It was said with a sort of boyish enthusiasm which was rather nice. I am convinced the remark had no deeper (!) significance.

Now that the Crown Prince is going to be back earlier, he will go to the Coronation instead of Prince Henry of Prussia. At least so the latter told me the other day. Prince Henry told me that the Emperor had wanted him to go, when it was thought that the Crown Prince would not be back in time, but now it is changed of course. Prince Henry is desperately keen to go over too, if only he is invited, and much hopes he will be.

Young Prince George of Greece, who is attached to the 'I Garde Regiment zu Fuss' and is such a nice simple youth, is also longing to be asked over to the Coronation. But I suppose his father will be the representative from Greece.

---

14 MO2c was the section of the Directorate of Military Operations at the War Office that dealt with Germany, Holland and Scandinavia.

I hear that the Emperor will be off to Corfu early in March. Princess Victoria Luise is to go too.[15] They will travel via Munich to Venice where the Imperial Yacht will be waiting for the 'Hohe Herrschaften'.

The Gala Opera was great fun the other day and a lovely sight. I am told that the Emperor was on the stage at the dress rehearsal the night before giving directions. The Emperor picked up a taxicab the other day and went for a short drive. History does not relate how much gold he poured into the man's palm afterwards!

FO 371/1123, f. 452

63

Conversation with the Emperor
(Russell, MA 4/11, 3 March 1911)

I have the honour to bring to your notice the tenor of a long conversation I had to-day with His Majesty the Emperor.

The occasion was the annual inspection in riding by His Majesty of the subaltern officers of the I. Guard Dragoons, which was followed by a luncheon at the officers' mess. By invitation of the Officer commanding the Regiment and by permission of His Majesty, I was present at the inspection and remained to luncheon afterwards.

Immediately after luncheon the Emperor called me up to him and conversed with me for nearly an hour. We were standing out of earshot of the remainder of those present.

After some remarks of a general nature, His Majesty passed to politics and in very vehement terms urged his passionate desire for a good understanding with England. The general drift of the Emperor's observations were to the following effect:– An exchange of naval information is no use whatever;[16] what we want is a proper political understanding. 'The matter is quite easy' His Majesty repeated several times. 'We all want it here in Germany.'

'Everyone knows that the alliance between Russia and France is merely to fight Germany and now you have gone and joined them. You had the choice of joining with us or with Russia and France and you chose the

---

15   Princess Victoria Luise (1892–1980), only daughter of Kaiser Wilhelm II.

16   After the 1909 naval scare, a regular exchange of naval information between Britain and Germany had been proposed as a means of avoiding such outbreaks in the future. Negotiations over this proposal rumbled on ineffectually for some years and eventually petered out.

latter. England and Germany together would ensure the peace of the world. We do not want to fight you. If we did fight you, who would reap the benefit? Undoubtedly the nations which had not taken part in the war.'

'France will not try to regain Alsace and Lorraine; if they did attempt such a thing, they would get a worse beating than they ever dreamt of.'

His Majesty then urged the decadence of the French nation in general and the French army in particular. He said that he had read reports of the health of the French army, which were deplorable. Infectious diseases were rife amongst the French soldiers. The number of cases of typhoid fever, mumps, etc., was appalling. These diseases did not exist in the German army. He had agents and watchers (*sic*) who told him all about these things. One of his officers had told him that on the French manoeuvres the ditches were full of men who were too weak to continue marching. The sanitary conditions in French barracks was [*sic*] terrible. It was reported to him that in quite a new barracks in France there was not a single w.c.!

Why, therefore, did we join with a dead nation like that[?] The Emperor said he was quite certain that the German ships of war were better than the British. If we joined with Germany it would thus be a great thing for us. Every German bayonet too would be on our side. To this I ventured to ejaculate 'and Your Majesty has a great many bayonets' to which the Emperor replied 'Yes and very good ones too.'

His Majesty urged that our panics in England were very undignified. There could be no panics in Germany, because every streetboy knew quite well that the French could not suddenly arrive in Berlin.

'All my life,' the Emperor continued, 'I have worked for a good understanding with England, but you do not help me. Look at Repington's letters to *The Times*, saying that you ought to practise the same tactics as the French, so that you can fight side by side against the Germans.[17] Excuse my saying so, but the few divisions you could put into the field could make no appreciable difference.'

'And then this question about Flushing; it is ridiculous. As if I wanted Flushing! Have I not enough to look after at home without bothering myself about Flushing. The hundredth anniversary of Waterloo is coming round very soon. We fought side by side a hundred years ago. I want our two nations to stand together again in front of the Belgian monument at Waterloo.

---

17 Charles à Court Repington (1858–95), former army officer, subsequently military correspondent of *The Times*. He was an ardent advocate of Anglo-French cooperation and, alongside Lord Roberts, campaigned for the introduction of national service in Britain.

'One of these days you will implore German help against the yellow races. You made a terrible mistake allying yourselves with Japan. Your prestige all over the world has suffered in consequence and you have given life to a new Power in the Far East.

'I have always been loyal and friendly to you. I wanted a coaling station. I asked you, if I took one, where would it be least inconvenient to you. Lord Salisbury said later on he would see me damned first.[18]

'We have now a wonderful situation which will never occur again. The German Emperor grandson to Queen Victoria. The English people ought to be proud of it. They ought to come round me and ask what they can do for me.' His Majesty appeared very hurt on the other hand that the British Regiment, of which he was Chief, should have been sent abroad to India.

His Majesty then referred in very reverential terms to Her Majesty Queen Victoria.

Returning to the earlier part of the Emperor's conversation, I might add the following observations:– Referring to a war between England and Germany, His Majesty said: 'What do I gain by a war with England? Do I want Australia? With its labour politicians? No thank you. Do I want India? What could I do with India? I can assure you that the Japanese are stirring up trouble for you there.'

I have only given the most salient points of a long conversation, perhaps not quite in the right sequence, but the whole drift of the Emperor's remarks gave evidence, in my opinion, of a passionate desire on His Majesty's part of a political understanding with England.

FO 371/1123, f. 88

64

Existence or Absence of Military Preparations in Germany
(Russell, MA 16/11, 27 July 1911)

I think that it is desirable that I should record my impressions at the present juncture with regard to the existence, or absence, of any unusual preparations of a warlike nature in this country.

I believe that a number of alarmist reports have recently appeared in French newspapers, chiefly referring to German military operations

---

18   Robert Gascoyne-Cecil, 3rd Marquis of Salisbury (1830–1903), Prime Minister of Great Britain, 1885–6, 1886–92, 1895–1902

near the frontier and the alleged calling out of a large number of additional reservists.

With regard to the former contention it must be conceded that manoeuvres are now in progress in the neighbourhood of Metz, but this is the season of the year in which large bodies of troops are normally brought together for purposes of training. The report regarding the calling out of additional reservists does not in my opinion rest on any solid foundation of fact. The orders for the calling out of reservists for their autumn training were issued in March last, were not in any sense abnormal and have not, I am convinced, been altered since that date.

It is impossible to predict in a situation like the present what the future may bring forth, but I think it may fairly be said that no indications of any unusual military activity are observable at this moment.

The time of year, no doubt, is an eminently favourable one for a sudden mobilization. The navy is fully armed and manned for the Manoeuvres. In the Army the youngest soldiers have nearly completed their first year's training and have thus been fully competent for some time past to take their places in the ranks. The reservists who are to be called for training this year are about to join their units. These are, however, quite normal phenomena.

On the other hand I have heard indirectly that no proceedings of any unusual character are to be noted on the railways. To my knowledge a number of officers holding important appointments here, among whom I believe may be included the Chief of the General Staff,[19] are absent on leave at the present time. There is less than the usual activity to be observed in and about the building of the Great General Staff, if one may judge by casual external evidence.

My French colleague[20] who has just returned from a tour in Eastern Prussia, assures me that he was received by his German brothers-in-arms with the greatest cordiality and perhaps with almost excessive conviviality.

He further states that the numerous French officers on leave in Germany, with whom [he] is in touch, do not inform him of any unusual proceedings.

This normal state of affairs may, however, of course change at a moment's notice. In the German scheme for mobilization no uncertainty exists, nor is there any need for undue haste. Everything which human forethought can provide for beforehand, has already been accomplished.

FO 371/1166, f. 191

---

19 Helmuth von Moltke, the younger.
20 Maurice Pellé (1863–1924), French Military Attaché in Berlin, 1909–12.

65

Penal Law
(Russell, Memorandum No. 1231, 23 August 1911)

(1). Passing under an assumed name is not in itself considered an offence under German law. It is, for instance, permissible to give an assumed name at an hotel. If, however, a theft or something of that sort takes place at the hotel and you are asked your name by an official, it is an offence (a minor one punishable with a small fine) to give a wrong name.

It is also a minor offence to enter your name falsely in any public register (birth, death, marriage, etc.)

(2). Being in disguise is not considered an offence if unconnected with another offence, unless it amounts to what is called 'Grosser Unfug' [public nuisance]. For instance, if a lady prefers to walk about in the Grunewald in male attire, there is no law to prevent her doing so. If, however, a man with a big beard walks down the Wilhelmstrasse in lady's clothes and causes a commotion, he can be punished.

(3). The same rules apply when the two cases are in conjunction.

[Postscript]

The rule with regard to attire is that men should wear 'sichtbare Hosen' [visible pants/trousers] and ladies 'unsichtbare Hosen' [invisible pants/trousers]!

KV 3/1

66

The Armed Forces of Germany and France
(Russell, MA 23/11, 22 September 1911)

With reference to Colonel Fairholme's[21] despatch of the 7th instant to Sir Francis Bertie[22] in which our Military Attaché in Paris points out the very admirable state of preparedness of the French army, it is perhaps unnecessary for me to submit that the German army is equally in a condition of immediate readiness for war.[23]

---

21 Colonel William E. Fairholme, British Military Attaché in Paris, 1909–12.

22 Sir Francis Bertie (later Lord Bertie of Thame) (1844–1919), British Ambassador in Paris, 1905–18.

23 Fairholme's report of 7 September 1911 is reproduced in full in G. P. Gooch and Harold Temperley, *British Documents on the Origins of the War, 1898–1914.* 11 vols (London, 1926–38), VII, pp. 635–7. It contents are accurately described by Russell in this despatch.

Having only a limited knowledge of the conditions in the French army, I am unable to make any remarks with regard to the relative value of the two forces and I can only confirm with strong conviction that one looks in vain for any sign of real weakness in the military strength of the German Empire.

This state of admirable efficiency is, moreover, not quite a new thing in Germany, as Colonel Fairholme informs us is the case in France, but has existed for many years. From this fact it cannot but have gained strength particularly as ceaseless efforts towards ever greater perfection have always characterised the activities of the German military administration.

There is, however, one factor which is in a sense a source of strength, which may perhaps constitute the sole really weak spot in the German armour. I refer to the amazing confidence in their superiority to all others and perhaps particularly to the French, which animates all ranks of the German army. Valuable and excellent though this sentiment is, it may also, if exaggerated, lead to an improper appreciation of the strength of the hostile forces and may cause even a temporary non-fulfilment of the high hopes entertained to act most adversely on the morale of the disappointed troops.

I am convinced that the Emperor is not adequately instructed with regard to the excellence of the French army. From numerous shreds of evidence it is clear to me that His Majesty encourages German officers who witness the manoeuvres, the work or barrack life of the French army to report adversely on all they see. The Emperor wishes to hear that all is not well with the French forces and it is doubtless not difficult to find bearers of such tidings.

Whether the German Great General Staff, which certainly strives honestly to obtain only the truth, is better informed on this matter than the Emperor, the Press and the man in the street is very difficult to say. From the small amount of evidence at my disposal, I am inclined to think that, though holding a juster appreciation than the rest of the nation, this body has not by any means truly estimated the new power of the French armed forces.

If there are tendencies in German tactics which are not in accordance with our ideas and which we even think may lead to unpleasant surprises for this formidable fighting machine, when applied to the test of war, these will doubtless correct themselves in the school of real experience before it is too late. If the French army has a lead in the matter of aviation, the German troops are also making rapid strides in the advancement of this science. If the material and handling of French artillery is superior and the cavalry and infantry are as good as in Germany, there are certain factors in the strength of the latter power which cannot be denied.

The vast resources in trained and untrained men at the disposal of the German Empire constitute an asset which it is hard to overestimate. The mobilisation of the German army is slightly more rapid than that of the French and the initiative will probably be on the side of the former power. The fixed determination to conquer at all costs which has entered into the flesh and blood of the German soldiers of all ranks, the incomparable qualities of the Staff and the certainty that the leaders, as in 1870, will work together in harmony for the general good regardless of personal ambition, are certainly powerful aids to victory. I do not know if these characteristics are present to a similar degree in the French army.

The German army, as all good armies should be, is at the present time keenly anxious for war. Though burning to vent their hostility on France, their feelings against us are, I think, bitterer still.

FO 371/1127, f. 87.

67

German Tendencies in the Matter of Naval and Military Aircraft
(Russell and Watson,[24] MA 24/11, NA 27/11, 6 October 1911)

[...]

As regards dirigibles, the younger officers of the army are inclined to ridicule the dirigible and put their trust in aeroplanes. [...]

AIR 1/7/6/77/3[25]

---

24   Hugh Dudley Richards Watson (1872–1954), British Naval Attaché in Berlin, 1910–13.

25   Both the top copy and all the office copies of this report appear to have been weeded. This one sentence, reproduced in a printed summary, is all that survives of what was undoubtedly an important document.

68

Nervousness in Germany Regarding Their Military Forces
(Russell, MA 26/11, 27 October 1911)

From the tone and substance of recent notices in the press, and from other indications of various kinds, I am inclined to think that the confidence of the German people in the perfection and invincibility of their military forces, and particularly in the matter of the superiority of these forces over those of France, has been slightly shaken during the last few weeks. This feeling has not in my opinion communicated itself in any way to the army. I refer only to the general public.

The bold and confident attitude of France during the Morocco negotiations has produced an uneasy feeling that the French army must be very efficient and very strong.[26]

I do not imply, my Lord, that there is anything approaching to a panic, and in the army the most unbounded confidence still reigns supreme. I refer more to a kind of nervous tremor which I believe to have passed through the civilian element of this country with regard to its military strength.

This feeling manifests itself by enquiries in the press as to whether the laws for universal service have been administered with sufficient stringency, whether the 90,000 young men who come of age each year and are fit, but are not called up to serve, might not perhaps with advantage have been given some military training, whether the provisions of the Quinquennial Law of 1911 were really adequate to the needs of the military situation in Europe, and similar questions of this nature.[27] And further, why was not the great might of the German Empire exerted at once to decide by war, or threat of war, the differences which existed between them and France.

The authors of articles on the manoeuvres appear to me to go out of their way to reassure their readers that all is, indeed, well with the German army, whereas formerly such consoling communications would have been considered quite superfluous.

---

26 This is a reference to the Second Moroccan Crisis, which broke out in July 1911 with the arrival of the German gunboat *Panther* at Agadir.

27 Quinquennial Law of 1911: the army bill, of five years' duration, that had been passed in 1911. At the time, as Russell's report recorded, there was no dissatisfaction with its provisions. In the wake of the Second Moroccan Crisis, the impetus for army expansion would gather force.

There exists, I think, also a feeling of indignant irritation at the possibility of France raising large bodies of coloured troops to be used against the German army on European battle-fields.

There would also appear to be a demand, as the supply is very plentiful, of articles on the armed strength of Great Britain. If these are couched in derogatory terms they are, I fancy, all the more palatable to the reading public.

I do not for a moment consider, my Lord, that the feeling I have referred to, which is in some respects akin to that which is now demanding an increase in the navy law, is sufficiently powerful to produce an agitation affecting in any way the systematic increase of the army which has already been fixed by law, particularly in view of the fact that more money may be required for the navy. I thought, however, that it was perhaps desirable that I should acquaint your Lordship with my opinion on the present state – even if only a transitory one – of the public mind on this subject.

The confidence of the army in itself is not, I am sure, as I have stated above, influenced in the least degree by the misgivings which appear to disturb the man in the street. The dominant feeling in the army at the present moment – and this feeling is not only confined to the army – is, I believe, one of intense hostility to ourselves. The chief origin of this sentiment is best illustrated by the remarks of some German officers, who recently assured my French military colleague that they could very easily and quickly have settled their differences with France over Morocco, if it had not been for the interference of the English.[28]

A remark made to me by a German Officer is also illuminating: 'What is the use of our having an army, as we do not use it?'

I am perfectly aware that I have failed in this despatch to substantiate my contentions by tangible evidence of any kind, but an opinion gained on the spot by numberless minor indications is perhaps not uninteresting.

FO 371/1128, f. 93

---

28 On 21 July 1911, in the Mansion House speech, David Lloyd George, the Chancellor of the Exchequer, had indicated that Britain would strenuously uphold its interests in the Moroccan negotiations.

69

The Imperial Manoeuvres of 1911
(Russell, MA 27/11, 31 October 1911)

I have the honour to forward herewith a report on the Imperial Manoeuvres of 1911.

Numerous German Princes and a larger number of foreign guests, even than usual, were present on this occasion.

The foreign Military Attachés, though treated with much hospitality, suffered under the usual disabilities with regard to the observation of the operations and on the last day were taken by their leaders, accidentally, as we were assured, for a ride into the country far from the scene of where the fighting was in progress.

[Enclosure]

Germany

IMPERIAL MANOEUVRES

The Imperial Manoeuvres took place in Mecklenburg-Strelitz and Pomerania on the 11th, 12th and 13th September and were carried out by the Guard, II, IX and XX (specially formed) Army Corps.
[…]

METHOD OF CONDUCTING THE MANOEUVRES

The scheme. Whereas the intention of the Directors of the Imperial manoeuvres in 1910 had been to produce fighting about fortified field positions, the object underlying this year's scheme was to practise the repulse of an invading field force.
[…]
It is apparent at once that the notion underlying the general idea was that, whilst Germany was occupied by a war with France, a descent was made on the north east coast of Germany by British forces. These forces, represented by Red, were organized in 3 armies and were marching on Berlin and Hanover. The resistance of the British invasion was at first only maintained by means of forces left to guard the coast, which were probably *Landwehr* troops.

The railway was then made use of to bring up 'freigewordene blaue Heerestelle', Blue troops which had been freed from southern Germany and Silesia to reinforce the Blue armies, which were already opposing the Red advance. On learning of the landing of the III Red Army the whole of the reinforcements were [...] diverted to oppose it, and were detrained at Prenzlau.

The Red Army was jokingly referred to as the British Army by the German officers throughout the manoeuvres; this accounts for the jubilation in the press and elsewhere at the defeat of the Red Army which seemed, without this explanation to be somewhat out of proportion. [...]

Failure to appreciate the effects of modern fire:– The general impression given by the conduct of the troops on the manoeuvres was that the effects of modern rifle fire was [*sic*] most inadequately appreciated. The mounted officers remained on horse back in the firing line, machine guns were leisurely carried about within 200 yards of the hostile infantry, cavalry patrols rode about under the close fire quite unconcernedly, and similar instances of an equally flagrant nature were of frequent occurrence during the 3 days operations. Observers must have wondered whether such proceedings were really serious or whether the troops were indifferent as to whether the conditions at all resembled those of war or not. [...]

REMARKS

Infantry:–

Characteristics and powers of endurance:– There does not appear to be anything new to be said about the characteristics of the German infantry. The points emphasized in previous manoeuvre reports need only to be corroborated. The marching powers of this arm, always admirable, were put to severe test on the Imperial Manoeuvres as the weather was hot, the dust all pervading and a serious lack of water existed throughout the area of operations. So little water was there, that when the troops came into bivouac, there was often only enough available to give them a little coffee. No other cooking was, therefore, possible and no further supply of water was available for drinking purposes, let alone washing. [...]

The spirit shown by the troops left nothing to be desired. I asked a Pomeranian Grenadier, whose battalion I knew to have marched well over

40 kilometres that day, if he was tired. 'The Pomeranians are never tired,' was the somewhat indignant reply.

The suggestion which has been made that the German infantry soldier is merely a machine is by no means a fair one. The fact that a large number of infantry soldiers carry a map in their boot, with which they follow the course of the operations, would alone appear to be a sufficient indication of the injustice of this indictment.

[…]

Fire control:– It is strange that German infantry does not appear to have advanced beyond the very elementary system of indicating targets which has been alluded to in previous manoeuvre reports (see Manoeuvre Report 1910 page 106. Indication and Recognition of Targets). The 'void of the battle field' did not exist in the actions which took place on the Imperial Manoeuvres this year and it is probably not fully realized what the nature of this void may be. It is not, therefore, thought necessary to legislate for it.

Fire was almost always delivered straight to the front, covering fire was seldom, if ever, made use of, no attempt was made to bring enfilade fire to bear on targets to a flank, or to make use of concentrated or distributed fire. Rapid fire was made use of on suitable occasions.

The German infantry has a good deal to learn from us in this respect.

[…]

Aircraft*

Two dirigibles of the M type (M II and M III) and 8 aeroplanes took part in the Imperial Manoeuvres.

Dirigibles: After some years experience with dirigible airships, it appears now, though it is difficult to state these facts with certainty, that military opinion in Germany is in favour of keeping a rigid and a non-rigid type and abolishing the semi-rigid airship (Gross M. type). If the evidence were not so strong in this direction it would be difficult to believe that the M. type which has apparently hitherto fulfilled its functions so well should be 'marked to die'. It further appears probable from views expressed by military men, that the rigid type (Zeppelin) is only retained now out of deference to the prominent services of the aged Count Zeppelin, and that on his death this type of airship will cease to be built.

[…]

Aeroplanes: The aeroplanes consisted of 4 Etrich-Rumpler (Taube) monoplanes[29] allotted to the Red and 4 Albatross biplanes[30] allotted to the Blue Army.

[…]

The following incident is said to have occurred on the Imperial Manoeuvres, which certainly illustrates the value of aeroplanes in the domain of reconnaissance.

False disposition of the Blue forces were marked on a map and a staff officer was sent out with a view to this misleading information falling into the enemy's hands. The officer in question was soon surrounded by hostile patrols who endeavoured to effect his capture. He escaped, however, pretending to let his map fall accidently [*sic*]. The map with the false dispositions on it was soon brought to the Red commander in triumph. The latter, however, determined to verify the information thus obtained and sent out an aeroplane to reconnoitre. The aviator returned in a short space of time and was able to prove that the information was entirely misleading. Lieutenant Mackenthun[31] on an Albatross biplane is said to have sailed over the whole of the enemy's front on the first day of the manoeuvres and to have returned within 35 minutes bringing back information which the cavalry could not have obtained in less than four hours. […]

(* Portions of this have already appeared in my XXVI [*sic*] of 6 Oct. 1911)
FO 371/1126, ff. 92–118

70

Recent Articles in *The Times* on the German Army Manoeuvres
(Russell, MA 29/11, 16 November 1911)

I have the honour to inform you that I recently received instructions from the War Office to report upon the effect produced in Germany by the publication of a series of articles on the German Imperial Manoeuvres, which have lately appeared in *The Times* from the pen of the military correspondent of that journal, and to ascertain to what extent lieutenant-

---

29 Etrich-Rumpler Taube [dove] was Germany's first mass-produced military aircraft. It was designed by Io Etrich, an Austrian, and manufactured in Germany by Edmund Rumpler.

30 Albatross Werke was founded in 1909. Among the aircraft it manufactured was a biplane version of the Taube, known as the Albatross Doppeltaube.

31 Walter Mackenthun (1882–1948), one of the first German military aviators. He received his pilot's licence on 7 March 1911.

Colonel Reppington [sic] was believed in this country to be associated with the British General Staff.

I replied at once that the Great General Staff was well informed with regard to this matter, and appreciated the fact that the military correspondent of The Times, though editor of the new Army Review, did not represent the views of our General Staff, but that the army in general did not realize to the same degree the personality of this brilliant military writer.

Since writing in this sense, I have had time to probe the matter further, and am now able to confirm the opinion I expressed in the first instance.

Some aspects of public opinion on the subject of these articles, as reflected in the press, are not, I think, without importance or interest.

Notices have appeared in the newspapers in this country stating that these articles in The Times had been inspired by the British military attaché in Berlin, and that he should in consequence not be invited to attend the Imperial manoeuvres on future occasions.

I might perhaps quote in this connection a matter which came to my notice, and which appears to constitute a notable exception to the rule that the General Staff here is well informed with regard to the authorship of the articles in question. The Bavarian military plenipotentiary in Berlin, Lieutenant-General Freiherr von Gebsattel,[32] informed me the other day that the War Minister had said to him, 'I suppose Russell did not really write those articles in The Times?' The indignant surprise contained in my comment on this remark caused General von Gebsattel to change his tone somewhat, and he hastened to assure me that it was of course only a bad joke on the part of the War Minister.

Writers in the newspapers here note with regret that the belief of foreign nations in the invincibility of the German army is no longer so firm as it used to be. The homage paid in the past to German military strength is now replaced by unfavourable criticism.

In most cases the authors of these articles hasten to assure their readers that there is no cause to apprehend that the German sword is not sharp and ready for immediate use. They assert, however, that a State which perpetually avoids war loses respect and prestige in the sight of its neighbours, and that a protracted attitude of defence engenders a disbelief in the offensive power of a nation. Germany has kept the peace so long, they declare, that the saying now is: 'So schnell schiessen die Preussen nicht' [The Prussians don't shoot so quickly].

---

32   Ludwig von Gebsattel (1857–1930), Bavarian Military Attaché in Berlin.

The letters of the military correspondent of *The Times* are alleged to have been written with the special purpose of inspiring confidence in France, and all foreign criticism of German military and naval armaments is asserted to be part of the policy of encompassing Germany ('Einkreisungspolitik.')

The present occasion is not an opportune one for examining the contents of Lieutenant-Colonel Reppington's [*sic*] letters in detail, but my own opinion with regard to them from a general point of view – and this opinion is shared by all my military colleagues who have read the articles – is that, though brilliantly written and containing much that is quite incontrovertible, they are too severe in many instances in their judgment of the German soldiers.

If I may venture to express an opinion with regard to the desirability of publishing these articles, I am bound to admit that I can only deplore that they should have appeared in public print. My reasons for this opinion are as follows:–

1. I consider that these articles have contributed to increase ill-feeling against us.
2. I do not think that it is desirable to afford helpful criticism to a foreign country.
3. I believe that these articles will be misunderstood to a great extent by the British public.

With regard to 2, I am convinced that these most ably written letters will be studied with care by the German Great General Staff, and that this observant body will not fail to find much food for reflection and suggestions for improvement in this trenchant criticism of the Imperial manoeuvres.

I should, perhaps, explain more fully the meaning I wish to convey by the third reason I gave above. I believe that the British public, too prone as it is to dismiss unpleasant truths, particularly when they have any reference to the armament and defence of their own country, will only too gladly accept this indictment of the German military forces and hasten to the conclusion that the German army is a bad one and may be taken as a negligible quantity.

That such an attitude is in the highest degree regrettable needs no demonstration.

FO 371/1126, f. 124

71

The Employment of Coloured Troops by the French in European Warfare
(Russell, MA 30/11, 21 November 1911)

I have the honour to inform you that at yesterday's resumption of the proceedings in the Budget Committee of the Reichstag the question of the so-called 'Black Peril' was discussed.

General Wandel, representing the Prussian War Office, attended the meeting and asserted that the 'Black Peril' was not so great as had formerly been believed by many people to be the case.[33]

In the near future, he continued, there could be no possibility of the French occupation of Morocco providing that country with any considerable accession of military strength. A long period must elapse before large bodies of troops could be raised in that region. On the other hand, it could not be denied that in course of time an increase in the military strength of France in Morocco might take place.

A National Liberal deputy then stated that he was able to assert from personal knowledge that the military qualities of the natives in question were by no means to be despised. He thought it therefore desirable to urge that one should be prepared for the necessity of taking precautions against this danger. This remark produced a strong protest from a Socialist deputy against any increase of armaments.

Another Socialist deputy protested later on that, so far from being able to draw troops from Morocco in time of war for employment in Europe, France would be obliged to keep European troops in Morocco.

In connection with the statements which had been made with regard to the military qualities of the population of Morocco the representative of the War Office then proceeded to give some information as to the achievements of the coloured troops employed by the French in the war of 1870.

The Secretary of State for Foreign Affairs, Herr von Kiderlen-Waechter,[34] then remarked that the figures given in the Reichstag as to the number of coloured troops taking part in the war of 1870–71 originated from the General Staff.

He further stated that the matter of universal service in Algeria was at present a question of an experiment, which had been strongly opposed by

---

33 Franz Gustav von Wandel (1858–1921), Deputy Prussian Minister of War, 1909–13.
34 Alfred von Kiderlen-Waechter (1852–1912), German Foreign Secretary, 1910–12.

the colonists. These latter foresaw a danger for themselves in giving the coloured men a military training and were of opinion that the chances of insurrections were increased by this means. Those who pointed to the Sikhs and Gurkhas must not forget the action of the sepoys in the great mutiny.

A member of the Centre then enquired if, as had frequently been urged, two army corps had been mobilised instead of sending the ship to Agadir, what would have been cost of such a mobilisation.

It was subsequently decided, however, in accordance with the wish of a majority of the members of the committee, that this question should not be proceeded with.

FO 371/1120

72

Aircraft in Germany
(Russell and Watson, MA 35/11, NA 37/11, 9 December 1911)

On October 6th, 1911, we had the honour to submit to Your Excellency a Report on Air Craft (Naval No. 27, Military No. 24).[35]

Since submitting that report we have taken some trouble to get more in touch with the authorities on airships in Germany, because our earlier experience had led us to think that the progress made in Germany with these vessels was probably greater than that in England.

As a result of our investigations, we have collected a considerable amount of information on the airships of Germany, and have ourselves by ascents in two types of airships, practically tested the claims of the manufacturers. The details of information collected will form the subject of a separate report. A special report on the flight of the Siemens-Schuckert Airship[36] under disadvantageous circumstances, as observed by us, has been forwarded in our report (Naval No. 36, Military No. 33 of 5th December).

2. In our report (Naval No. 27, Military No. 24) of October 6th, 1911, and in Report forwarded on Military Manoeuvres for September 1911,

---

35 See document 67 for all that remains of this report.
36 An experimental airship produced by a subsidiary of the Siemens company. Despite its successful trials, the Siemens company decided to concentrate on aircraft and did not develop this airship further. The airship was, however, purchased by the German government at the beginning of 1912.

we then stated therein that it appeared probable from views expressed by military men, 'that the rigid type (Zeppelin) is only retained out of deference to the pre-eminent services of the aged Count Zeppelin, and that on his death, this type of airship will cease to be built'.[37]

Information has now come into our possession, and we have since so reporting, acquired personal experience of a recent rapid increase in the power of Zeppelin airships, which renders it necessary to entirely revise the statement made on October 6th as to zeppelins; while the flight of the Siemens-Schuckert Airship must make us also preserve an open mind on the future of the Non-rigid airship.

The truth is that before the last few months the opinion largely held in Germany was that airships were useless and that aeroplanes would supplant them. This opinion we were voicing in our Report of October 6th.

Apart from the fact that we have since then got into touch with the manufacturers of airships, the feats of the new Zeppelin *Schwaben*, of the latest Parseval, and of the Siemens-Schuckert airships in regard to a considerable access of speed, reliability, and manoeuvring powers, have now shown conclusively that the airship is by no means dead, and that the energies and abilities of the various manufacturers, aided by the support of Government and wealthy people have made this movement into a very real one.

The aims held out for future airships show clearly that England must at once regard this German airship movement seriously, and examine how to get to the point Germany has reached.

The great point that some of the German airship manufacturers make is that there is no royal road to success in this matter; that it lies only through the acquisition of laborious experiments with every detail. They say openly that they are not afraid to show us things, hence our being able to acquire the experience we have, aided by extending hospitality to the Heads of the Airship firms.

They speak most kindly and with genuine regret of brother craftsmen, at the failure of the British Naval Airship, and state it is in their opinion impossible to build airships without many years of experience such as the Zeppelin and Parseval Firms now have in the brains and hands of their officials, workmen and nowhere else.

3. As stated, the details of some of the various German airships will be forwarded in another Report.

---

37 See document 69.

In regard to the question of the various uses for the different types of airships, we also propose therein to submit some remarks, but we may state briefly here that at the present moment, rigid, semi-rigid, and non-rigid airships of the chief firms are achieving such excellent experimental success that it seems possible that each may have its useful purpose, and that the construction of each type may be continued. Rather than an Airship Firm dropping out entirely, an amalgamation with others seems more likely.

4. We have, we trust, said enough to prove, coupled with our previous reports and the information to follow in [a] later report, that we are justified in thinking that the German airships are in a high state of development and that England will benefit by any opportunity of a closer study of the German state of progress, which can be achieved by getting into effective touch with the German firms, either through British firms inviting German firms to manufacture airships in England, or by the Admiralty and War Office ordering airships direct from German firms. We submit this with the greatest consideration in regard to those at work on this subject in England, but we deem it essential before it is too late, to point out that the German state of progress is very high in airship development and it is desirable for England to catch her up.

The question of how to achieve this connection is somewhat difficult, but we believe unless our proposals are acted on at once, the recent rapid development and consequent orders will somewhat close the door to British inspection of German airships, especially when the German Government come to realise what a valuable asset they have in the German airships now, as they will do very soon.

The present position is that we have a verbal assurance from the Parseval Company that they will allow Captain M. F. Sueter[38] R.N. and Major Sir Alexander Bannerman[39] to inspect their Firm's Works and Airships at Bitterfeld (three hours by train from Berlin); probably under greater restrictions as experts than we were under, but still we believe under conditions which should render the acquisition of useful information possible.

But apart from the actual acquisition of information on Parseval airships, we believe that this is the best way of getting a stepping-stone to a visit to Zeppelin airships by British experts. The question of what the

---

38   Murray Fraser Sueter (1872–1960), naval aviation pioneer; Inspecting Captain of Airships, 1910–12; Director of the Admiralty Air Department, 1912–15.

39   Sir Alexander Bannerman (1871–1934), Commander of the Army Balloon School, 1910–11; Commandant of the Air Battalion, 1911–12.

Parseval airships are capable of, and their use, is one for the future and for examination by experts.

In suggesting this visit, it becomes necessary to examine into what the Parseval Company want in allowing it. Their point has been made perfectly clear to us. They desire to get into connection, through our Government's assistance, if possible, with an English firm, and to make Parseval airships in England.

We submit our belief that the British Government will do well to assist this and so foster an agency for information and experience. In addition to this, we would submit that our acquisition of the large amount of experience and information on German airships has been entirely due to the assistance of the Parseval Company. The details of the airships obtained, and flights made, having been done through the agency of Kapitänleutnant von Simson (retired naval officer),[40] and our connection with the Company enables us to forward our reports on the stage of airship development in Germany.

Whether or not it is later deemed desirable to follow up the system employed in the construction of Parseval airships, we submit that the British authorities will be well advised to approach the examination of all German airships through the Parseval Company, helping them to such advantages in England as may be possible.

Zeppelin.

In regard to this firm it has been somewhat difficult to get into touch, as the Zeppelin Firm of Airship Manufacture is nationally funded, and is we believe in consequence, somewhat obliged to let no foreigners inspect their airships at the manufactory.

Through the Parseval Company and other influences this reluctance to let British officers see too much of their airships was partially overcome, and besides the Naval Attaché going in the *Schwaben* for a flight by booking passage as an ordinary passenger, he was allowed to travel in the steering position during the flight, and besides spend a day carefully inspecting the ship more closely than the ordinary public are permitted to do.[41]

The *Schwaben* is no longer the property of the Zeppelin Company, but is run by the Deutsche Luft Verkehrs Gesellschaft, which has the same directors as the Zeppelin Company.[42] (This is a similar method to

---

40 Hermann von Simson: manager of the Parseval Company, 1911–13.

41 The *Schwaben* (*L.Z.10*) was used as a passenger vessel offering a commercial air service. Accounts of her service differ, but it is generally agreed that she carried several thousand passengers in more than 200 flights.

42 Presumably a reference to the Deutsche Luftschiffahrts-Aktien-Gesellschaft, more commonly known as DELAG.

that pursued by Parseval Company and its affiliated Passenger Company.) Therefore the same reluctance to British officers seeing too much of the *Schwaben* is generally displayed.

Subsequent steps taken by us in direction of cementing the friendship made with the Heads of Firm, have resulted in our being able to state as our opinion that through the Parseval Company it is possible that we may be able to arrange for Captain Sueter and Major Sir Alexander Bannerman to see Zeppelin ships; but this would arise out of getting a connection with the Parseval Company. Or failing this, after visiting Parseval and while in Germany, they could perhaps go to Baden-Baden or other towns where *Schwaben* starts flights again in February next and book a passage. This is sometimes not easy, owing to the number of intending passengers. But this we may be able to arrange.

Naturally, the Deutsche Luft Verkehrs Gesellschaft require something, and as the Director (Herr Colsman)[43] has requested us to regard it as confidential, we request that his desire may be observed.

The Company wished last September to start an airship line Cologne–London, and probably Paris as well; but political exigencies forbade it.

Herr Colsman hopes to start it in 1912, possibly June, but naturally wants a connection in England, first with the Royal Aero Club or other authorities, and to found a Company who will build Halls for this large vessel on a combinative arrangement similar to what the Passenger Airship Companies do in Germany.

If the Admiralty and War Office take this matter up and give good support to Herr Colsman in England, we are of opinion that their experts will be given first opportunities of acquiring experience of a Zeppelin Airship.

We have heard that application for the Airship to go over will probably be made through the Foreign Office here, and that it is probable they will make no objection. The question as to whether the flight of German Airships to England is desirable from a political point of view is not ours to report on. What we are concerned with is that it will probably assist to bring the point of English development of Airships to the same standard as the German standard, by having a stimulating effect on English manufacturers.

5. We would submit therefore that we may be empowered to approach the Parseval firm, in the first instance to allow Captain M. F. Sueter and Major Sir Alexander Bannerman to visit their Works at the earliest

---

43 Alfred Colsman (1873–1955), business manager of the Zeppelin Company.

opportunity that the Firm will permit, and that such other opportunities as may arise out of such visit may at once be taken advantage of by prolonging their visit as may be necessary.

With regard to what the Parseval Company want in England, we would submit that we may at the same time be informed what the Government would be prepared to do for them, for our use in case the Firm take up the attitude of 'no advantages, no visit'.

6. In conclusion we would state that we believe our proposal contains the best way of increasing knowledge of airship capabilities and details of manufacture, and that it is in our opinion desirable to strike while the iron is hot, in view of the position we have gradually led up to.

We would point out that in Berlin alone, people are now so accustomed to airships that they hardly stop to look at them, except in so far as the recent excellent performances of the last two months by the *Schwaben*, Parseval VI, and Siemens-Schuckert make the more interested persons realize the progress made lately.

FO 371/1127, f. 312

73

A New Army Bill
(Russell, MA 36/11, 15 December 1911)

I have this day heard on reliable authority that the rumours which are being circulated with regard to a projected increase of the Army next year beyond the limits prescribed by the Quinquennial Law of 1911, are substantially correct.

I am moreover informed that a bill embodying proposals of this nature is to be submitted secretly to the Bundesrat,[44] before the Emperor leaves (on or about the 28 January) for the Mediterranean.

The alleged details of these proposals have also already appeared in public print (*Berliner Tageblatt* of the 11 December 1911) and are to the following effect:–

Two new Army Corps are to be created, the XX and XXI, at Allenstein and Mülhausen respectively.

The existing infantry regiments would suffice for the formation of the new Corps, but as, even after this year's Army Bill, there are still 32

---

44 Bundesrat: the upper house of the German parliament. It consisted of the delegates from the different federated states.

infantry regiments with only 2 battalions, the proposal is to create 18 new infantry battalions.

The number of machine-gun companies is to be considerably augmented and in any case 2 new Train battalions will have to be formed for the 2 Army Corps.

The intention moreover appears to be to abolish the four existing Cavalry Inspections and to replace them by the formation in peace time of the required number of Cavalry Divisions, which would also be furnished with artillery and machine-guns.

Cyclist detachments are also to be formed as part of the permanent peace organization.

The augmentation of the number of divisions would also demand an increase in the number of field artillery regiments. There are at present 94 field artillery regiments, and the normal number of two to each division would, if the number of divisions is, as proposed, to be raised to 50, necessitate the creation of 6 additional artillery regiments.

A further proposal is that the field and foot artillery should be placed under a common General Inspection, as was the case before 1874.

Finally there is to be an increase in the Technical and Communication Troops.

The cost of these new proposals is estimated at from 60 to 70 million marks (£3,000,000 to £3,500,000).

I ventured to call attention some seven weeks ago (in my despatch No. XXVI of the 27 October 1911) to the feeling of uncertainty which I believed to be pervading the German people with regard to the adequacy of their military forces.[45] This sentiment did not at that time appear strong enough to produce an agitation affecting the systematic increase of the Army as fixed by law, particularly in view of the fact that further sums of money would in all probability be required for additions to the Navy.

The events of last week appear, however, to have brought about an alteration in the temper of the German people and, whether an increase in Naval Construction is decided on or not, there seems little doubt that a large section of the public will loudly demand a stronger army and be prepared to render whole-hearted support to the proposals, which have been outlined above.

The result of the elections in January will naturally indicate the strength and quality of the popular voice in this matter. The 'Fortschrittliche

---

45 Document 68.

Volkspartei', the National Liberals and other parties are said to be in favour of an increase in the Army Law only. The Conservatives and Centre desire to see both services reinforced. The Social Democrats are opposed to any augmentation either of the Army or Navy.

FO 371/1125, f. 386

1912

74

Fortress Rayons on the Island of Wangeroog
(Russell, MA 3/12, 16 January 1912)

I have the honour to direct Your Excellency's attention to a notice (No. 4007 of the 6 January 1912), in the *Reichs-Gesetzblatt*, No. 4, of the current year, in which the intention of the German Government to establish fresh fortress rayons on the island of Wangeroog is promulgated. [...]

I venture in this connection to call attention to my despatch no. XXIX of the 7 December 1910 in which I endeavoured to sketch the evolution of the defences on the German North Sea littoral and to indicate the gradual accession of military strength which is taking place along that portion of the coast line.[46]

[...]

When in addition to the evidence of the activity referred to above, it is taken into consideration that the defences at Brünsbüttelkoog at the North Sea entrance to the Kiel Canal are reported to have been considerable strengthened during the past year and that fortification work at Emden is said to be provided for in the naval estimates, some notion may be found of the untiring energy with which military preparations are being pushed forward on the German North Sea shore.

FO 371/1372, f. 133

---

46 Document 60.

75

Certain Facts and Rumours of a Disquieting Nature
(Russell, MA 6/12, 5 February 1912)

I do not doubt that it is desirable that I should call your Lordship's attention to certain facts and rumours of a disquieting nature, of which I have recently become cognisant.

I am very unwilling to attribute to normal coincidencies [*sic*] a sinister significance they do not possess, but it is difficult to deny that the indications I am about to refer to are capable of a not unalarming interpretation.

I have been much struck of late by the increased activity at the Great General Staff. The distinguished officers of this thinking department appear to have even less time than usual at their disposal. The hours of work which are usually from 10 to 5, appear now to be from 9 o'clock in the morning until 7 or 8 o'clock, or even later, at night. One officer who lived with his wife and family at Potsdam, and came up to Berlin every day for his work, has found this arrangement no longer possible. He has been obliged to take up his residence in Berlin in order to be closer to his duties.

I might adduce further evidence in support of my contention, but it is perhaps sufficient on the present occasion, if I state my conviction that an unusual amount of work is in progress at the Great General Staff.

The Prussian Supply authorities have recently called for tenders for foreign oats (see *Handels-Zeitung des Berliner Tageblatts* of the 31 January 1912), whereas the invariable rule in the past has been for oats to be purchased only in Germany. This purchase of oats abroad as well as at home appears to point to supplies of this form of forage being required on a larger scale than is normally the case.

It has been reported to me on an authority, on which I must admit no special reliance is to be placed, that a number of senior cadets at the *Haupt-Kadetten-Anstalt* at Gross Lichterfelde are to be allowed to join their regiments immediately, that is to say considerably earlier than they would do in normal circumstances. I have taken steps to investigate this rumour, but cannot at present say whether it is correct or not.

The fact that a large sum of money (part of a total of £9,500,000 out of the new Prussian Loan of £21,000,000) is said to be spent at once on the acquisition of rolling stock for the Prussian railways has already been published in the press. It has of course been well known for some time past that the German railways would be somewhat short of rolling stock in the event of mobilization, though this deficiency would be obviated to a certain extent by the appropriation of all foreign railway vehicles, which happened to be in the country at the time.

In connection with the preceding financial matters, it must, moreover, be noted that the destination of a little less than half of the Prussian Loan just referred to, has been adequately accounted for. The question whether the remaining 10½ million pounds is required for purely remunerative, for warlike or any other purposes is left unanswered.

The abnormal activity at the Great General Staff may possibly be partially explained by the fact that it is the season for winter exercises, and that numerous schemes have to be set and much work corrected, which involves a considerable amount of labour additional to the ordinary routine.

The purchase of foreign oats on a larger scale than usual may be due to the failure of the crops last autumn and the prospect of a dearth of forage in the spring sending up the price of oats, may have made it desirable to lay up large stores of this commodity at the present time.

The rumour regarding the cadets at the 'Haupt-Kadettenanstalt' at Gross Lichterfelde may not be true. It may be urged that an increase of rolling stock on the Prussian railway system may have been a pressing requirement for some time past. The portion of the Prussian Loan which has not been publicly allocated to any special purpose, may be destined for purely remunerative requirements.

On the other hand, it cannot be forgotten that the voice of the German people has been calling loudly for increased armaments, the political situation in Europe is full of disquieting uncertainties, the feeling of this country against us is full of anger and bitterness and that therefore any indications which point to warlike preparations, however capable they may be of alternative explanation, are not to be left unnoticed

FO 371/1373, ff. 404–6

76

An Interview with the War Minister
(Russell, MA 10/12, 1 March 1912)

In accordance with the annual custom of presenting bound copies of the Monthly and Quarterly British army lists to the Prussian War Minister,

I had an interview today for this purpose with Lieutenant-General von Heeringen.

On receipt of the volumes, His Excellency begged me to convey to the Army Council his very grateful thanks for the same.

I then purposely led the conversation up to last year's Imperial Manoeuvres, as I was anxious to dispel certain illusions which I knew to exist in His Excellency's mind, and ventured to state my regret that the military correspondent of *The Times* should have expressed himself in public print about the German army in the terms that he did. The War Minister replied that they were perfectly capable of gauging the value of such utterances and that one must in these days be prepared to be exposed to criticism. His Excellency then added – and this is the point I wish to bring to Your Lordship's notice – that they had put together and compared all the foreign criticisms of their manoeuvres for the last two years and had found the views taken in 1910 and 1911 to be diametrically opposed to each other.

To the War Minister the interesting point was the varied character of the criticism, to me the fact that all this criticism had been examined and sifted was distinctly illuminating and confirmative of the opinion I expressed in this connection in a previous despatch, that the German military authorities would not fail to profit by the hard sayings concerning the army which had been spoken by the military correspondent of *The Times*.

With a view to eliciting, if possible, some light on the new proposals, I remarked that His Excellency would no doubt be having a very busy time in the Reichstag with the Military Estimates. The War Minister replied: 'My scheme for the army (meine Heeresvorlage) is being postponed until the regular estimates are passed.'

This last statement is interesting as indicating that a new scheme for the increase of the army is definitely prepared and is, so to speak, in the War Minister's pocket, and further that we must not expect to learn much concerning the nature of its provisions until after the annual army estimates have been passed in the Reichstag.

FO 371/1374, f. 468.

77

Notes on a Visit to Johannisthal
(Russell, Memorandum No 1427, 20 March 1912)

I proceeded to Johannisthal[47] in company with Captain Watson, the Naval Attaché, on Monday last, the 18th instant, in order to obtain information on a number of points concerning which we had been asked questions, and also with a view to notify any special matters of interest in the domain of aerial navigation which may be observed at this flying ground.

I submit below some notes on the points I noticed:–

I. Aeroplanes

(1) The Fokker monoplane.

After a number of enquiries as to an aeroplane with automatic stability, which had been referred to in M.O.2.(c)'s memorandum No. C.12/93 of 13.3.12., we made the acquaintance of a young Dutchman, named Fokker,[48] who is the inventor and constructor of the machine I was in search of.

This young man appears to be endowed in a somewhat remarkable degree with the qualities which go to make not only a skilful and daring aviator, but also a most successful constructor. His machine is called the 'Fokker-Eindecker'.[49] He had 3 of these machines in his shed at Johannisthal and 6 others, I understand, in course of construction.

I do not know whether he has means of his own or not, but I have heard the name of one man (Graf Montgelas) who is said to assist in financing the Fokker aeroplane.

A thirty-five to forty mile wind was blowing, not evenly, but in a gusty and treacherous fashion. No other aviator dared to fly; the day was decided to be much too bad. This young man, however, insisted on going up to show the remarkable stability of his machine. I desired him not to do so, if it was at all unsafe, but he scouted the idea of danger and maintained that he has often flown on much worse days.

---

47 Johannisthal: airfield about ten miles south-east of Berlin opened in September 1909.

48 Anton Fokker (1890–1939), Dutch aviation pioneer, most famous for the military aircraft he designed for Germany during the First World War.

49 Fokker-Eindecker: monoplane aircraft that would later be developed into a successful fighter plane.

He then gave us a most remarkable display, flying with the wind, across the wind and against the wind, turning with consummate ease and certainty. For a long time, quite a minute, he held up his hands and waved. In fact the conditions referred to in the above named memorandum appeared to me to be amply fulfilled.

There seems to be some quite unusual quality in this aeroplane, which during its flight made it again and again recover its equilibrium, yielding and accommodating itself to the wind.

I attach a description of the Fokker aeroplane, which furnishes a quantity of details that need not, therefore, be repeated in this memorandum.

I might, however, mention that this machine is taken to pieces and put together again with astonishing ease and speed. This is naturally a great advantage in a military aeroplane and most convenient for transport purposes.

The extraordinary steadiness in the air appears to be chiefly due to the manner in which the machine is constructed, the way the wings are set and the situation of the centre of gravity due to the special position of the engines.

Fokker is engaged at the present time, besides other work, in constructing an aeroplane for the Prussian Military Authorities, fulfilling the conditions required in Germany for a military flying machine. To use his own words, the German officers, who have seen his aeroplane, have been 'Kolossal imponiert' [greatly impressed] and I must admit that I am not surprised.

I strongly urge that the machines made by this young man not only be not lost sight of, but that some further action be taken in this matter. We have arranged to go down to Johannisthal shortly to witness further flights with the Fokker aeroplane and I hope also to be able to send you some photographs of the same.

[…]

WO 32/18984

78

Extraordinary Warlike Preparations
(Russell, MA 16/12, 19 April 1912)

I have the honour to call your Excellency's attention to the following items of information, which have recently come to my knowledge from a highly credible source, and which, when taken in conjunction with other indications of warlike preparations, are not without significance.

The Chilian Government has endeavoured during the last few months to place orders for 30,000 rifles, 5,000 carbines, and a quantity of small arm and big gun ammunition with a well-known German firm. This firm was, however, so occupied with orders for the German Government as to be unable to undertake this work themselves and were obliged to transfer the orders to two Austrian factories. Some orders for military saddlery and harness had likewise to be made over to Austrian manufacturers.

It is impossible not to infer from the above that all other factories of warlike stores in Germany must be equally engaged with work for the German Government, or the German firms in question would no doubt have transferred the Chilian orders to factories of their own (German) rather than of Austrian nationality.

I felt bound earlier this year to call attention to what I considered to be unusual activity at the Great General Staff, the celebrated thinking department where plans for war are studied and prepared.

I ventured on the same occasion to describe certain other facts and rumours, which were disquieting in a similar sense.

To these I am now able to add a report received from the British military attaché in Denmark to the effect that the German Government has been making extensive purchases of horses by means of Danish agents in Sweden, in consequence of which some 2,000 horses have recently been shipped to Germany.

Whilst the extraordinary preparations referred to above are in progress, the military authorities, who made and obtained a year ago their demands for the next five years, now put forward further proposals, involving an increase of the peace strength of the army by 29,000 men, an acceleration of the carrying out of the measures provided for in last year's law, and many elaborate and costly changes of organisation.

The naval demands are also in excess of the existing Navy Law.

If these demands and these preparations which I have referred to above are made only in the interests of the defence of the Fatherland, it is not easy to explain why they should have suddenly become necessary, when less than a year ago this was not the case.

If they are not intended purely for defensive purposes, there remains but one alternative; they must be designed for offence or rather aggression.

FO 371/1373, f. 409

79

Strategic Railways
(Russell, MA 19/12, 3 May 1912)

At the request of the Department of the War Office in London with which I correspond,[50] I have taken steps to enquire into the recent progress in construction made on the important strategic railway line Remagen–Jünkerath–Weywertz.

It appears from the recent official publications of the Prussian Diet that the rough work on this line is already finished, that the *Oberbau* or superstructure and the building of stations is in process of completion and that the last section of the railway … will be able to open for traffic on 1st July next.

The information given above is corroborated in the latest edition of the Imperial Railway Guide […] which has just been published. According to this publication the section Remagen–Dümpelfeld is already in working order.

The sections Dümpelfeld–Lisendorf (Jünkerath) and Jünkerath–Weywertz are noted as being still under construction ('noch in Bau'), but they are nevertheless entered in the Railway Guide, which leads one to conclude that they will be open for traffic during the course of the summer.

It is further noticeable that in connection with the list of trains on the line Remagen–Dümpelfeld, a note has been inserted to the effect that a fresh timetable will be issued on 1st July. This may doubtless be taken as an additional indication that trains will be running on the entire length of the line Remagen–Weywertz before the end of the current year.

The official publications issued by the Prussian Diet, which have been referred to above, unfortunately throw little light on the important strategic line Malmedy–Stavelot. It would be particularly interesting in this connection to learn how the work on Belgian territory is progressing, but no information is vouchsafed on this point. […]

FO 371/1375, ff. 394–4

---

50 Presumably MO2c.

80

Increased Strength of the German Army due to the Enactments of the Army Bill of 1912 (Russell, MA 21/12, 13 May 1912)

The new Army Bill was read a third time in the Reichstag on Tuesday last the 21st instant, on which occasion this Bill and the new Navy Law Amendment Act were voted 'en bloc'.

There was a solitary and formal protest against these Bills by a Socialist Deputy on the occasion of the third reading, but no other member spoke and the measures passed amid considerable enthusiasm.

The anticipations uttered freely in the press and elsewhere to the effect that these measures would be passed before Whitsuntide, have thus been realized. The sanction of the Federal Council and the signatures of the Emperor and Imperial Chancellor are now alone necessary before the Bills become law.

If there could possibly have been any doubts as to the Emperor's attitude with regard to this matter, they are now set aside by His Majesty's action in conferring high orders on the Ministers who were chiefly instrumental in framing these measures.

The smoothness of the passage of these Bills through the various stages of the Budget Committee of the Reichstag and the insignificance and futility of the opposition shown to them, have been fully commented on in the European press and the various aspects of these measures have been so freely discussed, that there appears to be little to add on the present occasion.

I am anxious, however, with your permission, Sir, to lay some stress on the quality of the very considerable accession of military strength which will come to the German army from the enactments of the Army Bill of 1912.

The army on the whole, if I gauge the feeling of this body correctly, is satisfied with the quality and quantity of the proposals for its expansion and improvement, but a few dissenting voices outside this force, including that of the new German Defence League (*Wehrverein*) have been raised in condemnation of what is considered to be the inadequacy of the reforms contemplated.[51]

---

51 *Wehrverein*: generally known as the German Army League, this was a right-wing pressure group, formed after the debacle of the Second Moroccan Crisis, to campaign for greatly increased expenditure on land armaments.

To satisfy these malcontents, the whole organization of the army would have to be revolutionized, whereas the changes about to be introduced are grafted on to the stem of the present organization with but little disturbance to the existing order of things. The skilful manner in which the units have been selected for the formation of the two new army corps is a case in point.

I will now very briefly summarize the most salient advantages of the changes to be introduced:–

The two new army corps would no doubt have been formed in any case on mobilization, but their previous creation in time of peace furnishes them with a cohesion and a power of smooth and efficient working, which they could not possibly have possessed, had they been hurriedly made up on the outbreak of war.

The formation of the new, VII, Army Inspection, which is to have its head-quarters at Saarbrücken and is to be composed of the XV Army Corps at Strassburg and the XVI Army Corps at Metz, adds to the German military forces, from the point of view of war organization, a new 'Army' complete in all respects.

The formation of 17 new battalions of infantry, of 6 new squadrons of cavalry and of 41 new batteries of field artillery and other augmentations involving altogether an addition of nearly 29,000 men to the colours, doubtless constitutes a considerable reinforcement and one, moreover, which brings about a corresponding increase in the number of men passing annually to the reserve.

The increase of establishments in the case of 123 battalions of infantry will promote the efficiency of these units in time of war, as fewer reservists will be present in the ranks.

The addition of numerous new appointments for seconded officers and the creation of Landwehr Inspections, though the Budget Committee in both these cases reduced somewhat the numbers originally demanded, makes a considerable increase in the amount of officers available on mobilization and enables the work of preparing for mobilization to be more perfectly performed.

The creation of the various other formations and the increase of establishments, which I enumerated in my despatch No. XVI of the 19 April 1912,[52] obviously form an accession of strength to the army, the advantages of which it is hard to overrate.

---

52   Document 78.

Whilst considering the material increase in strength of the army, which will be brought about by the provisions of the Bill under review, it is desirable not to lose sight of the moral effect, which these new enactments will no doubt also produce.

I have ventured on previous occasions, with perhaps somewhat tedious persistency, to state my belief that the German people had been considerably shaken of late in the former proud confidence they possessed in the invincibility of their military forces. But it is surely permissible now to conclude that, with the introduction of the new army reforms, a measure of this former consciousness of strength will be restored.

When to this returning confidence we add an uncomfortable feeling in German hearts that the army of the Fatherland is gaining a reputation of being unwilling to fight, an intense irritation at what is considered French arrogance and the apparent inevitable hostility to ourselves, we obtain a sum of national sentiment, which might on occasion turn the scale, when the issue of peace or war was hanging in the balance.

FO 371/1374, ff. 364–7

81

The Neutrality of Belgium and Holland
(Russell, MA 22/12, 24 May 1912)

I have the honour to forward herewith a translation of an article, which appeared in the *Vossische Zeitung* of 19 May 1912, from the pen of Herr Georg Gethein, a member of the Reichstag and a well-known Radical leader and free trader.

Though the article contains no arguments, which have not been used before and though it would be idle to credit the author with any special acquaintance with the strategical ideas of the German General Staff, the remarks Herr Gethein makes are perhaps not without interest as an expression of opinion from a man of his standing, experience and party.

I do not think that many people would be prepared to quarrel with the author's contention that the value of international treaties has in the last few years depreciated in a very lamentable manner and that the smaller states are in danger of suffering from this decline in the morality of nations.

I desire particularly to draw attention to the author's observations with regard to the interest of Germany in preserving the independence and neutrality of Holland, without, however, in any way associating myself with the views expressed.

The effect Herr Gethein considers the Rhine Navigation Laws are having on relations between Holland and Germany is also interesting. Herr Gethein has doubtless studied the question in all its bearings, as he was a prominent member of the Central Committee for German internal waterways from 1894 to 1908.

FO 371/1376, ff. 410–15

82

The Emperor and Colonel Repington's Articles on the German Imperial Manoeuvres
(Russell, MA 23/12, 27 May 1912)

I fear that the mischievous consequences resulting from the publication in *The Times* last autumn of Colonel a Court Repington's articles on the German Imperial manoeuvres are likely to be even more far reaching than I have ventured on several occasions in the past to predict. (Please see my despatches No. XXIX of 16 November 1911 and No. X of 1 March 1912.)[53]

For some time past we have been in the habit of sending eight British officers (exclusive of the Military Attaché) each year to attend manoeuvres in various parts of Germany. This practice has been of the greatest possible value to the General Staff and to the army as a whole, as the lessons learnt in this manner have been widely disseminated.

It is much to be regretted that this desirable precedent is unlikely to be continued in the future and that only a much smaller number of our officers will probably be allowed to be present at German manoeuvres.

That this is the case and that it is the direct result of Colonel Repington's articles was brought to my knowledge in the following manner.

After a luncheon following on the annual *Schrippen Fest* or commemorative festival of the Instructional Infantry Battalion at Potsdam this morning, the Emperor took me by the arm and led me out of earshot of any bystanders. His Majesty then commenced a violent diatribe against press correspondents in general and Colonel Repington in particular. His Majesty said that the military correspondent of *The Times* had written

---

53   Documents 70 and 76.

the most horrible things about the German army and had been making untold mischief in America, France and other places by his writings on this subject.

The Emperor then recalled the fact that at my intercession last year he had cancelled his previous decision and had after all allowed eight of our officers to attend manoeuvres in Germany. 'And then,' as His Majesty remarked, 'this sort of thing happens.'

I told the Emperor that Colonel Repington was not now an officer in the British Army. His Majesty replied that he was, or at least had been.

I then endeavoured to explain that the British officers, whom His Majesty had been kind enough to allow to attend manoeuvres last year had nothing whatever to do with the articles he was referring to, nor would British officers be permitted to write to the public press on such a subject. His Majesty spoke, however, so volubly that it was difficult to cause him to pay any attention to my statement of the case.

The Emperor then continued to describe the indignation of his officers at the writings of the Military Correspondent of *The Times* and added: 'Write and tell your War Office that I will not stand these correspondents.'

I was determined not to surrender without an effort to the Emperor's apparent intention of not allowing any British officers to attend at German manoeuvres this year and I, therefore, remarked as soon as I was able to do so: 'But surely Your Majesty will allow our officers to be present at your manoeuvres as usual?' To which he replied: 'Only as few as possible!'

Although I did my best, even to the extent of interrupting His Majesty to a greater extent than is perhaps compatible with customary deference, I was, I fear, unable to explain to, or adequately convince His Majesty that Colonel Repington's articles were merely the result of journalistic enterprise and had nothing whatever to do with the British officers attending manoeuvres. I fear that the Emperor is unable to disassociate the two ideas in his mind and is, therefore, determined to reduce the number of our officers attending manoeuvres in this country to a minimum.

I am consequently forced to the conclusion that we cannot possibly ask for more than two, or at the utmost three, of our officers to attend manoeuvres in Germany this year.

His Majesty spoke to me in a friendly manner across the table at luncheon before this conversation took place and in bidding me farewell he showed cordiality, but with regard [to] the matter of press correspondents, among whom he apparently most unfortunately also includes British officers attending manoeuvres, he was exceedingly angry.

I am somewhat at a loss to explain why the Emperor should suddenly have referred to a subject, which one might reasonably have supposed to have been buried long ago. Certain requests concerning the attendance of British press correspondents have recently been made to the Embassy here from the Imperial Foreign Office and it is possible that this matter may also, therefore, have been brought to His Majesty's notice. If this was the case, it might no doubt account for the Emperor being occupied with the subject today, but I have not had an opportunity of speaking with His Majesty since the offending articles appeared and am inclined to think that he has been nursing the grievance till this moment occurred when it was possible to air it unreservedly.

This question, however, which is perhaps only interesting from the point of view of Imperial psychology, is at any rate less important than the fact that the request for British officers and press correspondents to be allowed to attend manoeuvres in Germany this year is likely to be somewhat embarrassing.

FO 371/1376, ff. 88–91

83

Airships for the Italian Government to be forwarded to the Aegean Sea.
(Russell, MA 29/12, 28 June 1912)

During the course of a visit to the works of the Parseval Airship Company at Bitterfeld today, made chiefly with a view to inspecting the reconstructed military airship, P. II. (formerly known as P.L.8.) I came into possession of certain points of information, which I consider I should not fail to bring to Your Excellency's notice.

The chief interest and importance of the intelligence gained on this occasion seems to consist in the light it throws on the future course of Italian hostilities against the Turks.

The facts I learnt are to the following effect:–

(1)   The Italian Government has within the last few days placed an order for one complete airship and all the parts except the hull (cars, engines &c.) of two others with the Parseval Airship Company. (The hulls of the two latter are to be constructed in Italy.)

(2)   This work is to be finished in 8 weeks from the present date.

(3)   The Parseval Airship Company has promised to execute the order within the period mentioned.

(4)   These airships are to be capable of a speed of at least 17 metres per second and a considerable additional sum is to be paid for each metre of speed per second developed in excess of the velocity mentioned.

(5)   The dirigibles are to be capable of carrying more than a ton's weight of explosives in addition to the crew and other necessary adjuncts. A special space is to be arranged for in each car for the storage of shells.

I was further informed that these airships are to be sent to the Aegean Sea, a statement, which I am inclined to think, may be accepted as being in accordance with fact. There seems in any case to be little likelihood of these three dirigibles with their special construction being required at such short notice for the Campaign in Tripolis [*sic*], where an airship and a number of aeroplanes are already available.[54]

The projected airships, it will be observed, are to be capable of a high rate of speed and are evidently intended mainly for purposes of dropping shells. If they are to be sent to the Aegean Sea, it seems to be difficult not to infer that they are to be used against the forts at the mouth of the Dardanelles. No other objective in the special circumstances and in view of the particular design of these aircraft, appears to be either so likely or so suitable.

We are thus furnished with evidence pointing to the intention on the part of the Italians of making an attempt to force the Dardanelles and also to the fact that this enterprise is likely to be undertaken in rather more than two months time from the present date, that is to say, during the course of the month of September.

FO 371/1377, f. 158

---

54   As a result of the Italo-Turkish War (September 1911–October 1912), Italian forces had been fighting in and around Tripoli for many months in their efforts to conquer Libya.

84

Orders for New Construction received by the Parseval Airship Company
(Russell, Memorandum No 1520, 2 July 1912)

1) *Italian Government.* See my despatch No. 29 of the 28th June 1912.[55]

2) *Turkish Government.* One of the Directors of the Parseval Airship Company is about to proceed to Constantinople. This action is doubtless taken with a view to negotiations with regard to the sale of airships.

3) *Russian Government.* The Russian military authorities ordered a Parseval airship some six months ago, but the actual instructions to commence work have not yet been received.

4) *Prussian Government.* P.L. 8 in future to be known as P.II, has been reconstructed for the Prussian military authorities, and is now practically ready for her trials. The Directors and Engineers of the Parseval Company are not entirely satisfied with this reconstructed vessel, particularly as it is only fitted with 4-cylinder engines, which are believed to be inferior to those of 6 cylinders. There is little doubt, however, that though not of equal capabilities to the P.L.II or P.III, this airship will be a very useful one.

Another order has just been placed with the Parseval firm by the Prussian Government for a new airship, which is to constitute an advance on all previously constructed dirigibles of this type. It is to be very similar in design to the P.L.13, which was recently sold to Japan, and which has given quite admirable results.

I gather that the German military authorities are at present opposed to the notion of equipping Parseval airships with machine-guns. (This does not apply to the Zeppelin type.) The designers of the new Parseval airship had proposed to mount machine-guns on the bulwarks of the car, one on the port and one on the starboard side, but this was not approved of by the Prussian military authorities.

The new system of hanging the car appears to work admirably.

The Prussian Government has, I understand, shown great consideration to the Parseval Company in not pressing for the completion of its own orders, so as to enable the firm to make rapid progress with the work for the Italian Government.

---

55 See document 83.

War Experience. The experts at the Parseval works inform me that they hear that the Italians have been able to achieve far greater results in the domain of reconnaissance with dirigibles than they have with aeroplanes. This is naturally a prejudiced view and I only mention it for what it is worth. I was informed that the hull of an airship in Tripolis was on one occasion perforated with 30 bullets, without the efficiency of the vessel being in any way impaired.

Photograph. I attach (to original only) a photograph of the Prussian military airship P.III.

AIR 2/196

85

The Emperor's Views on Espionage
(Russell, MA 31/12, 16 September 1912)

I have the honour to bring to Your Lordship's notice some fragments of a conversation, which the German Emperor held with a Russian officer during the recent meeting at Baltic Port on the subject of espionage. The officer in question was Major-General von Tatistscheff, His Majesty's Personal Aide-de-Camp in Berlin. The sentiments expressed on this occasion are perhaps not without interest, as shedding some light on the Emperor's attitude with regard to the matter referred to.

The substance of the Emperor's remarks were not disclosed to me by Major-General von Tatistscheff himself, but by Colonel Basaroff, my Russian military colleague in Berlin, to whom the story had been related by the Emperor of Russia.

The question of espionage was rather naturally much on the *tapis* at Baltic Port in view of the trial of Captain Kestewitsch, which was proceeding at that time.[56] The Emperor of Russia was very anxious that Captain Kestewitsch should be exchanged for a German officer, who had been convicted of spying and was then serving a term of imprisonment in Russia. The German Emperor was not, however, in favour of the proposed exchange.

Whilst discussing this subject with Major-General von Tatistscheff the German Emperor remarked that it was of little interest to him whether it was a Russian, an English or a French spy who was arrested. What

---

56 Captain Kostevitch, a Russian cavalry officer, was convicted of espionage and sentenced to two years' imprisonment in a fortress.

affected him, however, was that a German should have been prevailed upon to betray his country.

His Majesty continued that when large sums of money were offered, the temptation was very great. And in this connection the English were by far the worst offenders. They spent such vast sums of money on secret service, 'that it was impossible to compete with them'. The somewhat naïve admission contained in this last sentence is not without a touch of humour.[57]

For purposes of such 'competition' as His Majesty referred to, considerable sums of money are as a matter of fact voted annually by the Reichstag.

In the Military Estimates for 1912 the sum set aside for 'secret expenditure' (Geheime Ausgaben) amounted to 37,500 M (£1,875) and a somewhat similar sum has been voted each year for some time past.

In the Naval Estimates and *Novelle* for 1912, 200,000 Marks (£10,000) were voted for secret expenditure, thus making up a total of nearly £11,900 available for this purpose in one year. It was reported in the press that when Admiral von Tirpitz was questioned by a Social Democratic Deputy during the deliberations in the Budget Committee of the Reichstag as to the employment of the fund entitled 'secret expenditure', the Minister for Marine denied that it was made use of for special spying work in foreign countries, asserting that it was only applied to 'defend against foreign spying'. (See Captain Watson's No. 42 of 15 May 1912.[58])

In addition to the sums referred to above there is a fund for 'unforeseen contingencies' in the military estimates, the use of which is not clearly explained and which need apparently not be accounted for to the Reichstag. This sum amounted in 1912 to 60,000 M. (£3,025). It is impossible to say, My Lord, to what precise uses these sums are applied, but it is clear that there is plenty of money available in Germany for defence against foreign espionage.

FO 371/1378, f. 254

---

57   The idea that the British Secret Service Bureau was well funded would have come as a surprise to Captain Mansfield Smith Cumming, who headed it.

58   This report is reproduced in full in Matthew S. Seligmann (ed.), *Naval Intelligence from Germany: The Reports of the British Naval Attachés in Berlin, 1906–1914* (Aldershot, 2007), pp. 430–1.

86

The German Press on the Subject of the British Manoeuvres
(Russell, MA 32/12, 20 September 1912)

There is, I am happy to say, no exact equivalent in the English language for the German word 'Schadenfreude', but a display of this particular sentiment is observable in the German Press this morning, which imagines it has found cause for ridiculing the British Army.

Die Post, the organ of the Pan-Germans, commenced in this morning's issue an article headed 'The manoeuvre achievements of our adversaries' with the following words: 'Hardly have we recovered from the hearty and refreshing laughter produced here by the comic opera and stage effect which brought the French manoeuvres to so speedy a termination, when the news comes from London that the British manoeuvres have similarly been brought to an abrupt close. Once again, therefore, the whole of Germany resounds with positive Homeric laughter. In France, it must be admitted they still preserved their sense of humour and the capture of the French Blue Commander was held to be a good joke, which might all the same have had very serious consequences … In England the story cannot be told in a few words.' Then follows a would-be graphic account of the alleged confusion in the British ranks, which, as was asserted, was the cause of the manoeuvres being prematurely terminated.

In the *Berliner Tageblatt* too which is, as a rule, not entirely ill disposed towards us, reference was made last night to the completely inextricable muddle ('volkommen unentwirrbares Kuddelmuddel') which is stated to have taken place amongst our troops.

Other newspapers have published articles in a similar strain, but except as instances of the sentiment I alluded to above, they are not worthy of any notice.

FO 371/1378, ff. 267–8

87

Military Precautions in Germany
(Russell, MA 37/12, 15 November 1912)

I had the honour in a recent despatch to refer to the supreme readiness of the German army for war. (See my MA Germany No. XXXV of 31 October 1912.) This admirable state of preparedness, which may truthfully be said to be permanent, is enhanced during periods of crisis by the adoption of certain military measures and precautions, which could not fail to add momentum to the startling rapidity with which a mobilization would inevitably be carried out in this country.

Though the German Government is doubtless most earnestly and sincerely desirous of avoiding war at this juncture, such wise and prudent action as I have referred to above, is being taken at the present time.

The notices to reservists, giving precise instructions as to the place each man is to proceed to on mobilization being ordered were issued to all concerned some 7 or 8 days ago. There is, however, nothing unusual in the actual issue of these instructions, which are, as a rule, sent annually in January to each reservist. The only aspect of the case which is unusual, is the fact that the notices have been sent out at the present time. I desire to emphasize this fact, as it might possibly be inferred from a recent telegram in *The Times* from the correspondent of that journal in Berlin (see *The Times* 14 November 1912) that the issue in itself of these notices was an extraordinary measure. During the Morocco Crisis last year instructions of this nature were similarly sent out at an earlier date than usual.

There are strong rumours, which I have not as yet been able to substantiate definitely, of unusual purchases of grain and other food stuffs by the German Government as well as the retention in German territory of rolling stock from Dutch and Belgian railways. This latter course was also adopted during the critical months of 1911, although heavy demurrage had to be paid as long as the railway carriages were kept in Germany.

I have also heard that another measure which was resorted to during the period of crisis last year, has again been adopted at the present juncture. I refer to the formation of war staffs. The officers concerned are informed as to the composition of the staffs of which they are to form part on mobilization and are further instructed to make themselves acquainted at the earliest possible date with other officers in whose company they are to serve.

I may also add that unusual activity is observable in the building in which the Great General Staff carries on its labours. The officers arrive earlier than is their wont and lights may be seen burning long after the usual hours of work.

The measures I have outlined above do not, I am convinced, foreshadow any present or immediate intention of resorting to hostilities, but must merely be considered as the prudent, it might almost be said, necessary precautions demanded by the uncertainty of the present political situation.

FO 371/1379, ff. 121–2

88

Detraining Stations on the Eastern Frontier of Germany
(Russell, MA 39/12, 22 November 1912)

I had the honour in a previous despatch (MA Germany No. XV of 1st June [1911][59]) to forward to Your Excellency a list of the detraining stations (*quais de debarquement*) on the western frontier of Germany, which was made out in accordance with the latest information in possession of the French General Staff.

I am now able to submit similar information with regard to the eastern frontier of the German Empire, and, as on the previous occasion, I am indebted for these details to the courtesy of my French military colleague here in Berlin.

The situation of the various detraining stations will be clear from a study of the accompanying map 'A', short red lines indicating the position in each case. The adjoining figures (also in red ink) give the approximate length of the available platforms in metres. In places where a doubt exists as to the accuracy of the details supplied, signs of interrogation have been inserted.

The information given on the map represents, I understand, quite accurately the condition of affairs at the commencement of 1911.

It is perhaps also interesting in this connection to study the territorial organization of the German army, which, in accordance with the provisions of the Peace Strength Law of June 1912, has been altered

---

59   Sadly, no copy of this report appears to have survived.

since 1st October last by the addition of two new Army Corps. I venture, therefore, to attach another map ('B') which illustrates the subdivision of the Empire into Army Corps Districts and gives the stations of all units.

It will be clear from this map that the new XX Army Corps has been inserted between the I and XVII on the north-eastern frontier and the new XXI occupies a position in Alsace-Lorraine on the French frontier between XV and XVI Army Corps.

FO 371/1379, f. 160

89

Some German Tendencies in the Employment of Aircraft
(Russell, MA 42/12, 10 December 1912)

I have the honour to forward herewith a paper I have written on the subject of 'some German tendencies in the employment of aircraft'.

I am able to do little more in this document than enumerate a number of theories held in Germany on the proper method of employing dirigibles and aeroplanes in war time. In the absence of any satisfactory war experience from which to draw deductions, these ideas are of necessity still very much in a fluid state and have not as yet crystallized sufficiently to enable a positive affirmation to be given as to the effect they will have on German aeronautical strategy and tactics.

The German military authorities with characteristic insight into the causes and success and failure in war, though working feverishly to improve the aeronautical power of the army, fully realize that it is not machines alone which can decide the fate of nations, it is the army itself: the man and officer; not arms alone, but 'die Kraft des Gemüthes [the power of the spirit]'.

[Enclosure]

Some German Tendencies in the Employment of Aircraft

I. General

It is realized in Germany that the advantages of the airship over the aeroplane are that the former, having a greater carrying capacity, is able to transport a large supply of ammunition and offensive stores as well as a more numerous crew, that it is able to remain in the air without moving, that it can manoeuvre by night and in a fog, that it can carry a wireless installation more easily and that its crew is not subjected to undue stress and fatigue.

The aeroplane on the other hand is more mobile, is more easily transportable, is less vulnerable and does not require costly sheds which are a necessity for the dirigible airship.

It is contended, however, that one form of aircraft cannot replace the other. It is essential for a modern army to be in possession of both airships and aeroplanes. The German theorist indeed goes a step further than this, as he alleges that two kinds of airships are required: the large rigid Zeppelins working from fixed strategical points and the lighter non-rigid Parsevals which accompany the field army, take shelter in transportable sheds and can, if required, be dismantled and packed on a wagon.

German military thought condemns the notion that aircraft can in any way replace cavalry. 'Not aircraft or cavalry, but aircraft and cavalry' is a catchword frequently uttered and written. Commanders, however, appreciate the fact that, whereas formerly information concerning the enemy came in slowly and piecemeal, a complcte and accurate statement of the hostile dispositions may now be brought to them at very early stages.

Some thinkers assert that after a few weeks of war all aircraft and pilots will be *hors de combat*. The advantage will then lay with the country which has the greatest reserves and the best means of production.

The tendency of the young military aviator to deride the airship is rapidly becoming a thing of the past, owing to the remarkable achievements of the German dirigibles in recent times.

II. Dirigibles

The Germans, like the French, consider the dirigible may be used for:

1) Strategical reconnaissance.
2) Reconnaissance by night.
3) Communications.
4) Offensive action.

1) *Strategical reconnaissance.* The fact that the majority of the German military airship sheds are situated on either the eastern or western frontiers of the Empire, (viz: Strassburg, Metz, Cologne, Königsberg and Thorn) appears to give a clue as to the manner in which this form

of aircraft will be employed on the outbreak of war. It may indeed be inferred that the proximity to the frontier will admit of early strategical reconnaissance by which it will be hoped to obtain accurate information of the progress of the hostile mobilization, places of concentration, initial movements, lines of advance and other valuable intelligence.

Very similar inferences may be drawn from the strategical positions of the projected naval airship sheds at Hamburg, Kiel, Wilhelmshaven and Emden.

It is realized that this aerial reconnaissance will by no means be conducted unopposed, and to enable the airships to combat their foes, they have been provided with offensive weapons.

Machine-guns or marksmen are to be placed on the top of the rigid Zeppelin airships for purposes of firing at hostile aircraft. The Parseval or *M* ships may be furnished with machine-guns or marksmen in the car.

The suggestion is also put forward that each airship should be accompanied by a flotilla of aeroplanes, which would assist in the struggle against aerial enemies. A writer on this subject maintains that in a combat with a single aeroplane an airship has one advantage in that it can rise more quickly and thus prevent the aeroplane getting above it. But if a number of such efforts have to be undertaken in rapid succession, the airship from loss of gas would soon have no course left but to take refuge in flight. The airship and the aeroplane, however, as the same writer continues, will not as a rule have a fair start, but will in all probability approach each other with great suddenness. The airship travelling at the rate of 80 km (50 miles) an hour and the aeroplane at 120 km (75 miles) an hour will rush towards each other at a combined velocity of 200 km (125 miles) an hour and it may easily happen that the aeroplane will pass over the airship.

2) *Reconnaissance by night.* The airship can travel by night as well as by day and, if winds are favourable, can approach their objective without the use of engines and therefore without noise. The hours of darkness or periods of fog can thus be utilized to pass over dangerous places or to reach particular localities unseen.

3) *Communications.* German writers in the newspapers and elsewhere claim that wireless telegraphy has been used from dirigibles with complete success. All experiments of this nature, have, however, been guarded with the greatest secrecy and little is known of the results achieved. (Note: on December 10th 1912 a Telefunken station was established at Johannisthal for purposes of communication with the Naval Airship, *L.I* which is at present stationed at that place and making daily flights. The radius of action of this station is said to be 150 km (nearly 94 miles).[)]

4) *Offensive action.* Great secrecy has also been observed with regard to the trials connected with the projection of projectiles and explosives from airships. German writers claim that great proficiency and accuracy has been obtained and that it is no longer necessary for an airship to come to a stop before dropping explosives, etc. (See below: Aeroplanes (d) Offensive action.)

Other methods of offensive action have been referred to above under (1) Strategical reconnaissance.

III. Aeroplanes

Although it can hardly be said to lie in the genius of the German people to make good aviators, very great advances have been made during the past year in training pilots and gaining experience in the science of aeroplane work.

The Germans consider that the aeroplane may be used for:

a) Reconnaissance.
b) Observation of fire.
c) Communications.
d) Offensive action.

a) *Reconnaissance.* The radius of action of an aeroplane is considered to be about 200 km (125 miles). The chief forms of reconnaissance are thought to be flying along roads to locate troops on the march, the exploration of positions, location of bivouacs or places of assembly, discovery of situations of concealed artillery, etc.

The aeroplane is not considered suitable for close reconnaissance or small enterprises at short distances. The commander allotting a task must, it is said, realize that, in order to reach the prescribed service height of 800 metres (880 yards) some ten minutes are required. Any exploration, therefore, within a radius of 10 km (6½ miles) is not worth while, when other means are available.

On the other hand it is realized that an aviator may be able to report the advance of an enemy in half an hour, when he is still more than a day's march distant.

b) *Observation of fire.* It is doubtful whether the Germans have advanced as far as the French in this particular function of aircraft. Any experiments made have been guarded with secrecy, but there is no doubt that the matter is receiving the diligent attention of the military authorities.

c) *Communication.* The Germans consider that for carrying messages aeroplanes should only be employed where long distances are concerned.

Wireless telegraphy from aeroplanes, though eminently feasible and successful in the brains of the German writers on this subject, is probably still quite in its infancy.

d) *Offensive action.* Aeroplanes, it is thought, may be employed in fighting airships, but not against living targets on the ground, as the effect, owing to the limitations of weight carried, cannot, except from a moral point of view, be of any decisive value.

On the other hand it is hoped that aeroplanes may not be without use in dropping explosives on to railway lines, field fortifications, ammunition stores, magazines, etc.

Until quite recently the throwing of bombs from aeroplanes was not considered likely to be productive of much effect, as the machine was obliged to be in motion during the act of projecting explosives. It is now claimed, however, that appliances are available which enable projectiles not only to be discharged from an aeroplane at a particular moment and in the desired direction, but also to make it possible for the pace and height of the aeroplane and the effects of the wind to be neutralized. These appliances will also be made use of in the case of airships. Arrangements are, it is said, moreover possible by means of which the sudden loss of weight no longer affects the stability of the aeroplane.

With reference to offensive action against other aircraft, it is still a matter of theory whether the aeroplanes will fight one another first or make their initial efforts against the hostile airships.

It is suggested that aeroplanes should be posted during war time at important strategical points, such as bridges, stations, etc., to combat any airships which approach. In order to enable this work to be performed efficiently a good service of intelligence would also be required.

Another proposal, perhaps rather a fantastic one, for defending important strategical points is to stretch wires suspended from captive balloons. A strong wind, however, would doubtless drive off the captive balloons and render these arrangements innocuous.

e) *Most suitable moments for aeroplane work.* The early morning and late afternoon hours are considered the most suitable times for aeroplane work, owing to the comparatively quieter, cooler and heavier condition of the atmosphere.

Great heat, it is alleged, thin, oppressive air, very boisterous or strong wind, rain and mist often make ascent difficult or impossible. The clearness of the air and the position of the sun are of course realized to be of great importance to the observer.

f) *Instructions for the action of one's own troops on the appearance of an aeroplane.* These are to the following effect:–

The first question is to which side does the aeroplane belong. As it is impossible even with expert knowledge and the best glasses to make out particular colours or flags, and as all aeroplanes of modern armies are of similar appearance when at some height up, the question is a peculiarly difficult one. Smoke signals have been suggested as a possible solution of the problem.

(i) *If hostile.* If it is ascertained that the aeroplane is hostile, the duty of the commander and his subordinates is to make observation as difficult as possible to the aviator in question. If no overhead cover is available, immobility and adaptation of colour to surroundings are important points to look to. Rifles, lances, flashing accoutrements, dust and single horsemen riding apart are likely to betray the whereabouts of troops. Guns, entrenchments, etc, must be made to resemble the surrounding background by being covered with bushes, twigs, etc.

Firing at an aeroplane flying at the service height has little prospect of good effect. Fire may only be opened if the aviator is undoubtedly hostile and one's own troops are not likely to be endangered by the descending projectiles. In the case of musketry fire, even when employed on a large scale, one can only rely on chance shots striking the aeroplane, owing to the height and rapidity at which it is moving. Even hits do not necessarily involve a landing or a rapid fall.

Even the fire from field guns is not very dangerous to the aeroplane. The angle of elevation of the gun is limited, opening of fire usually not quick enough and often impossible with regard to the front of one's own position. Guns specially adapted for this purpose are likely to be the most effective. (Note. Details of such guns have been given in previous reports. A.R.)

(ii)   *If friendly.* If the aeroplane is recognised as belonging to one's own side, assistance should when necessary and feasible, be offered if a landing is contemplated. This is usually best effected by sending forward an officer to regulate the keeping of the ground. It may also be desirable to furnish a mounted man to forward messages to the addressee. Sometimes the messages are thrown down. For this purpose a cylindrical tin box attached to a small red parachute are [*sic*] made use of. It is often difficult to find these messages, if the fall of the parachute is not very carefully watched by several people.

A spot where a landing is contemplated, must at once be cleared of vehicles, piles of arms, etc.

A landing place must be at least 400 metres (440 yds) long and must be clear of formidable unevennesses such as large holes, ditches, stumps of trees and swampy ground. The spot must not be surrounded with woods or houses. The selection, therefore, of landing and starting places requires some judgement.

To make a landing specially easy, it is a good method to place a man on the most suitable spot for landing with a white flag and up wind about 200 metres (220 yards) of another man with a red flag. Both these men must make themselves visible by waving their flags.

When landing in a strong wind, the run is often twice as long as usual. Landings in a side wind, especially with small monoplanes are to be avoided. It is desirable to land in the neighbourhood of roads, towns, railways and more particularly of telephones.

If it is very dark, a fire of straw is useful to assist the landing or better still the use of signal lamps. If a searchlight is used, only the ground below not the aviator must be illuminated.

g) *Observation from aeroplanes.* An experienced German aviator declares that observation from an aeroplane is very easy and that it is not affected by the pace of the machine as soon as one has risen a few metres from the ground. It is very difficult, he continues, for columns or large bodies of troops to escape the notice of an aviator appearing suddenly. On the other hand motionless bodies of troops in small numbers, particularly when clothed in field service uniform, are impossible to recognize from an aeroplane in flight. In fact the aeroplane, he asserts, is not suited for the recognition of such objects.

h) *Instruments, etc. carried on an aeroplane.* The following instruments, etc, are carried on a military aeroplane:– Compass, map in roller case, clock, barograph, speedometer, aneroid barometer and cylinders for throwing down messages.

i) *Cost of aeroplanes.* The average cost of aeroplanes in Germany at the present time may be said to be 20,000 to 30,000 Marks (£1,000 to £1,500) of which some £400 to £500 are involved by the engines.

k) *Expenditure of fuel.* Each hour of flight involves the consumption of 20 to 30 litres of petrol and 2 to 4 litres of oil. The tanks carried on a military aeroplane provide for about 3 to 4 hours flight.

l) *Comparative merits of monoplanes and biplanes.* This vexed question is by no means settled yet. The monoplane is generally considered the faster and to maintain its equilibrium better. The biplane has a greater carrying capacity, is somewhat slower, but is more easy to land with even on very uneven ground.

m) *Aims in the construction of future aeroplanes.* The chief aims sought for in the construction of future aeroplanes are as follows:–

(i)   to increase the stability of the machine in the air so that there be less dependence on wind and weather.

(ii)   to increase the carrying capacity.

(iii)   to accelerate the powers of rising from the ground and cause landing on uneven ground to be safer.

(iv)   to make machines which are dismantled and put together again in a very short space of time.

(v)   to produce engines which, though lighter, are more powerful and more reliable.

FO 371/1370, f. 124

90

A Bill for the Provision of Aircraft
(Russell, MA 44/12, 18 December 1912)

I have the honour to call Your Excellency's attention to the persistent rumours, which have been current of late both in the press and elsewhere, with regard to the probability of an almost immediate issue of Supplementary Military Estimates as well as of a Bill for the provision of aircraft.

The special objects mentioned in connection with the rumoured military expenditure have been the creation of cavalry divisions in peace time, the formation of field howitzer regiments, the provision of an increased establishment of horses for field artillery batteries, etc.

A 'communique' has, however, now been published in the *Norddeutsche Allgemeine Zeitung*[60] of the 17th instant to the effect that all reports regarding the issue of Supplementary Military estimates are without foundation and that money is only to be demanded for the provision of aircraft.

It is further added that detailed information concerning the Aircraft Bill cannot be published at the present time, as the work of preparing this measure is still unfinished.

FO 371/1379, f. 314

---

60 *Norddeutsche Allgemeine Zeitung*: a semi-official newspaper that presented the views of the German government.

1913

91

A New Army Bill
(Russell MA 3/13, 10 January 1913)

I had the honour in a previous despatch (my No. XLIV of 18 December 1912[61]) to refer to certain rumours, which had been current with regard to the probability of an almost immediate issue of a Supplementary Military estimate as well as a Bill for the provision of aircraft.

I quoted, however, on the same occasion a 'communique', which had been published in the *Norddeutsche Allgemeine Zeitung* of the 17th December 1912, which appeared to dispose of any rumours regarding a new Army Bill, as it declared that money was only to be demanded for the provision of aircraft.

On the 8th instant, however, *Die Post* published an article, which asserted that a new Army Bill was to be laid before the Reichstag at a very early date, probably even during the month of January. The writer in *Die Post* explains that the new proposals are being framed with a view to filling the 'gaps' in the German army, which are still left over from the last Army Bill. The changes contemplated involve:–

1) an increase in the establishment of infantry companies,
2) the creation of third battalions for those regiments which have only two,
3) the formation of cavalry divisions in peace time,
4) training for the *Ersatz* Reserve,
5) the provision of various artillery requirements,
6) the formation of another army corps from redundant units.

---

61 Document 90.

This intelligence published in *Die Post* has naturally evoked a considerable amount of comment from the remainder of the German press. No attempt appears to be made in these utterances to deny absolutely the likelyhood [*sic*] of some such proposals, as have been outlined above, being formulated, but there is a strong body of opinion which inclines to the belief that the notice in *Die Post* is both premature and exaggerated. The difficulty of finding the necessary funds is also not lost sight of.

All the information I have points to the fact that a new Army Bill is undoubtedly contemplated in the near future, but it is difficult at present to obtain intelligence as to its precise scope and character.

The fear has been expressed to me by Germans on several occasions lately that the new measure, if passed, will probably not go far enough and that 'gaps' will still be left in the German army.

FO 371/1648, f. 1

92

Prussian Railways and Mobilization
(Russell, MA 4/13, 11 January 1913)

I venture to think that a certain statement made in the Reichstag on the 9th instant by Herr Wackerzapp,[62] the President of the Imperial Railway Office, is of considerable importance and should not pass unnoticed.

The debate in the Reichstag on the occasion referred to was upon a Socialist interpellation concerning the recent dislocation of traffic on the Prussian railways.

The question of mobilization was mentioned several times during the course of the debate. The non-Socialist speakers were desirous of being informed whether there was any danger of a deadlock on the railways in the event of war, whilst the Socialists expressed their determination to convince the public of the disturbance of business which war would involve.

Herr Wackerzapp concluded the debate on the subject with a reply, which was to the following effect:–

'I desire to state that the dislocation of traffic in the Rhenish-Westphalian coal district has nothing whatever to do with the political situation. Railway carriages were neither kept back at that time for a

---

62   Michael Wackerzapp (died 1922), head of the Imperial Railway Office.

threatened mobilization – in such an event quite other measures would be taken – nor was the deadlock referred to brought about by causes of this nature. Any statements to the contrary are pure invention. Equally untrue is the assertion that in the case of a real outbreak of war our mobilization would be in any way interfered with by such a deadlock. The disturbance only occurred in the forward and backward movements of goods trains. This difficulty, in the event of war, would disappear automatically, owing to the different traffic regulations which would be introduced at once.' (Applause.)

It may no doubt be inferred from the last sentence quoted above, that the regulation of the traffic on the railways would pass immediately into the hands of the military authorities on the outbreak of war.

It may also be accepted as a certainty that the railway arrangements for a mobilization, prepared with infinite pains by the Great General Staff in peace time, will not be found wanting when submitted to the test of war.

FO 371/1648, f. 380

93

Influences working for further increases in the German Army, etc.
(Russell, MA 5/13, 23 January 1913)

With reference to Captain Watson's despatch, Naval Attaché, No. 2 of 20 January 1913,[63] I venture to submit for Your Excellency's consideration the following remarks, which are made more from a military as opposed to a naval point of view, and which appear to me to be relevant to the subject of the position of the German naval expansionist party and to form a necessary supplement to the matter under discussion in that letter.

Captain Watson refers to the present exhaustion which he observes in the offensive powers of the naval expansionist party in Germany, and enumerates the causes which have brought about this state of affairs. I desire to draw attention to further causes which I believe to be contributory to the weakened state of this party. As I have ventured to reiterate on previous occasions, the German nation has lost some of its former confidence in the supremity [*sic*] of its army, and the army

---

63   This is reproduced in full in Seligmann, *Naval Intelligence from Germany*, pp. 473–80.

itself has likewise been affected to a certain degree by the prevailing sentiment of disquietude. Hand in hand with this feeling, there exists in the minds of the Germans the knowledge that, situated as they are, their very existence depends on their army, as British existence depends on the British navy. The Germans, therefore, desire passionately that the army should be the first care of the state. In the days when the Germans were supremely confident in the invincibility of their army, they felt it permissible to indulge in the 'luxury' of a large navy. I believe, however, that it is very universally felt in Germany that the main attention of the Government should now be devoted to the army, and to this feeling may be chiefly ascribed the demands for another Army Bill, which are so prevalent at the present time.

To add fuel to the flames of the declining confidence which I have described comes the reflection that the alliance with Austria cannot now furnish her ally with the same measure of military support, as it might have done in the past. In the event of a great European war, a strong Turkey might have neutralized the power of Servia, but Germany's Austro-Hungarian ally can no longer count on such timely assistance from the dismembered Ottoman Empire. Servia indeed and perhaps not Servia alone, might fall on the flank and rear of an Austrian advance against Russia.

To be prepared, therefore, against all eventualities, the Austrian Army will be obliged to divide its forces and some 30 or 40 per cent of its strength will cease to be available for use against Russia. This loss of strength, the Germans say, they themselves must make good, adding that 'their own troops' are moreover 'the best allies'. They have too, they assert, the necessary supply of men, if only the state would choose to make use of them.

There is one more aspect of this affair, which it is important not to lose sight of. Notwithstanding the uncertainty as to the true quality of the German military strength, which exists in the country and to a lesser degree in the army, and notwithstanding the most markedly more friendly attitude adopted recently by the German press, there is in Germany a war party, composed chiefly of very senior officers, who consider that war is absolutely indispensable for the health of the German army and who attempt to urge their views upon the Emperor both in and out of season. The animosity of these warriors, which has been mainly brought about by the representations of the naval expansionists, is chiefly directed against Great Britain. From the west of Germany rumours have reached me of this party being in great strength and of being passionately desirous of war, but of war particularly with England. Outside this party, which certainly does not express its views to me, I find the German officers to be most friendly towards us.

Captain Watson states his opinion that, notwithstanding the agitation of the expansionist party, the German Government is not likely to embark immediately on an increase as a reply to a large British naval programme, nor do I think that the representations of these officers and others, who desire a war with Great Britain, will throw sufficient weight into the scale to induce this department to adopt a different view.

I venture, therefore, to endorse Captain Watson's opinion that the moment for a large British naval increase and for any further measures which may bring an accession of striking power to our army, is a peculiarly favourable one, though perhaps of a fleeting nature, and to submit for your consideration, Sir, that the influences at work to bring about further increases in the German army are both powerful and widespread.

FO 371/1649, ff. 78–80

94

Rumours of Mobilization of the German Army
(Russell MA 10/13, 9 February 1913)

There is little need to practise the calling up of reservists in Germany. The places of mobilization are in almost all cases in close proximity to the homes of the men and the proceeding would take place with ease and regularity.

[…]

With regard to […] my disbelief in a general mobilization of the German army at the present time, it is perhaps unnecessary for me to enlarge on this aspect of my case, beyond stating my belief that war is not wanted at this juncture by the responsible heads of the German Army and that, therefore, no step would be taken deliberately which would be bound to cause uneasiness in Europe and might precipitate hostilities. The Emperor was heard to say a few days ago that, as far as he was concerned, there should be peace in Germany until after his jubilee, and from remarks made quite recently by the Chief of the General Staff to a colleague of mine, there seems little doubt that this influential officer is equally undesirous of war at the present time. My Russian colleague here, Colonel von Basarow, tells me that in his country the 1st of March is considered as a very critical date. The Austrian Army will then be ready in every respect for war and will have to decide whether to cross the Rubicon or not. I could not but infer from my conversation with Colonel von Basarow that he considered war between Austria and Servia to be absolutely inevitable at an early date and further that this view is shared by a large proportion of his brother officers in their own country.

FO 371/1649, f. 186.

95

Russell to Henry Wilson
(30 March 1913)

[...] I had a very nice talk with the Emperor the other day, whose charm, I must say, is quite unequalled. We did not, however, talk of matters of political moment. We laughed though very much and that is always pleasant.

The *Army List* I gave the Emperor of course suggested to H.M. the 'Royals' and he let himself go on the favourite grievance of his regiment being abroad so long and his never being able to see them.[64] H.M. has often spoken to me about it before and he really resents it bitterly.

I cannot help laughing (inwardly on this occasion) at H.M.'s attitude on this subject, as it is really impossible for us to change the roster: and it is in a way rather nice of him. He really has a great feeling for the regiment.

I think therefore that it is of great importance that the Royals should show some special mark of their appreciation on the occasion of the Emperor's Jubilee in June this year. I wrote consequently some considerable time ago both to General Lindley,[65] the Colonel, and Makins, the O.C. in South Africa, to remind them of the approach of this auspicious occasion and to suggest to them that they should take some action in the matter. I think a silver statuette of a Royal might be the solution and, if possible, a deputation to present it.

I do not know whether the Royals are going to be back by June, but I presume not. Perhaps, however, there might be some officers on leave in England who could form a deputation.

---

64   The Kaiser had been Colonel-in-Chief of the 1st Royal Dragoons since 1894.
65   Major General Hon. John Edward Lindle, Colonel of the 1st Royal Dragoons, 1912–19.

Perhaps you will very kindly ask Charles Sackville-West[66] and let me know what you think about this matter.

[...]

SHC G173/21

96

Accelerated Mobilization of the German Army by the Provisions of the Army Bill of 1913 (Russell, MA 19/13, 12 April 1913)

An exceedingly important point to consider in connection with the Army Bill of 1913 is whether the proposed measures are capable, or not, of bringing about an acceleration in the mobilization of the German army.

The famous dictum of Napoleon: 'Ask me for anything but time!' is illustrative of the supreme importance even of hours where military operations are concerned.

That the Army Bill of 1913 is intended to furnish the army with 'increased and ever ready fighting powers' and facilitate the transition from a peace to a war footing is set out in the preamble to that measure. There are without a doubt certain changes projected, which I have the honour to submit below for Your Excellency's consideration which cannot but tend to facilitate and accelerate mobilization, but to precisely what extent it is not easy to determine.

The augmentations of the peace establishments are some of the changes I refer to. In the infantry there are at present three establishments, the higher, the medium and the lower. The 'medium' and the 'lower' are now to be abolished by the 1 October 1913 and the former 'higher' is to become the 'lower' and a new 'higher' is to be created.

Exclusive of officers, the existing higher establishment of an infantry company is 160. This is now to become the lower establishment. The future higher establishment is to be 180.

The existing higher establishment of an infantry battalion is 640. This is thus to become the lower and the new higher is to be 732.

If we add to 732 the customary 8% for recruit[s] over establishment, (58.56), say 60, we find that there are only 258 reservists required to bring a battalion up to its proper war strength of 1,050. At present 360 men

---

66   Charles Sackville-West, 4th Baron Sackville (1870–1962): also known as 'Tit Willow', worked in MO2.

are required. There can be no question that the process of mobilizing a battalion is facilitated by the proposed change.

252 Prussian, 3 Saxon and 3 Württemberg battalions are to be brought up to the new higher establishment. Thus no less than 2/5th of all the infantry battalions of the German army – and they are chiefly the ones stationed on the western and eastern frontiers – are to be placed in this enhanced state of readiness. All the remaining battalions too on the present medium and lower establishment are to be brought up to the future lower, formerly higher, establishment.

Similarly the establishment of every cavalry regiment is to be increased by 5 non-commissioned officers, 25 lance corporals and men and 30 horses.

All batteries of Horse, Field and Foot artillery too are to have increased establishments and will thus be more ready for war. The batteries of Field artillery on the frontiers can now move out against an enemy at practically a moment's notice with 6 guns, 3 ammunition wagons and 1 observation wagon, which would be sufficient with which to take the field at the commencement. (Horse artillery batteries are to be provided with teams for 4 ammunition wagons.) The remaining wagons, etc., could be mobilized later and sent to join their units.

In the same manner the infantry and cavalry of the frontier Army Corps could march out at extremely short notice and, though there are many reasons for believing that the Germans would not undertake any operations on a large scale until they had concentrated in as full a strength as possible, the advantage of being able to advance immediately, over the frontier if necessary, with a considerable force of all arms cannot be gainsaid.

The collection of the necessary horses was one of the considerations in the opinion of foreign critics, which was likely to retard German mobilization, but the existing state of affairs will be remedied to no small an extent by the acquisition of the 27,000 horses proposed in the Army Bill.

As I have stated above, it is difficult to estimate the exact extent to which mobilization will be accelerated by the measures referred to and it is only possible to hazard an opinion. I venture, therefore, to state that I think the German mobilization may possibly be shortened by one day. (The railway and other arrangements have already reached such a degree of perfection that it is not easy to affect enhanced rapidity.) This is a marked acceleration, but, as I understand from my French colleague, the General Staff in his country are not seriously perturbed by this consideration.

FO 371/1648, f. 136

97

Development of the German Airship Fleet
(Russell, MA 23/13, 12 June 1913)

It is clear from the fact that the German Government proposes to spend some 60,000,000 M. (£3,000,000) during the financial year 1913 on the service of aeronautics, that considerable developments may be expected to take place during the next ten months in all that pertains to the efficiency and completeness of this arm.

I will deal on this occasion only with the evolution of the airship fleet, which seems likely to make very marked advances during the current year.

If the trials are successful, two new Zeppelin airships are to be handed over to the military authorities in the immediate future, and one new dirigible of the same type to the Navy. The airships in question are the following:–

For the Army

1. The dirigible which is to replace $Z.I^{67}$ and which is undergoing her trials at the present time.
2. A new dirigible to be called $Z.V.^{68}$

For the Navy

1. A new dirigible which will probably be called $Z.II$ which is expected to be completed before the end of the summer, and which will at first be stationed at Johannisthal.

In addition to the above reinforcements, the airship fleet in possession of the military authorities will receive, probably before next autumn, the addition of a new Schütte-Lanz dirigible, the reconstructed $M.IV$ and a new Parseval to be called $P.IV$. It will thus be observed that the total additions to the Government fleet of airships during the current year will consist of 3 Zeppelins, 1 Schütte-Lanz, 1 M. or Gross airship, and 1 Parseval, raising the total number of State-owned dirigibles to 17.

---

67 *Z.I* (known to the Zeppelin Company as LZ 3), the army's first Zeppelin airship, was purchased in 1908 and, as this report implies, was decommissioned in 1913.
68 *Z.V* (known to the Zeppelin Company as LZ 20): military airship, made its maiden flight in July 1913.

A new airship dock is expected to be completed at Potsdam at an early date, when trials with the new Zeppelins will be undertaken from that place. A number of airship sheds are to be erected shortly, one double one at each of the head-quarters of the airship companies, which will probably be ready to use by the 1st April, or at the latest by 1st July, 1914. It appears that the first of these sheds will be completed at Hannover.

In view of the rapid construction and occasional destruction of airships in Germany, as well as the somewhat puzzling changes in nomenclature and the secrecy which is endeavoured to be observed in this matter, it is not a little hazardous to attempt an accurate enumeration of existing German dirigibles. I venture, however, to attach a list, which is as complete and accurate as I can make it, of the State-owned and privately-owned airships in Germany at the present time. There are other dirigibles in process of construction in the Zeppelin and Parseval yards, concerning which no information is at present available. It is reported in the press that these consist of one Zeppelin and five Parsevals for passenger service, all of which may be classed as powerful craft. There are also some privately-owned airships, which are practically of no value, and are, therefore, not included in this list.

Irrespective, therefore, of existing or future orders for airships, it appears that Germany will possess before the end of this year no less than seventeen State-owned and twelve privately-owned dirigibles of high power, carrying capacity, and speed.

ADM 116/1278

98

The Passage into Law of the Army Bill of 1913 and its Effect on Public Opinion
(Russell, MA 25/13, 4 July 1913)

As Your Excellency reported in your despatch No. 241 of 30 June 1913, the Reichstag passed the final stages of the Army Bill and of the Financial Bills connected with it on 30th ultimo. The Federal Council in a plenary sitting yesterday, 3rd July, gave its sanction to these Bills and the Emperor's signature was obtained the next morning.

The Army Bill of 1913 has thus become law. No considerable amendments of any kind have been made to the original proposals of the Government and even the creation of the full number of cavalry regiments demanded in the draft of the Bill has now, as I ventured some time back to predict would be the case, received the sanction of the Reichstag. I intend to bring the precise nature of these amendments to Your Excellency's notice as soon as information on this subject has been published officially.

Between 1911 and 1913 the military authorities have come forward three times with large demands and on the first two occasions, when they had obtained all they required, had expressed themselves as finally satisfied. On the third occasion, however, a series of proposals exceeding anything of the kind which had ever been previously laid before the Reichstag, were formulated and have now also, as stated above, been added to the statute book. For how long the heads of the Army will consider that the military needs of the Empire are fulfilled by the improved conditions brought about by the new Bill remains to be proved.

In the Army there is, I am convinced, but one sentiment of satisfaction and relief that there is now no uncertainty as to the introduction of military measures, which were considered immediately and imperatively necessary.

The man in the street wonders, I think, in his inmost soul as to whether augmentations on so vast a scale were really called for, but is prepared to bow to the will and superior knowledge of those set in authority over him.

The press speaks with many tongues. On the whole the military proposals meet with approval and are but faintly criticised, but the method of providing funds for these changes causes much doubt and uncertainty and a full measure of heartburning.

The War Minister[69] will probably sleep quietly in his bed and the other members of the Government will doubtless have few, if any, regrets or misgivings with regard to their military demands which have just become law, even if they feel that the ship of state is hardly under control in the matter of financial policy.

That the sacrifices of the nation have been met with unquestioning and willing enthusiasm can certainly not be said to be the case. That the German army is receiving no mean accession of strength, that the new provisions will make this military machine more ready for war and more capable than ever of carrying out its ingrained and traditional policy of the offensive, should the decision be taken at any time to draw the sword, stands beyond dispute.

FO 371/1648, f. 201

---

[69] Since 7 June 1913 this had been Erich von Falkenhayn.

99

New Formations in the German Army
(Russell, MA 28/13, 28 July 1913)

I have the honour to forward herewith, for transmission to the War Office, a list of the new formations, etc., which are to be created in the Prussian, Saxon and Württemberg armies by 1 October 1913.

The precise nature and extent of these changes and the means by which they are to be affected, have been brought to the knowledge of the army by a lengthy order in *Armee-Verordnungsblatt* No. 15 of 4 July 1913.

With a view to lucidity and for purposes of limiting the compass of this despatch, I have, instead of reproducing elaborate tables, etc., contented myself here and there by referring to the above-quoted publication, which is at all times accessible to the Department concerned at the War Office.

It will be observed that the changes enumerated below constitute a very formidable array and involve an accession of strength to the German army which it is difficult to overestimate, guaranteeing moreover, to this remarkable fighting machine a perfection of organization and a readiness for war, which has perhaps never been surpassed by any military force.

Whether the real objects of the Army Bill of 1913, which I conceive to be those of gaining such a commanding lead over France as to outdistance competition and even more of obtaining complete security against the rising power of Russia, have been accomplished even for a period by the projected army increases or not, can hardly be judged as yet with any degree of certainty. There can, however, be no doubt that the military strength of Germany is about to be enhanced in a manner which is deserving of very serious consideration, but whether at the same time the financial sinews of the Empire have not been unduly strained by the consequent increase of taxation and the industrial life of the nation been sapped to some extent by the withdrawal of so much manhood from productive work is, my Lord, another more open question.

FO 244/818

100

Some Notes on the System of Subsidizing Mechanical Transport Vehicles in Germany (Russell, MA 30/13, 5 September 1913)

The system of subsidizing mechanical vehicles belonging to private firms, with a view to their employment by the military authorities in time of war, has been in force in Germany since the year 1908.

During the first period of five years 825 (Prussia 743, Bavaria 82) military mechanical transport trains, each consisting of one motor wagon and one trailer, were subsidized and during the current year an additional 135 trains (Prussia 120, Bavaria 15) were similarly registered, bringing the total number nearly up to one thousand.

The number of trains subsidized during the years under review were as follows:–

Year.	Prussia.	Bavaria.
1908	166	9
1909	176	51
1910	140	12
1911	141	15
1912	120	15
1913	120	15

The total cost for the first period of five years amounted to 5,000,000 Marks (£250,000).

The breweries appear to have furnished the largest number of subsidized vehicles and the brick industry the second largest number. 16 German firms in all, of which 3 are Bavarian, are in receipt of state aid of this nature.

During the first period of five years: i.e. from 1908 to 31 March 1912 only mechanical transport trains, consisting of one motor wagon and one trailer, of a total carrying capacity of 6,000 kg were subsidized for a total sum of 8,000 M. (£400). This year in Prussia in addition to 80 similar new mechanical transport trains, 80 single motor wagons of a carrying capacity of from 4,000 to 5,000 kg were also subsidized. The state aid is henceforth to be 7,800 M. (£390) for each mechanical transport train and 5,000 M. (£250) for each single wagon.

On mobilization these trains and wagons, which have been continually under military surveillance, would at once be requisitioned for the army.

According to the most recent regulations (*Kraftfahrtruppen im Felde* – Mechanical Transport Troops in the Field) which were issued last March, the marching capacity of motor transport is laid down to be 8 times as great as that of horsed transport, the daily minimum march being given as 60 km (37½ miles) and the average 100 km (62½ miles). The mechanical transport allotted to the Cavalry Divisions is expected to be able to accomplish 125 km (76 miles) in the day. Great care is, however, enjoined in the case of protracted marching and it is laid down as a principle that every mechanical transport vehicle is to cease working for one day in the week, when it can be thoroughly examined and overhauled. The reduction in the depth of columns is of course also a further advantage entailed by the use of motor transport. The carrying capacity of one Line of Communication Mechanical Transport Column, consisting of 10 military mechanical transport trains, is laid down to be equivalent to that of one supply park ('Fuhrpark-Kolonne') or two supply columns ('Proviant-Kolonnen') or 2 Infantry or Artillery Ammunition Columns.

The supplies for one German Army Corps for one day could thus be carried by 9 military mechanical transport trains with one in reserve. (i.e. 10 in all.)

In cases of emergency these wagons can also be made use of for the transport of personnel, one train being capable of taking 55 fully equipped infantry soldiers.

German military opinion appears to incline to the notion that in the actual vicinity of the fighting troops horsed transport will still have to be employed.

It will, I think, be clear, My Lord from the preceding notes that by means of this wise system of subsidizing motor transport vehicles in times of peace, the German government has not only supported an important and growing industry but has also made a valuable contribution to the readiness and efficiency of the army for war.

FO 371/1652, f. 311

101

Summary of Military Estimates for 1914
(Russell, MA 41/13, 27 November 1913)

[…]

The chief impression left on the mind after a study of the Military Estimates for the ensuing year, is that every patriotic German must feel that, in the words used in the Reichstag yesterday by the new War Minister, Lieutenant-General von Falkenhayn,[70] his country will 'have a chance of winning in the great life and death struggle, when it comes', as it is one which 'in its preparations neglects nothing which may favourably affect the issue'.

FO 371/1654, f. 133

102

An Article by General von Bernhardi on Germany's
Financial and Economic Preparedness for War
(Russell, MA 44/13, 11 December 1913)

I have the honour to forward herewith a translation of an article by the well-known military writer, General of Cavalry F. von Bernhardi, on Germany's financial and economic preparedness for war. This essay appeared in the November number of *Der Greif*, a new monthly periodical which made its first appearance in October last.

Bernhardi is convinced that the German Empire is fully equal to meeting the financial strain even of a prolonged war; the recent additions to the war treasure will, moreover, in the author's opinion, greatly facilitate the work of overcoming the first financial difficulties during mobilisation.

The writer of the article under review considers the problem of food supply during war time as a difficult but not an insoluble one, and suggests measures for improving existing conditions. He believes that the industrial state of Germany during a war would present less favourable features than the question of the people's food supply. For this state of affairs the general also suggests remedial and precautionary measures.

---

70 Erich von Falkenhayn (1861–1922), Prussian Minister of War, 1913–15, Chief of the Great General Staff, 1914–16.

There are three conditions on the importance of which the general lays special stress:–

1)   That the trade routes to the Balkan States and Turkey should be kept open.

2)   That the German navy should be supreme in the Baltic.

3)   That a wise diplomacy should exclude the possibility of a war being forced on Germany. German statesmen must, on the other hand, foresee an inevitable war, prepare for it systematically, and seize the initiative at the most favourable moment.

Such policy as this certainly does not present any new features to Bismarck's[71] fellow-countrymen.

The English of the attached translation is a little rough in places, but the meaning is, I think, quite clear throughout.

FO 371/1654, f. 233

---

71   Otto von Bismarck (from 1871 Prince Bismarck) (1815–98), Minister-President of Prussia, 1862–90; Chancellor of the German Empire, 1871–90.

1914

103

Teaching at the German Staff College
(Russell, MA 1/14, 5 January 1914)

Some information from a reliable source relating to certain tendencies in the strategical and tactical instruction, which is being imparted at the present time to the students of the Staff College here in Berlin, has recently come to my notice. As the promulgation of unsound doctrines to the future leaders and staff officers of the German Army would appear imprudent, to say the least of it, the nature of the teaching at the establishment in question cannot be without significance. I venture, therefore, to submit below for your Excellency's consideration the main details of the information referred to, which I have endeavoured to summarize as concisely as possible:–

The Staff College students are taught when considering a war between Germany and France to assume:–

1)   that no part of the German forces will march through Belgium; such violation of the last named country's neutrality is said to be both impolitic and unnecessary;

2)   that if Great Britain takes part in the contest, her forces will in all probability not arrive in time to influence the result of the first great battles; it might, however, be conceivably necessary to detach a small body of troops to crush (*sic*) the British expeditionary force;

3)   that the French forces will invariably move preceded by a strategic advanced guard which will in every case be 10 kilometres (6½ miles) in advance of the main columns.

With reference to (1) it is no doubt wise to be careful not to reveal any strategical secrets to a number of young and somewhat untried officers, but the possibility of a German advance through portions of Belgian territory as an alternative suggestion might surely be admitted by the instructors at the German Staff College. This does not, however, appear to be the case. The Staff College students are doubtless unaware of the numerous disembarkation stations which have been constructed within the last few years in Germany in close proximity to the Belgian frontier (see my MA Germany No. XV of 1st June 1911), to mention only one indication of German strategical intentions, or they would be less ready than they are to accept the teaching imparted to them. I am in a position to state confidently that more advanced military students on the General Staff carry out schemes in which every conceivable strategical alternative is considered. It is curious therefore that the Staff College teaching should be of so narrow a kind. The question of the insufficiency of roads to admit of the deployment of the large German forces, if Belgian territory is not to be made use of, is apparently easily answered on paper by moving two or three Army Corps one behind another on the same road and assuming that the troops will also to a large extent move across country.

With regard to (2) it would doubtless appear a little imprudent to an impartial observer to show such scant consideration for British diplomatic promptitude and for the effect which would be produced by the British expeditionary force.

The assumption referred to in (3) viz. that the French forces would always move in the particular cut and dried formation described above might conceivably have been correct 10 years ago. It is certainly not so now. The doctrine that the French will invariably move in this fashion enables the young German student to defeat his enemy on paper on every occasion with the greatest possible ease. Training of this kind is undoubtedly unsound.

The main inference to be drawn from the above is that the strategical and tactical training at the German Staff College is narrow and old fashioned. It is strange that this should be the case, when the training of the more senior officers on the General Staff is superlatively good. It appears only to be explicable by the fact that in certain departments of military work the Germans allow themselves to continue year after year in the same groove. Such instances as the obsolete methods of fire control and disregard of the effects of modern weapons seen on German manoeuvres, which I have frequently commented on in previous reports, are cases in point.

It is interesting, I almost said satisfactory, to find that there are some weak spots in the German armour.

FO 371/1985, ff. 448–449A

104

Military Opinion on the Zabern Incidents (Russell, MA 3/14, 23 January 1914)

Civil bodies, such as the Upper Chamber of the Diet of Alsace-Lorraine, have means of giving public expression to their opinions on the recent events at Zabern[72] and have not failed to take advantage of the opportunities at their disposal. The corps of officers of the German Army is less articulate. I have been at some pains, therefore, to investigate the feeling which exists among German officers with regard to the incidents in the Reichsland, which have caused so much stir even beyond the confines of the Empire. I cannot say that I am entirely surprised to have found complete unanimity on the subject. The German officers appear to be quite incapable of admitting any opinion on the matter except their own extremely partisan view. The mere suggestion that the behaviour of Lieutenant von Forstner[73] might have been somewhat provocative or that Colonel von Reuter[74] may possibly have displayed a slight excess of zeal in the performance of his duties brings on an argument not unaccompanied by heat. Numerous officers have assured me that in circumstances similar to those in which Lieutenant von Forstner found himself, they too would undoubtedly have drawn their swords on a lame and unarmed cobbler.

The large number of letters and telegrams of congratulation received by Colonel von Reuter on his acquittal recently, nearly all of which, I gather, were from military bodies and individuals, testify to the sympathy evoked by this officer's conduct among the soldier element of the population.

---

72 Zabern (Saverne) was an important garrison town in northern Alsace. In October 1913 a major incident erupted there that called into question the place of the German military in the Prusso-German constitutional system. The trigger for the so-called Zabern Affair was the use by a junior army officer of the derogatory term 'Wackes' to describe the local population. When news of this insult leaked out there was considerable public anger and some protest. The local garrison, for whom sensitivity was clearly an alien concept, then overreacted and, taking the law into their own hands, arrested a number of protesters. The incident caused some disquiet in Germany as a whole and was debated in the Reichstag. The Chancellor's indifferent defence of the army's actions led to a motion of no confidence in him being passed.

73 Günter von Forstner (1893–1915), the young lieutenant whose words started the incident. He was tried by court martial and sentenced to six weeks' imprisonment, but this was quashed on appeal.

74 Adolf von Reuter (1857–1926): Forster's commanding officer.

From all I have heard the officers in the provinces are, if possible, even more bigoted on this subject than those who are quartered in the vicinity of the metropolis. There can in fact be no doubt that the whole corps of officers of the German Army from top to bottom are unanimous in the approval of the conduct of their comrades at Zabern.

The opinions held by German officers on current affairs, even when the matters in question concern the Army very intimately, are perhaps only of evanescent interest, but when taken as indications of the attitude of mind of the whole military caste in Germany, the nature of these views is not without significance.

The prevailing ideas in military circles described above indicates primarily an uniformity of thought in the corps of officers which, even if at times in a mistaken direction, is in itself a sign as well as a source of strength. It is in part this sentiment which spurred on the German leaders in the past to march to the sound of the guns, with a view to supporting their comrades at all costs. It is one of numerous proofs that the German soldiers will again 'pull together', as they have done before on many a stricken field. And this surely is no small matter.

Whatever then may be one's view regarding the justice or injustice of the prevailing military sentiment over the Zabern incidents, it is difficult to withhold a measure of one's admiration from the singlemindedness and solidarity which have been displayed on this occasion by the whole corps of officers in Germany.

FO 371/1985

105

Airships and Airship Sheds
(Russell, MA 8/14, 20 February 1914)

I have the honour to call Your Excellency's attention to the present stage of development of the German airship fleet, which, regardless of loss and disaster as well as of adverse opinion from some quarters, is being relentlessly re-enforced by dirigibles of ever increasing range, carrying capacity and speed. [...]

It will be observed that there are in existence and under construction 20 State owned and 13 privately owned airships. Of these 14 Government and 3 private dirigibles (*Victoria Louise*,[75] *Sachsen*[76] and *Hansa*[77]) are actually 'in commission' at the present time and the remainder could be rendered fit for service at short notice. There are in addition other dirigibles in process of construction in the Zeppelin and Parseval yards, concerning which no information is at present available.

There are 35 existing sheds (of which one is not available at the present moment) including the 4 transportable halls, which are the property of the military authorities and are used chiefly for manoeuvres purposes. 9 more sheds are either under construction or are projected for the immediate future. Of the 35 completed sheds, 15 belong to the Government. It is reported in the press, with what truth I am unable to state, that it is proposed to build airship sheds also at Darmstadt, Munich, Stuttgart and Emden. Should all these projects materialize, Germany would be in possession of no less than 48 airship sheds.

It will be clear from the above that the airship industry in this country is being carried on with unfaltering zeal and determination.

FO 371/1987, f. 204

106

Prussian-Hessian Railways
(Russell, MA 12/14, 6 March 1914)

I have the honour to forward herewith an official document (Reichstag Publication No. 1305 of 22 January 1914), in which a proposal is formulated for dealing with the congestion of traffic, which it is anticipated must take place on the Railway Line Strassburg–Basle, if remedial measures are not resorted to at an early date. It is suggested that either a third and fourth set of rails be laid along side the existing double line or a new independent double line be constructed to run approximately parallel and comparatively close to the present Strassburg–Basle Railway.

It is not necessary at the present time to examine more closely into the details of this proposal, it is merely desirable to note that the plan exists, as, though no military considerations are referred to in the document in

---

75 *Victoria Luise*: the Zeppelin airship LZ 11 was a commercially run airship named after the Kaiser's daughter. It was requisitioned by the military at the start of the First World War.

76 *Sachsen*: the Zeppelin airship LZ 17. It was requisitioned by the military at the start of the First World War.

77 *Hansa*: the Zeppelin airship LZ 13. It was requisitioned by the military at the start of the First World War.

question, from a strategical point of view the additional railway facilities proposed would be of considerable value.

Details with regard to recent railway construction in Prussia are given in I. Volume of *Anlagen zum Staatshaushaltsetat für das Etatsjahr 1914*, which has just been published. It appears from this document that at the end of the financial year 1912 the length of line available for traffic on the Prussian-Hessian Railways was 38,850.20 km (24,281 miles). In addition to this 239.31 km (149 miles) of small gauge lines were in use.

358.01 km (223¾ miles) of line have been added during the period April 1913 to March 1914 and thus at the commencement of the financial year 1914, there were available for traffic 39,208.21 km (24,508 miles) of ordinary gauge and 239.31 km (149 miles) of small gauge lines. It is proposed during the ensuing year to add a further 589.60 km (381 miles) of line.

Of the additional line constructed during 1913, most of which was in the great industrial district on the Rhine about Cologne and Essen and was doubtless destined for purely commercial purposes, the only sections which may be said to be of strategical importance are the following:–

On the Western frontier:

Ahrdorf–Blankenheimwald	29.94 km (18 miles)
Malmedy to the frontier near Stavelot	3.70 km (2¼ miles)

On the Eastern frontier:

Scheidemühl–Jablenewo	18.56 km (11¾ miles)
Carlshof–Deutschfeld	39.26 km (24½ miles)
Kolzig-Schlawa–Kl. Gräditz	61.47 km (38 miles)
Hultschin–Deutsch Krawaru	14.37 km (8¾ miles)
Bad Jastrzemb–Loslau	21.18 km (13 miles)

The railway facilities for conveying troops to the eastern frontier are doubtless not considered by the authorities to be as satisfactory as they might be, but an attempt to remedy this state of affairs is evident from the work of construction carried out in 1913 as well as from the additional lines projected during the current year. In this connection I would specially mention the following sections which are to be completed during 1914:–

Flatow–Deutschkrons with branch line to Jastrow	63 km (39 miles)
Angerburg–Gumbinnen	64.97 km (40½ miles)
Arys–Lick	35.24 km (22 miles)

There are other minor sections projected in this part of Germany, which I have not referred to, but which will contribute in a measure to the capabilities of the railway systems in the eastern districts of the Empire.
FO 371/1988, f. 266

107

Feeling in Germany towards War
(Russell, MA 13/14, 13 March 1914)

I have the honour to forward herewith a translation of an article, which appeared in the *Berliner Tageblatt* of 9th instant and to which Your Excellency made a reference in your despatch No. 100 of 10th March 1914. Your Excellency's statement with regard to the article in question was as follows:–

> Even the radical *Tageblatt* which generally is opposed to all forms of chauvinism, printed yesterday an article by an anonymous writer, who is described editorially as a 'prominent personage experienced in all branches of international politics', in which it was urged that a stop must be put once and for all to Russia's pretensions, if necessary by the sword. I am forwarding in a separate despatch a translation of this article, which presents certain features of interest, in view of the political complexion of the *Tageblatt* and the weight which the editor, whilst deprecating the idea of preventive war, attaches to the opinion of this writer …

The agitation in the German press on the matters dealt with in the attached article appears to be subsiding and the journalists of all nations have done their best to explain the origin of this newspaper campaign, its purpose and the extent of Government participation in it. It is important, therefore, to proceed a step further and investigate as to whether the journalistic phenomena which have occurred, are indications of increasing inclination for war in Germany and what effects, if any, this raging in the press has had on the temper of the German people. The writer in the *Tageblatt* is doubtless correct in ascribing to the Emperor intentions of a highly pacific order and in describing His Majesty's entourage as taking the cue from their Chief.[78] The Government has certainly no desire for hostilities at the present time. The Crown Prince, however, with light-hearted enthusiasm would lead his country into warlike operations without a moment's hesitation, but whether he would be equally bellicose, if he came to hold a responsible position, cannot now be foretold.

There is in Germany, I am convinced, a reserve of latent patriotism and national enthusiasm, which does not invariably appear on the surface, but which is almost boundless in quantity and at times highly inflammable in quality. These feelings deep down in German hearts have been profoundly stirred, I believe, by the recent articles in the newspapers, but I do not think that the result will be a demand for further increases in the Army, as has been suggested in some quarters. The Zabern incidents left the honours of the day entirely in the hands of the military party and the conservative element in the country has been strengthened by the issue of those events.

It is realised in Germany that a war with Russia is not likely to become an easier undertaking as time goes on; the rapidity of German mobilization has probably reached its utmost limit whereas the time required by Russia for the same operation will doubtless continue to decrease.

These and other considerations, as well as numerous causes, which are somewhat too elaborate for discussion on the present occasion, have in my opinion brought about an increase in the war party in Germany, though the writer in the *Tageblatt* denies the existence of any such body. To sum up the situation I would state that I do not consider that Germany stands on the threshold of war, nor do I believe that war is likely to take place at any particular time. I maintain, however, that circumstances might easily arise, which would inflame public opinion to such an extent that the issue of war or peace would be at the mercy of accident. The feeling in the country might be so strong that the Emperor and his Government, however pacifically inclined, would not be able to prevail against it and any false diplomatic step or any real or imaginary injury to German honour might precipitate hostilities at the shortest notice. It is imperative, therefore, for Germany's potential enemies to maintain their preparations for war on the highest possible footing.

FO 371/2092, f. 30

---

78   While there was an element of truth in this in relation to the Kaiser, the same cannot be said for this characterization of the imperial entourage, which contained some highly belligerent individuals.

108

The Prince Henry Circuit of 1914
(Russell and Henderson, MA 18/14, NA 23A/14, 1 June 1914)

We have the honour to report that, in compliance with an invitation from the Committee of the Prince Henry Circuit of 1914, we attended this aeronautical meeting, which was held in the west of Germany between the 17th and 25th ultimo.
[…]
A detailed report of this meeting will be submitted to Your Excellency at an early date.
FO 371/1988, f. 373

109

The Prince Henry Circuit of 1914
(Russell and Henderson, MA 19/14, NA 24/14, 10 June 1914)

[…]
General Impressions. In flying with 'heavier than air' machines, the Germans appear to have arrived at a point which we reached a year or two ago. They are making exhaustive trials of aeroplanes most suited to their military needs, but have not yet settled on the best type of machine. They are still learning to fly and have not yet seriously considered the question of 'fighting aeroplanes'. It seems to be the intention eventually to establish a Government aircraft factory not only for the purpose of constructing their own machines, but also with a view to training their own aircraft mechanics for the supply of whom they at present have to rely on private firms.

Although it might have been thought that it hardly lay in the genius of the German people to produce a race of really first class aviators, the contrary appears to be the case. The standard of skill and dash among the flying officers has risen during the last year in a truly remarkable manner and the spirit which obtains in the flying battalions may certainly be said to leave nothing to be desired. The attitude taken towards accidents fatal and otherwise is a thoroughly virile one as might indeed have been expected from a nation which is so essentially manly and which is always preparing itself for war. Officers who are killed at their work are regarded as though they had lost their lives in action. Very little sentiment is permitted. Relentless prosecution of the art of flying is the order of the day.

The organisation of the meeting was truly German in its thorough completeness, as will be clear from a study of the pamphlets which were issued prior to the event to all concerned. [...]

Type of Flying Officer. The type of flying officer has been referred to above under 'General Impressions'; it was remarkably different from the usual well-known heavy Teutonic type. The flying officers are fine-drawn, lean, determined looking youngsters, among whom a fine spirit prevails.

Supply of flying officers. We were told that there is great competition for the Flying Service, owing chiefly to the monotony of regimental service and the almost total absence of opportunity for enthusiastic and energetic officers otherwise to distinguish themselves. For 40 vacancies recently there were 800 candidates.

Type of aeroplane most favoured. As a result of the 'Circuit', it may safely be said that the monoplane is least in favour. All the completely successful machines, with one exception, were biplanes, and although some of the accidents which occurred to the monoplanes might perhaps equally have happened to biplanes, still the accidents to monoplanes were to the accidents to biplanes during the Reliability Flight as 6:4.

Although it was admitted that monoplanes were very stable in the air, the complaint was that they responded sluggishly to the balancing lever with the result that the process of landing was always connected with a certain amount of risk.

We heard rumours to the effect that monoplanes would be given up.

[...]

AIR 1/626/17/32

110

Proclamation of a State of Imminent National Danger (Russell, MA 20/14, 1 August 1914)

As your Excellency reported in your telegram No. 111 of today's date, a state of imminent national danger ('drohende Kriegsgefahr') has been proclaimed by the Emperor this afternoon throughout the Empire except Bavaria, where, however, a similar ordinance has also been issued.

It appears from the official pronouncement in the *Norddeutsche Allgemeine Zeitung*, published tonight and dated 1st August, 1914, that the military measures to be taken consequent upon this proclamation are the following:–

(1.)   All the necessary steps on the frontier and for the protection of the railways.

(2.)   Limitation of postal, telegraph and railway traffic to meet military requirements.

Further consequences of the proclamation of the state of imminent national danger are:–

(3.)   Proclamation of a state of war ('Kriegszustand') throughout the Empire.

(4.)   Prohibition of publications regarding movements of troops and measures of defence.

The state of war ('Kriegszustand') has the same significance as the state of siege ('Belagerungszustand') in Prussia. See article 68 of Reichsverfassung.

The state of war having also been declared this afternoon, certain further ordinances have been issued regarding the prohibition of the export of foodstuffs and certain articles and materials, prohibition regarding publication of news of military interest, &c., &c.

I am forwarding direct to the War Office copies of two editions of the *Deutscher Reichsanzeiger*[79] which contain the further ordinances referred to.

FO 371/2160, f. 330

---

79   *Deutscher Reichsanzeiger*: an official newspaper that published details of government appointments as well as official decrees and ordinances.

Bibliography

Manuscript Sources

Liddell Hart Centre for Military Archives, King's College, London (LHCMA)

Ian Hamilton Papers

National Archives, Kew (TNA)

Admiralty Papers (ADM)
Air Ministry Papers (AIR)
Colonial Office Papers (CO)
Committee of Imperial Defence Papers (CAB)
Foreign Office Papers (FO)
Secret Service Bureau Papers (KV)
War Office Papers (WO)

Royal Archives, Windsor Castle (RA)

Papers of King Edward VII
Papers of King George V

Surrey History Centre (SHC)

Earl of Onslow Papers

Memoirs and Contemporary Accounts

Gleichen, Edward, *A Guardsman's Memories: A Book of Recollections.* London, 1932.

Russell, A. V. F. V., 'Reminiscences of the German Court', *The Fighting Forces* 1 (1924), 58–71.

Waters, W. H.-H., *'Secret and Confidential': The Experiences of a Military Attaché.* London, 1926.

Waters, W. H.-H., *'Private and Personal': Further Experiences of a Military Attaché.* London, 1928.

Waters, W. H.-H., *Potsdam and Doorn.* London, 1935.

Select Secondary Sources

Andrew, Christopher, *The Defence of the Realm: The Authorized History of MI5.* London, 2009.

Barraclough, Geoffrey, *From Agadir to Armageddon: Anatomy of a Crisis.* London, 1982.

Boghardt, Thomas, *Spies of the Kaiser: German Covert Operations in Great Britain during the First World War Era.* Basingstoke, 2004.

Ferguson, Niall, *The Pity of War.* London, 1998

Fergusson, Thomas G., *British Military Intelligence, 1870–1914: The Development of a Modern Intelligence Organization.* London, 1984.

French, David, *British Economic and Strategic Planning, 1905–1915.* London, 1982.

French, David, 'Spy Fever in Britain, 1900–1915', *Historical Journal* 21 (1978), 355–70.

Gooch, G. P. and Temperley, Harold, *British Documents on the Origins of the War, 1898–1914*, 11 vols. London, 1926–38.

Gooch, John, *The Plans of War: The General Staff and British Military Strategy, 1900–1916.* London, 1974.

Herrmann, David G., *The Arming of Europe and the Making of the First World War.* Princeton, 1996.

Herwig, Holger H., *'Luxury' Fleet: The Imperial German Navy 1888–1918.* London, 1991.

Higham, Robin, *The British Rigid Airship, 1908–1931: A Study in Weapons Policy.* London, 1961.

Hilbert, Lothar Wilfred, 'The Role of Military and Naval Attachés in the British and German Service with particular reference to those in

Berlin and London and Their Effect on Anglo-German Relations, 1871–1914.' PhD thesis, University of Cambridge, 1954.

Hiley, Nicholas P., 'Entering the Lists: MI5's Great Spy Round-up of August 1914', *Intelligence and National Security* 21 (2006), 46–76.

Hiley, Nicholas P., 'The Failure of British Espionage against Germany, 1907–1914', *Historical Journal* 26 (1983), 867–89.

Hiley, Nicholas P., 'Re-entering the Lists: MI5's Authorized History and the August 1914 Arrests', *Intelligence and National Security* 25 (2010), 415–52.

Judd, Alan, *The Quest for C: Mansfield Cumming and the Founding of the Secret Service.* London, 1999.

Kennedy, Paul M., 'Great Britain before 1914', in Ernest R. May (ed.), *Knowing One's Enemies: Intelligence before the Two World Wars.* Princeton, 1984, pp. 172–203.

Kennedy, Paul M., *The Rise of the Anglo-German Antagonism, 1860–1914.* London, 1980.

Marder, Arthur J., *From the Dreadnought to Scapa Flow.* 5 vols. Oxford, 1961–70.

Mombauer, Annika, *Helmuth von Moltke and the Origins of the First World War.* Cambridge, 2001.

Monger, George, *The End of Isolation: British Foreign Policy 1900–1907.* London, 1963.

Morris, A. J. A., *The Scaremongers: The Advocacy of War and Rearmament, 1896–1914.* London, 1984.

Seligmann, Matthew S., '*Hors de Combat?* The Management, Mismanagement and Mutilation of the War Office Archive', *Journal of the Society for Army Historical Research* 337 (Spring 2006), 52–8.

Seligmann, Matthew S., 'Military Diplomacy in a Military Monarchy? Kaiser Wilhelm II and the British Service Attachés in Berlin 1903–1914', in Wilhelm Deist and Annika Mombauer (eds), *The Kaiser: New Research on Wilhelm II's Role in Imperial Germany.* Cambridge, 2003, pp. 176–94.

Seligmann, Matthew S. (ed.), *Naval Intelligence from Germany: The Reports of the British Naval Attachés in Berlin, 1906–1914.* Aldershot, 2007.

Seligmann, Matthew S., *Spies in Uniform: British Military and Naval Intelligence on the Eve of the First World War.* Oxford, 2006.

Steiner, Zara, *Britain and the Origins of the First World War.* London, 1977.

Stevenson, David, *Armaments and the Coming of War: Europe 1904–1914.* Oxford, 1996.

Vagts, Alfred, *The Military Attaché.* Princeton, 1967.

Williamson, Jr., Samuel R., *The Politics of Grand Strategy: Britain and France Prepare for War, 1904–1914.* Cambridge, Mass., 1969.

Index